Victorian and Edwardian Town Halls

Frontispiece Building Rochdale town hall, W. H. Crossland, 1866–71

Victorian and Edwardian Town Halls

Colin Cunningham

Routledge & Kegan Paul
London, Boston and Henley

First published in 1981
by Routledge & Kegan Paul Ltd
39 Store Street, London WC1E 7DD,
9 Park Street, Boston, Mass. 02108, USA and
Broadway House, Newtown Road, Henley-on-Thames, Oxon RG9 1EN
Set in Monophoto Baskerville, 11 on 13pt
and printed in Great Britain by
BAS Printers Limited, Over Wallop, Hampshire

British Library Cataloguing in Publication Data

Cunningham, Colin

Victorian and Edwardian town halls.
1. Municipal buildings—Great Britain
—History—19th century
I. Title
725'.13'0941 NA4435.G7

ISBN 0-7100-0723-X

Contents

Illustrations

Preface

My intention in writing this book is not to convince myself or my readers that town halls are all great works of art. They are not. Some few are, but they are very much in the minority. They do, however, form one of the largest and most significant types of Victorian buildings. The development from the small market-space-and-assembly-room to the great municipal palace took place entirely within Victoria's reign; and their very ubiquity makes town halls both a significant part of the nineteenth-century urban landscape and interesting as expressions of local pride and local character.

In short, to set town halls as a class alongside the select examples which mark the path of architectural development in the Victorian and Edwardian periods is largely to miss their point. Almost by definition they are backward-looking (though occasionally quite daring in detail), for they are statements in brick and mortar of urban consciousness and of pride and confidence in their towns. They have to mirror the history of their town as well as proclaim its wealth and future, and this is generally most easily done by the use of motifs with an established history. What makes this class of buildings worth studying is their significance in the developing townscape, not only in relation to the growth of their town, but also in the field of competition between towns. Each of these buildings was designed to be both a focus and a showpiece for its town as well as a functional creation. A whole vocabulary of forms appeared, that gained in clarity and credibility as it found increasing currency. What is fascinating is the way in which this vocabulary was employed by a great variety of architects, of the whole range of ability, to put across the municipal message and to house the increasing variety of municipal offices.

It is possible to trace a development of styles that roughly parallels the general development, though more often the late survival of a particular variety is more startling than the early adoption of any new fashion. From the full range of Italianate-classical and unarchaeological Gothic of the 1830s springs a numerous progeny of bulbous and undisciplined mid-Victorian buildings of vaguely Renaissance character. Alongside these there are the few last monuments of romantic classicism soon to be almost submerged in a rising tide of Gothic that was supposed to echo all the virtues of the olden days of merchant venturing. Yet, despite the prevalence of the Gothic, surely the most widespread and varied of the styles of town hall architecture, the classical strain continued here and there. In the late 1870s a dash of Queen Anne opened the way to a renewed eclecticism and the surface riches of Jacobethan, which provided all the freedom in planning that was once the prerogative of Gothic while allowing for as much grandeur in ornament as the various town funds allowed. Again this new fashion did not entirely obliterate its predecessor, but both Gothic and eclectic styles were swamped in the closing years of the century by the rise of Edwardian baroque. This suitably imperial and authoritarian mode seems almost to admit a difference in the relationship between the urban bureaucracy and the town it served. The style was fully established by the late 1890s and remained almost *de rigueur* until 1914 when the Great War brought an end to the comfortably bourgeois society that had for nearly a century expressed its communal self-satisfaction in stone and marble.

Though the town hall as a type is not as closely definable as, for instance, the bank or the school, I believe there is a spirit underlying the collection of buildings surveyed here that has something to teach us about Victorian attitudes to urbanisation and the attendant problems of community that were, dimly perhaps, recognised as the century progressed. The question of status seems to me intimately bound up with the problems of community consciousness and urban development; and it is in that light that we should consider these buildings. They answered complex and constantly developing functional and emotional needs, and they provided the expanding towns with a succession of buildings, good, bad and indifferent, that were always showy, often vulgar and domineering but very seldom dull when seen in relation to the town that built them.

I need to thank more people than I can name for help in completing this work, and am grateful for this opportunity to do so. In particular I am grateful to the Frank Gott Foundation for a grant towards the original research and more recently the British Council and the Open University for grants that have enabled me to complete the work. My thanks are also due to William Thompson of Leeds University who encouraged me to begin this study and to the late Professor Arnold Noach without whose constant advice and help I would never have completed the task. I am grateful, too, to many friends and colleagues for advice and especially to the late Professor Jim

Dyos and to Dr Stefan Muthesius. Most particularly also I am grateful to my wife and family for endless patience and to all the many town hall keepers, serjeants at mace and other town hall staff who made me welcome and showed me over town halls up and down the country.

Introduction

'There stood a thing out in the middle of the place, about 25 feet long and 15 wide, being a room stuck up on unhewn stone pillars about 10 feet high. It was the town hall.'[1] Cobbett singles out the town hall of Great Bedwyn, one of the fifty-six rotten boroughs of the 1832 Reform Bill, as typifying the system he so disapproved of. Town halls are certainly symbols, and this one at Great Bedwyn was simply a humble version of a common type which did literally consist of an upper room used for meetings and below it a space, usually open where market stalls could be stored. Brackley and Dursley provide typical examples of a kind that became common in the late seventeenth and eighteenth centuries, and which is still familiar from most parts of the country. They may reach heights of elegance as at Abingdon, or remain small and workaday as at Whitby. There are even odd variants such as the octagonal structure at Barnard Castle. The type has a long history in such examples as the market house at Tetbury (1655); but, though many of these buildings survived as working town halls of the nineteenth century, they are of a totally different kind from the town halls of Victoria's reign. Those grew up to fulfil the needs of the rapidly developing towns, that were for the first time urban centres such as we would understand. In them new wealth, new patrons and a new language of architecture opened the door to a rich and sometimes strange variety of buildings. Yet all the new generation do share with Great Bedwyn and the rest an important symbolic function. This symbolic function is of some importance not only as providing the unifying theme of what is in other ways a disparate type, but also because it is at bottom the symbolic value of the buildings that is the excuse for their elaborate decoration and for the series of useless and extravagant towers without which a nineteenth-century town hall seems hardly to deserve the name.

A symbol must be of something; and the nineteenth century did see a real change here. True, town hall balconies were still used for announcing the results of elections as at Great Bedwyn; but it was only in the nineteenth century that town living and local secular control of that living became the norm. The 1851 census is the first to record over 50 per cent of the population living in towns where previously the majority had lived in villages with the manor house or parish church as the symbols of power and stability. Throughout the nineteenth century the growth of towns and cities was as much due to immigration from (or absorption of) rural areas as to the natural increase of the urban population itself. Towns were new—the very word urbanisation hardly belongs to the nineteenth century—and lavish municipal palaces are one of the products of the newly developing consciousness brought about by the growth of urbanisation. Yet even this urbanisation was only a stage in a slow evolution with deep historical roots; and the new town hall did not spring suddenly into being. The individual history of each town to some extent affected its type of town hall; and the variety of history means that within the nineteenth century we have to consider buildings with something like twenty different titles as falling within the umbrella of town hall.[2] Not all town halls fulfilled all the functions, and new business might lead either to a new type or to modification, while local pride might retain an outmoded building. The very title Town Hall can be misleading if one compares those at Birmingham and Bradford, for example; while at Manchester in 1878 there was some controversy as to whether the new building, the epitome of a town hall, should even be called by this name.

It is, however, possible to distinguish a few types of building whose functions during the nineteenth and early twentieth century are, or may be, subsumed in the municipal buildings. One of the oldest of these types is the Moot Hall, some few of which survive. The actual title has a fine Anglo-Saxon pedigree suggesting the independent yeoman spirit and native Englishness that was so prized by the nineteenth-century burghers. The actual building was, of course, originally connected with the organisation of towns and with local jurisdiction, which thus forms one element in the history of the town hall type. The Newcastle moot hall of 1810–12 is an example of the attachment to this title. A closely connected type of medieval origin is the Guildhall, a more popular title in the nineteenth century because of its connections with trade. London, York and King's Lynn, for example, continued to use and modify medieval guildhalls for nineteenth-century municipal functions. Other towns, such as Nottingham, retained only the title for what were essentially office buildings. However, both these types originally contained a large hall for meetings which survives as an essential part of a town hall, though there may be some doubt whether it should be seen more as an ancestor of the council chamber or of the great hall.

Another distinct medieval strain comes in the Market Hall, though covered markets were then a rarity. This type, it seems to me, represents one of the earliest service building of the municipality, and we should remember that the granting of a market charter is, often enough, one of the first liberties of a borough. The provision of service buildings of different types is very largely a nineteenth-century development, but the public market survived as a very important part of the essence of township. The market-and-town-hall is the type of building castigated by Cobbett, but the type survived well into the nineteenth century. There are many examples of market halls adjoining or built on to town halls. Cardigan (1858), Castle Cary (1856), Mansfield (1835–6) and Darlington (market and public offices, 1863–4) are only a handful of examples; and we even find the market-and-town-hall appearing as the focus of completely new towns, as at Middlesbrough (1846). The complexity of municipal life and its building meant that separate markets became more and more common, and as such form no part of this survey. However, it should be noted in passing that they were often enough made the excuse for civic display, as at Bolton (1851–5), and the market-and-town-hall type was the most frequent predecessor of the town hall proper. It could either be extended, as at Salford (built 1825–7, extended 1849, 1862, 1875–8 and 1908), or completely rebuilt as two or more separate buildings, as at Barrow-in-Furness.

One final aspect of pre-industrial municipal building is the court house. Legal jurisdiction over its own district was an important stage in the development of urban independence; and a courtroom was an essential building. Pontefract town hall (1656 and 1782) and Worcester guildhall (1721) are fine examples of buildings in which the courts are the central feature. In assize towns the courts might require more accommodation, and later very often a separate building; but the capture of the West Riding assizes was a major factor in the design of the Leeds town hall as late as 1850.[3]

These three functions—meetings, markets and magistracy—have a long history, but there is another aspect of the urban community that helped to form the notion of a town hall. The assembly room is a creation of the eighteenth century, and can be linked to the rise of the middle classes. It is important for the town hall proper because it introduces the element of entertainment and jollification which seems an essential feature. Many eighteenth-century assembly rooms survived throughout the nineteenth century, and were often privately controlled. At Colchester a new private one was proposed as late as 1882. However, a number of these assembly rooms were built by the corporations, as at Worcester, and even more passed into their hands, as at Kidderminster; and they are the direct ancestors of the great halls of Leeds, Manchester and Liverpool. Like them, their use was in effect limited to a certain class of citizen, or rather to a certain socially acceptable type of activity.

A sort of cross between the assembly room and the market is to be found in the numerous corn exchanges put up in the nineteenth century (most of them date from the first half of the century). These again were usually privately owned but attracted a clientèle from a very precise social range and usually doubled as assembly rooms for the same group of local farmers and middle-class gentry. This was by and large the same social stratum that provided the ratepayers in the first half of the nineteenth century; and their aspirations in building seem to have been similar, whether in their capacity as shareholders in a Corn Exchange Company, or as town councillors. There are a number of cases too where exchanges are incorporated into new town hall buildings, though sometimes on rather specious grounds as a means of condoning extra expenditure. Mansfield (1835–6) and Rochdale (1866–71) are examples of both these attitudes. At Blackburn the first proposal to provide an exchange and club rooms in 1846 was the first step towards achieving the new town hall (1852–6). The failure to provide adequate space in the town hall led to the revival in 1859 of the public company which erected its own exchange premises (1865) directly opposite the town hall in a contrasting Gothic dress. In spite of such close connections, however, I have excluded corn exchanges, and their larger cousins, such as the royal exchange in Manchester or Bradford's woollen exchange, from this survey on the grounds that they generally retained their independence of the corporation and their special function rather longer. None the less it would be hard to think of the civic architecture of Leeds without Brodrick's corn exchange; and his success with the town hall was undoubtedly a factor in winning him the competition for the corn exchange. Also the variety of activities such buildings could house was a lesson that was not lost on later town hall builders.

The multi-purpose public hall, however, is an important part of the nineteenth-century and early twentieth-century town hall. Still it has to be remembered that the purpose was not quite as diverse then as now. When the celebrated Blondin applied to perform on the tightrope in the newly opened Leeds town hall, he was refused, 'it not being suitable'. There certainly was a need in the nineteenth-century towns for a large hall for meetings and entertainments of a wholesome kind. Theatres were emphatically not an acceptable alternative, and nineteenth-century piety would not allow the use of church buildings as we do today. This approach to the function of the hall underlies the undeniable earnestness about the town halls with their regular, and often loss-making organ concerts. It is echoed in the constant protestations, which we have to take as sincere, that the erection of a town hall would elevate the taste of the populace. There are a number of buildings with the name town hall that consist of nothing more than the public hall; and the many commemorative halls were often seen as an adjunct to or extension of the town hall. Though many were privately built, most of them passed into municipal ownership and need to be considered as part of the town hall movement.

The various municipal banquets were perhaps not quite in accord with this seriousness, and, as the halls became larger and filled with galleries and permanent seating, banquets became increasingly difficult to house. Thus we find, in the larger towns at least, the development of the separate banqueting hall. Sometimes, as at Barrow-in-Furness it even precedes the great hall. Examples such as that in the Birmingham council house fully live up to the expectations of civic splendour that hark back to the wicked extravagance of the unreformed corporations, but which form such an enduring, even endearing, element of our community consciousness. Whatever our feelings, it is worth remembering that, though these more private glories were authorised by the smaller circle of elected councillors who were also those who had the most enjoyment of them, they are none the less a major feature of many of the larger town halls. Even the comparatively modest Hove town hall (1880–1) had both a great hall and smaller banqueting hall as does the small size copy of Leeds town hall at Morley (1892–5).

These banqueting halls have really to be considered along with the mayor's apartments. Indeed they are very often built en suite. Here is a relic of the mansion houses of the greater cities, and the Manchester town hall does squeeze in a complete mansion house between the banqueting hall and the offices. The puritan ethic may rebel at such extravagance, but it was clearly felt essential that the elected head of a town should be able to receive formal visitors in surroundings that reflected credit on the town as a whole. The second Middlesbrough town hall (1883–8) is a considerable rarity in originally having no mayor's parlour at all.

The public or display elements of the town hall are generally the features which dictate its character. However the developing bureaucracy brought an inevitable and enormous increase in the amount of office and other space required. At the top of the scale came the committee rooms which were increasingly necessary as the pressure of business built up. Originally a single committee room would have been considered sufficient, as in Hansom's Birmingham town hall, but gradually the number increased. They needed to be substantial rooms and were usually well appointed which allowed them in some cases, particularly around the turn of the century, to double as part of the entertainment suite. This was not possible with the huge number of rooms required to house the growing army of clerks. A glance at the growth of municipal legislation shows the extent of the explosion, and by the last quarter of the nineteenth century town halls needed to house town clerks, borough treasurers, borough surveyors and engineers, rating departments, gas, water and sewage offices, medical officers, market inspectors, nuisance inspectors, highways departments and the whole paraphernalia of school boards and even Poor Law guardians, not to mention providing adequate storage for documents. In architectural terms this might mean a plethora of separate buildings, but the complications of scattering public servants were often enough the excuse for building huge centralised town halls or civic centres. The range in size is as great as the towns from humble Urban District Council offices to the monstrous municipal buildings of Birmingham or Liverpool. After 1882 they were joined by a further type, the County Council Offices, which lie outside the scope of this book, though examples such as Wakefield or Durham share many of the features of town hall building.

Closely allied to the office provision is the provision of the services themselves. It was not until the latter years of the century that separate buildings were provided for these, even in quite large towns. Two of the most important were the police and fire services. A fire station within the town hall was particularly common, and Rochdale provides a delightful example with its own iconography of phoenix and salamander corbels. A police station with cells would be essential if the town hall contained court space, and the Leeds town hall police station is still occupied as such. In a classical design these things could relatively easily be tucked away in the podium, but there were frequent problems with ventilating the cells and providing exercise yards and police parade space that did not impinge on the grander side of the building. The result was that, as the municipal machine expanded, these services were more frequently housed in other buildings. Often enough police station, fire station, public hall and municipal offices would form a coherent range of buildings in the city centre. This type of civic centre is most common in the twentieth century, but the public buildings at Cheetham Hill in Manchester provide an early example. They begin with the Cheetham Hill town hall of 1853–5, include the Prestwich Board of Guardians' Offices (1861) and end with a large public hall and baths of 1892. Perhaps more typical of this period is the magnificent baroque town hall at Lancaster (1906–9) which is flanked by a smaller and jollier little fire station that was none the less part of the same design.[4]

Another service that fitted well with the intentions of the public hall element was the reading room or news room and, later, library. At first these might well have been provided privately; but again legislation brought them within the municipal orbit, and several fine town halls, such as Rochdale, contain or used to contain libraries. Technical schools and schools of design were also quite acceptable in town halls, but usually there was only space in the smaller towns or in sub-districts of greater cities such as Newtonheath in Manchester (town hall and school of art, *c.* 1875). Other services were equally essential but less easy to house in the civic centre. Baths and wash-houses needed to be closer to the habitations of the lower orders and are only coupled with town halls in smaller townships such as Yardley near Birmingham (1898). The same was true of mortuaries and town yards.

A building to house all or even a fair proportion of these facilities would be large enough to require a living-in caretaker; and a dwelling for him was yet another of the problems the architect had to solve.[5] There might well need to be space for a flat for a police or fire superintendent as well, who would require more substantial accommodation. Thus the full-grown town hall was an extremely complex building. Problems of planning and construction led to an infinite variety of solutions. A good deal of ingenuity was required to fit all this into a rigidly classical plan, though the Leeds type had a successful progeny into the late 1880s. Gothic certainly gave more scope for irregular layout, and allowed for easier extension, but it lacked that obvious association with splendour and wealth that made the classical style almost *de rigueur* for banks. This seems a pity, for the best of the Gothic town halls and towers are without equal, but one senses a certain relief in the compromise of eclecticism ushered in by the adoption of the Queen Anne style at Leicester (1874–6). Eclecticism reached a peak in Sheffield town hall (1891–7), but the very freedom of the eclectic buildings seems to have led to less imaginative solutions; and as the proportion of office space grew in relation to the show element it seems to have become more difficult for a town hall to be a symbol clearly distinguishable from any large insurance office. Perhaps for that very reason towers seem to become almost more important in the closing years of the nineteenth century. Equally it is not surprising that the eclecticism of buildings such as Sheffield town hall was quickly superseded by the much grander Edwardian baroque of Belfast (1898–1906) or the designs for Plumstead municipal buildings (1899). However though this style itself allowed for considerable extravagance, opportunities for real display, as at Cardiff (1900–4) came rather more rarely. Though the baroque town halls that close this period can provide superb townscape, they do not often rise to the levels of comfortable vulgarity that make the best mid-nineteenth-century town halls such as Burslem a sheer delight.

I

The emergence of municipal democracy and the need for a town hall

Not until the eighteenth century in Britain did the town hall become a regular feature of the urban landscape, standing usually at the head of the market place. Grand town halls such as that at Liverpool (John Wood I, 1749–54) were very much a rarity, though some of these more elaborate buildings still dominate their town centres, as at Newark (John Carr, 1773) or Berwick-upon-Tweed (1754). The growth of municipal democracy in the nineteenth century, however, provided scope for building town halls that have remained landmarks in their town centres until very recently. Only in the late 1960s did the splendid tower of Leeds town hall begin to be dwarfed by the growing forest of tower blocks; but there are still many towns like Wakefield where the town hall tower even today stands as the dominant landmark visible for miles around. The story of these buildings forms an integral part not only of the history of architecture but of the understanding of the urban scene on to which our present life is still being grafted.

The growth of municipal democracy and legislation that provided the excuse for these buildings parallels the spread of urbanisation in the nineteenth century. It has been argued that the legislation itself, being mostly permissive, did relatively little to improve the general state of the towns. However the developing legal code secured the existence and power of the corporations. Then, as the problems of concentration of population brought home the need for detailed management, corporate power was increasingly extended with a corresponding need for ever larger corporate buildings. Birmingham provides a paradigm of the development. At the start of our period a Roman temple, with the Commissioners' business catered for by a single committee room in the basement, was seen as entirely appropriate for the Birmingham town hall (Fig. 1). By the 1870s Birmingham needed what was basically a wall of offices; but it

1 Birmingham town hall, J. A. Hansom and E. Welch, 1831–5; extended by C. Edge, 1835–54

still included a complete floor given over to the mayor and banqueting halls and council chamber (Fig. 2).[1] Within a very few years of the completion of this council house it became necessary, in 1884, to expand and build over the whole block with more offices round a huge courtyard. There was still an element of display in the midst of the functional offices, for one floor was given up to the art gallery, distinguished from outside by a handsome two storey portico and its own idiosyncratic tower. Even then the building could not keep pace with the growth of staff, and the council house–art gallery complex was barely complete before a further large extension was planned in 1899. This huge block was delayed until 1906 and completed in 1919. It in turn was followed by an even more grandiose civic centre scheme in the 1920s, only part of which was ever built. At the same time the original town hall was entirely renovated, or rather reconstructed, inside. Finally the 1960s saw a yet more extensive development which remains unfinished today.

From the first beginnings of the elected corporations development has been continuous and there is no particular reason, municipal or architectural for drawing a line at any one point. I have confined myself to buildings erected or planned between 1835 and 1914, since the development of municipal legislation within that period

2 Birmingham council house, R. Yeoville Thomason, 1874–9

represents a growth virtually from scratch to what is still recognisable as completeness. Edwardian municipal architecture is distinct from Victorian, but its dominant baroque style was fully established by the turn of the century and so needs to be considered along with municipal building in the various Victorian styles. Though the same civic pride can be traced in municipal building between the wars, it belongs to a very different architectural tale. The town hall story begins in 1835 with the Municipal Reform Act at a time when new elements were finding their way into the forms of architecture. Strict Greek revival and the outright picturesque were on the wane, and the seriousness of Pugin and the solidity of Barry's Travellers' Club were coming into their own.

The Municipal Reform Act did for the corporations what the Great Reform Bill did for parliament. In the eighteenth century 'the corporation was looked on as a body providing, at least in large cities, a dignified figurehead for public occasions, possessing various regulative powers which had become or were rapidly becoming entirely obsolete, often administering justices' justice of the urban variety, maintaining a small and usually loathsome gaol, managing corporate property or distributing legitimately or corruptly the usufruct of that property.'[2] Certainly the unreformed corporations were unrepresentative. They were usually Anglican and Tory, often elected for life, and even where there was municipal democracy it was restricted to freemen whose privilege was often the gift of the corporation. Far too many industrialists, like James Aspinall Turner and Joseph Potter (later to become the first two mayors of Manchester), were excluded from direct participation in their own municipal democracy. So it was hardly a surprise that the group of Whig barristers who formed the 1833 Royal Commission on Municipal Corporations found that 'in most cases all identity of interest between the corporations and the inhabitants had ceased'.[3] They castigated non-resident freemen and cited various malpractices: the Recorder of Lancaster did not once attend Quarter Sessions between 1810 and 1832; the magistrates of Malmesbury were often illiterate; the corporation of Leicester once spent £10,000 of corporate funds on securing a parliamentary election.

The Act of 1835 established at once 178 municipal corporations,[4] which were to be governed by an elected council. They would have the right to levy a rate and the duty to publish accounts. All property rights of freemen were to be abolished,[5] and any income vested in the new corporation. This was a major advance and formed the basis for municipal unity until the last reorganisation. However, though it opened up the possibility, it did not provide the impetus for town hall building, since there were really two aspects of corporate control of a town only one of which was altered by this Act. Legal jurisdiction has to be distinguished from the provision of services. After 1835 the new municipal boroughs had legal jurisdiction through their petty sessions and borough courts.[6] These had of course to be housed, but in most cases there already was a court house; and courts alone were too firmly linked to the national judicial system with its external authoritarian symbolism to give rise to buildings with that element of specifically local involvement that marks a town hall such as Leeds. The other essential excuse for building was the housing and provision of services, and that for the time being remained outside the control of most corporations. The managers in this sphere were the innumerable boards of Commissioners set up under various Local Acts to supervise paving, streets, town improvements, markets and the like. By about 1835 a more or less complete urban code was established; and, although in most cases the corporation could expect some representation (the numbers of freeholders qualifying for election was not generally all that large), it was the Town Commissioners who provided and regulated the services. Under the 1835 Act they might hand over their powers to the new corporations 'if they pleased'. Most did not, and as late as 1884 forty-four boroughs were still controlled by commissioners.

Thirty-three survived until 1893 when they were merged into the newly formed Urban District Councils whose offices form a class of poor relations of proper town halls.

Certainly the functions administered by the established boards of commissioners provided a need for communal buildings, and a number of commissioners did in fact erect town halls. The first Manchester town hall (*c.* 1819–45) is a good example. However these buildings needed to be individually financed by public subscription. Even more frequently, where the need for markets or public rooms was generally felt, a public company would be set up with the express purpose of building and running the premises. Frequently these became the town hall when the commissioners were absorbed into the corporation or the public company bought out. Salford, Kidderminster and Bishop Auckland (Figs 3, 4, 66) are only a few among many examples, and in the smaller towns privately financed town halls of this sort are probably as common as those built by the corporations themselves. This indicates a real need for some such buildings, and, significantly, even these publicly financed buildings show the same desire for display as the later corporate palaces.

Without the 1835 Act, however, no corporations as such would have been able, had they ever needed, to put up the sort of town hall that later became common. The date of incorporation of each town is often important, therefore, in the history of each town hall, and may even be the excuse for immediate building. Rochdale, for instance, was incorporated in 1856, and a town hall sub-committee was already at work by the end of 1858.[7] The rush to build cannot be dismissed as the chance megalomania of the early mayors. There was also a genuine and widespread desire for a symbolic centre expressive of the new status which is still seen in towns created municipal boroughs at the end of the period. Morley held its competition within six years, and completed its town hall within ten years of its incorporation. Leigh was even quicker with incorporation in 1899 followed by plans for a town hall in the same year. The resulting building is still the chief focus of a borough created by the administrative decision to amalgamate four local urban districts.

The Municipal Reform Act was only the start of a process, and needed almost immediate modification; but only the Local Government Acts of 1882, 1888 (with the creation of boroughs of county status[8]) and 1894 materially altered the spread of municipal corporations. The 178 corporations established in 1835 were increased by 38 in 1882; 155 boroughs were given freedom from County Council jurisdiction in 1888; and by 1903 there were 313 municipal boroughs in England and Wales. The bulk of the general municipal legislation did not need to deal with the status of the borough. Individual towns could apply for a charter of incorporation from the Crown as they felt necessary, and such applications were usually granted provided the town met certain criteria of urbanisation. Most municipal legislation had to do with

3 Salford town hall, Richard Lane, 1825–7

4 Kidderminster corn exchange and public rooms, Bidlake & Lovatt, 1853–5; town hall (to right), J. T. Meredith, borough architect, 1876–7

services. To begin with much of the progress was haphazard. Each set of improvements needed to be authorised by a local act of parliament, which until 1835 usually originated with the vestry and established the board of commissioners. This was an expensive business and smaller communities were slow to seek new Local Acts. However the quantity of such Acts increased dramatically from the 1850s on, and in terms of town hall building had very tangible results.

Another important factor was the development of the control of local finance. Municipal corporations had the right to levy rates for disposal as they wished and also enjoyed the profits of any municipal undertakings such as the gas works, which were often taken into municipal control. It was also possible for them to issue stock, and after about 1860 to borrow money from government on easy terms for urban improvements which included the building of town halls.[9] Most smaller towns had to apply to the Local Government Board for specific loans for town hall building, and their applications were scrutinised by inspectors at a public enquiry. Applications were occasionally referred back, but seldom rejected outright. The Limited Liability Act of 1873 meant that markets and public halls erected by subscription companies could be more securely funded and on rather easier terms; though such companies could and did go bankrupt, as at Kidderminster. It was usual in such cases for their premises to be taken over by the council which was, of course, in no such danger. The very permanence of the corporations meant that they had no inhibitions about contracting debts on a building that would not be repaid for a generation or more.

The growing importance of the new corporations and of the vestries, and above all the increasing size of their membership, positively required meeting space and offices for the attendant clerks. In most towns this was arranged by one or other of the boards of commissioners or later the council; but in London (where there were thirty-eight separate vestry boards in 1880) the vestry hall existed as a separate type. The buildings were almost always classical in design to express their freedom from ecclesiastical control (cf. Figs 5, 6);[10] but their general arrangement with large hall, committee rooms and offices was identical with many small town halls. Vestry halls performed all the functions of town halls in many London boroughs until the local government acts of the 1880s turned their parishes into boroughs and the buildings, or their replacements, became town halls. Thomas Allom's Islington vestry hall of 1856–8 (Fig. 6) is typical of the earlier buildings, and Mile End (1860–2) and Paddington (1853) are similar. Many vestry halls, however, date from the 1870s which underlines their connection with the control of services. St Clement Danes, St George's Hanover Square, Hampstead, Bermondsey, Kensington and Kensal Town all planned or built vestry halls between 1872 and 1878; and others such as Fulham and Lambeth were altering or enlarging older buildings at the same time.

5 Chelsea vestry hall, unsuccessful competition design by Henry and Sidney Godwin, 1858 (*Builder*, vol. XVI, 1858)

6 Islington vestry hall, Thomas Allom, 1856–8 (*Building News*, vol. III, 1857)

These buildings are mostly unmemorable, though they excited the same fierce interest and competition as their provincial counterparts. The Kensington vestry hall competition drew sixty-two designs in 1877, and Fulham as late as 1885 drew sixty-three. A number of important architects were involved. Sir William Tite, for instance, was a prominent member of the Chelsea vestry when their hall was built. Charles Bell took second prize for the Hampstead vestry hall in 1876; and Charles Barry assessed the Westminster vestry hall competition in 1880, for which competitors included J. P. Seddon. The buildings, however, suffered from being of necessity rather small in a large urban concentration. Site values were high, sometimes approaching 50 per cent of the total cost, and the vestries had not the same financial freedom as the boroughs. Kensington vestry hall in 1880 cost only around £40,000, and usually the allowances were between £10,000 and £20,000 (£18,000 at Kensington). For that price it was not possible to erect a building that could compete with the larger banks, warehouses and government offices, and so these vestry halls fail in one important aspect of town hall building, that of forming the townscape. Their almost uniform adoption of red brick and Portland stone dressings under a roof of green Westmorland slates was not, in London of the 1870s, distinctive enough to mark them out. From the 1880s they were largely replaced by new buildings now called town halls; but again though the possibilities were there, the sites usually prevented the buildings from contributing significantly. The use of Portland stone facing tended to mark them out as authority's buildings (e.g. St Pancras, 1892 or Bethnal Green, 1909–10), but it was generally only in the outer boroughs such as Croydon that they could compete satisfactorily with their neighbours. One might contrast the success of Deptford's cheerful little building on a relatively unpromising site with the totally insignificant Holborn town hall.[11]

Provincial Town Commissioners, on the other hand, might have more scope. A specific Act of Parliament was needed to establish them, but it did give them a job to do and the means and power to do it. If that job required a building it could be as grand as they deemed necessary, as at Kidderminster or Eye (Fig. 7). Francis Goodwin's town hall in Manchester was just such a building, though it is worth noting that it took twenty years to build. A town hall was not the primary requirement, the services provided by the commissioners were; and there seems to have been more reluctance on the part of the boards of commissioners, who after all administered a specific rate, to indulge in lavish spending. This is clearly seen at Mansfield where the town hall of 1835–6 (Fig. 50) is fitted into the schemes of the Improvement Commissioners established by an Act of 1823. They resisted plans for a town hall when they were first proposed in 1831; and took no action until the citizens got plans drawn and arranged a public subscription which netted £8,000 within a week. The actual building was put up by a town hall company who bought the site from the commissioners, but it stands on land bought by them in 1823 as part of a plan to improve the Nottingham road. It contained, besides an assembly room and an exchange, committee rooms, a market, shambles and a lock-up. In fact it was a complete town hall and in 1838 the commissioners were persuaded to lay out the open space in front of it that is still the centrepiece of Mansfield.

To begin with, commissioners and councils needed simply a room to meet in, but their advisers and clerks increasingly needed accommodation. Individual boards of commissioners often had very specific tasks such as paving or lighting or provision of water. However even before 1832 it had become common practice to introduce general Improvement Acts, and the resulting Improvement Commissioners had a wide field of action. The various local acts are too numerous to mention in detail, but dealt with bridges, ferries, roads, subways, paving, lighting, gas supply, water, railways, buses, trolleys, trams, canals, drainage and many other aspects of local government including control of the machine itself. There was even a detailed model

7 Eye town hall, E. B. Lamb, 1856–7 (*Building News*, vol. III, 1857)

in the Town Improvement Clauses Act (1846) to bring some measure of uniformity. National acts such as those which governed the provision and control of gaols and established various lighting, watching and scavenging duties in the 1820s and early 1830s also provided uniformity. As the century progressed there was a considerable body of general legislation that affected the municipal corporations. Among the earlier important items were the Public Health Act (1848), the Police Act (1856), the Municipal Corporations Act (1857) and after 1850 many others such as the Public Libraries Act. Although most of the legislation was permissive, and hence did not always lead to effective action, the taking of any action at all would increase the size of the municipal bureaucracy. The growth was particularly marked from the 1860s on when the flow of legislation became a real flood. Town halls of the 1870s and later reflect this growth and the way in which the corporations were steadily swallowing independent local enterprises.

Water and gas companies were among the first to be taken over by corporations and the supervision and collection of payments required a considerable staff. The gas office, for instance, was by far the largest 'working' space in the Birmingham Council House extension of 1884. The various building acts required inspectors and storage of deposited plans from the 1860s on. The 1870 Education Act meant an immediate need for school board offices, which, though often separately housed,[12] were none the less municipal buildings; and the ensuing provision of school buildings meant a great increase in the borough surveyor's (or architect's) office. The Tramways Act (1870) would have necessitated a similar growth in the borough engineer's department, though where a corporation was directly involved in transport there were usually separate offices in or near the depot. In 1875 there was another Public Health Act and an important Housing Act, not to mention the first of the Electric Lighting Acts. Local government, as we have seen, was itself modified in the 1880s; and the 1890s saw yet further duties laid on the corporations by the Housing of the Working Classes Act, more public health acts and so on. The welter of legislation in itself necessitated a growth in the corporation's legal department, the town clerk's office. And for each expansion of the municipal buildings themselves there needed to be a corresponding growth in the estates and surveyor's offices and in the corps of porters and attendants under their chief the town hall keeper.

This mass of regulations, coupled with a steady growth of urban populations that did not begin to ease until the 1890s, provided not only an excuse but a genuine necessity for building. This can be clearly seen at Middlesbrough where the municipal buildings of the 1880s form four sides of a large quadrangle (Figs 13, 31). Behind its uniform gothic façade was a veritable warren of segregated departments with ten entrances and no less than thirteen staircases, but without any complete means of internal circulation. Leeds town hall (1853–8) (Fig. 8) was the last of a more formal type containing little in the way of offices. There the allocation was not planned at the outset, and a list of 1858 mentions only town clerk's, borough surveyor's and borough treasurer's offices in addition to the courts, mayoral accommodation and great hall. As early as 1864, though, when finishing work on the town hall was still going on, Brodrick offered plans for the development of the adjacent site as municipal buildings. Though his plans were refused, the need to build was only resisted until 1876 when a major competition resulted in yet another huge pile of buildings that was itself quickly followed by a further block. The pressure on town hall accommodation was such that in Manchester in 1863 it was decided to stop letting any rooms in the

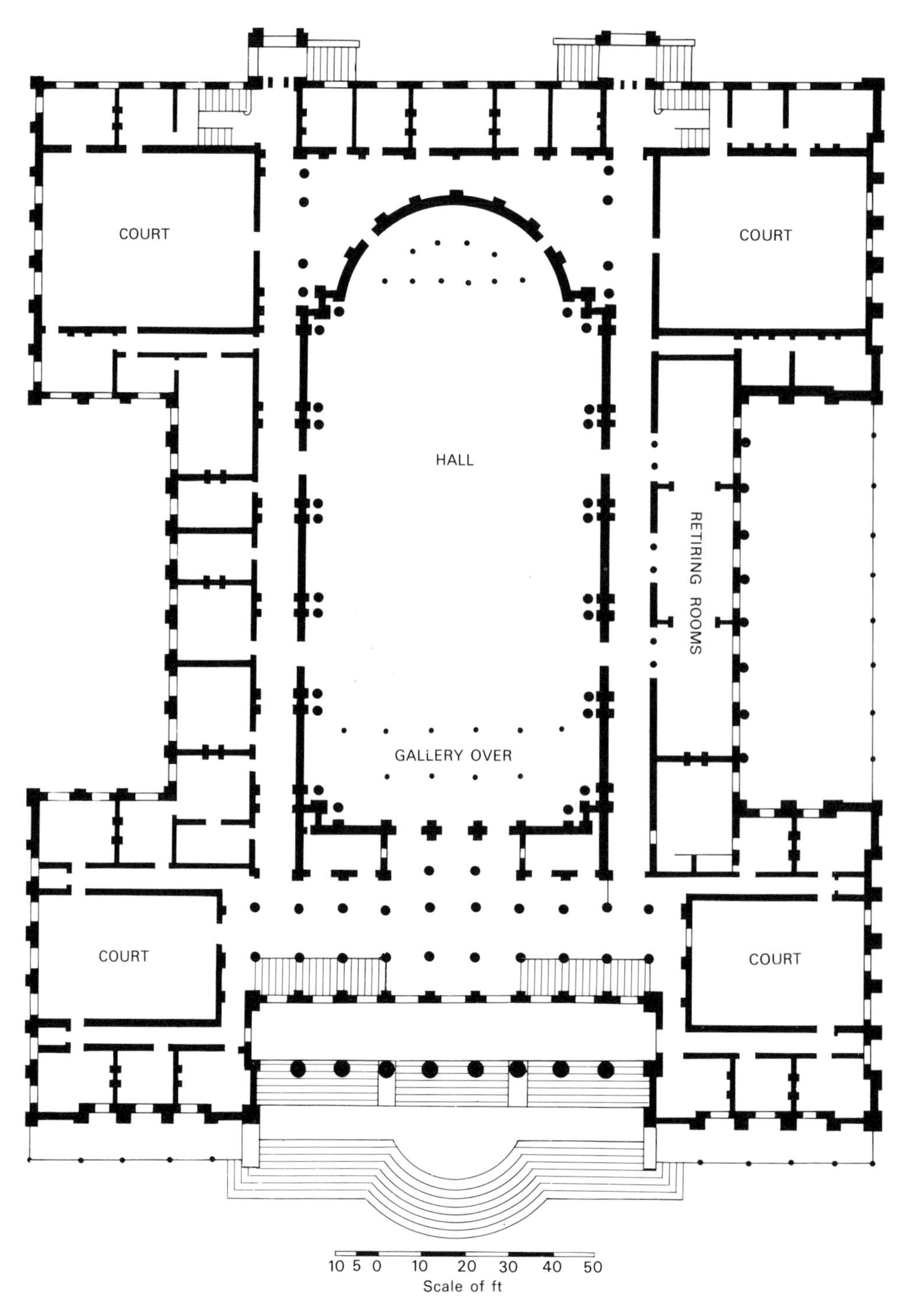

8 Leeds town hall, competition plan scheme 1, ground floor, Cuthbert Brodrick, 1852 (redrawn from an original in Leeds City Archives)

town hall as the outside use of the committee rooms made it impossible to conduct the business of the corporation. Manchester also called in an architect in 1864, at a very early stage in the planning for the new town hall, to consider whether enough accommodation could be provided on the rather cramped site proposed. That it could was amply proved by Waterhouse's ingenious building that sufficed until well into this century (Fig. 9).[13] Other towns were not so fortunate or efficient, and the problem of town hall extensions is a frequent one. At Bolton the adoption in 1863 of a design based closely on the Leeds town hall led to considerable problems at an early date. The building was completed in 1873 but by the 1890s its accommodation was stretched to the limit, and the problem was only solved by the very expensive expedient of doubling the size of the building in an exactly matching style. This was in fact delayed until the 1930s, but by then the town needed a further range of buildings that forms the present semicircular backdrop to the town hall. In the interim various departments were scattered in different offices around the town.

This sort of difficulty was clearly recognised by the end of our period, and provision for future extensions was frequently specified in the architect's brief. This was so at Sheffield where E. W. Mountford built a large town hall in 1891–7 (Fig. 15) and a short while later extensions were added, to his designs (1902ff. and 1912). Generally there was a longer gap and often a different architect, as at West Hartlepool. Barrow-in-Furness was realistic in specifying (1877) that competitors should design a building that could be built in parts. The extensions that would complete the courtyard still have not arrived. The need to allow for extensions was one of the main themes of an article on municipal buildings in 1892,[14] where it was even inferred that Waterhouse had deliberately allowed for extensions at Manchester by surrounding the great hall with space that could be built up if necessary. Happily this suggestion has not been taken up.[15] Generally speaking, however, the town hall builders made the greatest impact when they found the determination to complete their building regardless of the extension problem. In an age when architectural fashions followed one another in such swift succession, and when it would normally take about a decade from conception to completion of a major town hall, it was better to establish the character of one building and leave it to later architects to devise other structures as a complement or a foil. The possibilities can best be seen at Manchester where the town hall extension and library (1925ff.) form one of Vincent Harris's best contributions to civic building, and the town hall extension does not detract in any way from the Waterhouse pile. Within our period a similar problem occurred at Liverpool. After the completion of the St George's hall (Fig. 17) and after the eighteenth-century town hall had been modified as far as possible, the corporation surveyor John Weightman designed a separate block of municipal offices for a site half way between the two

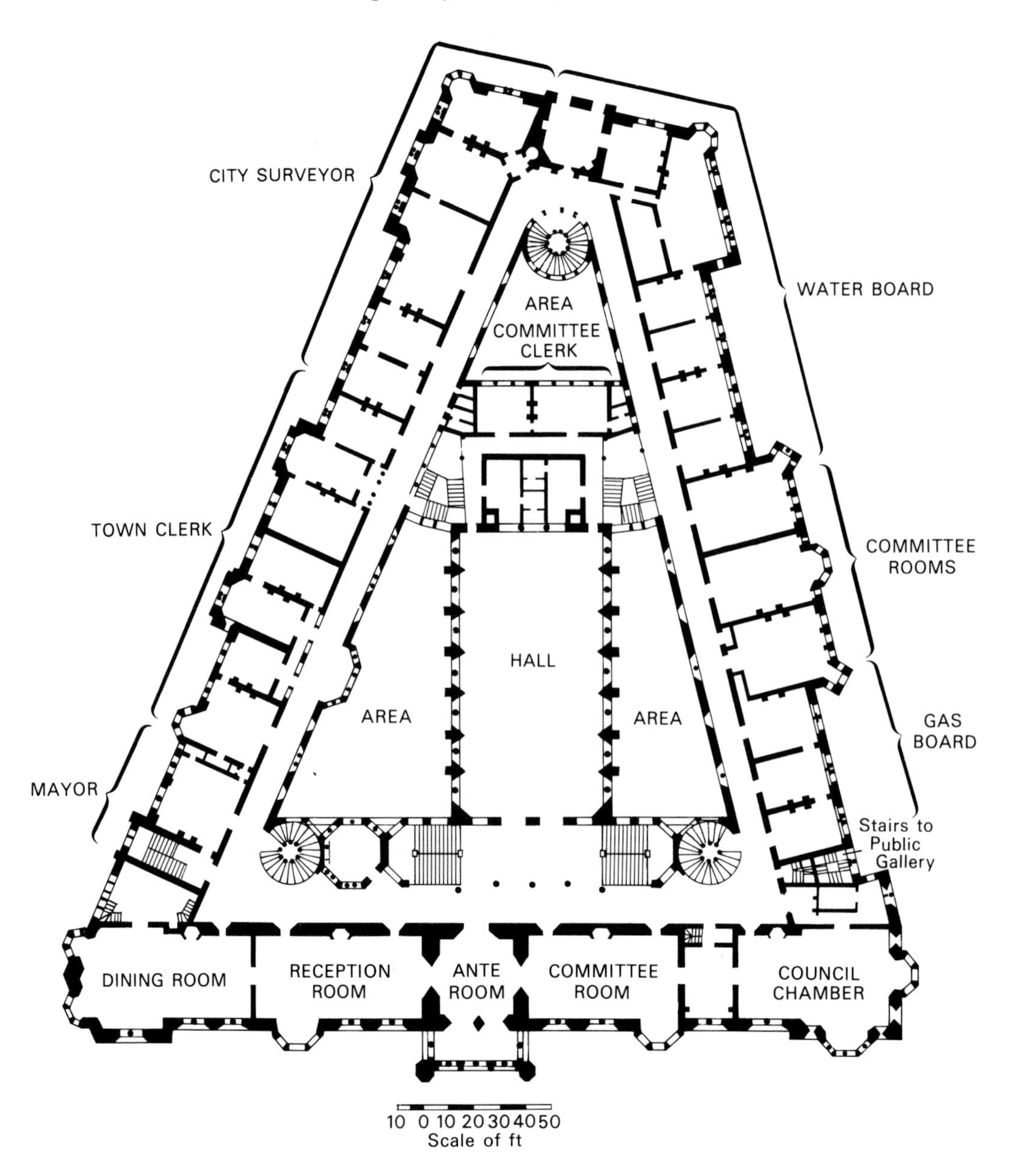

9 Manchester town hall, second stage competition plan, principal floor, Alfred Waterhouse, 1868 (redrawn from *Builder*, vol. XXVI, 1868)

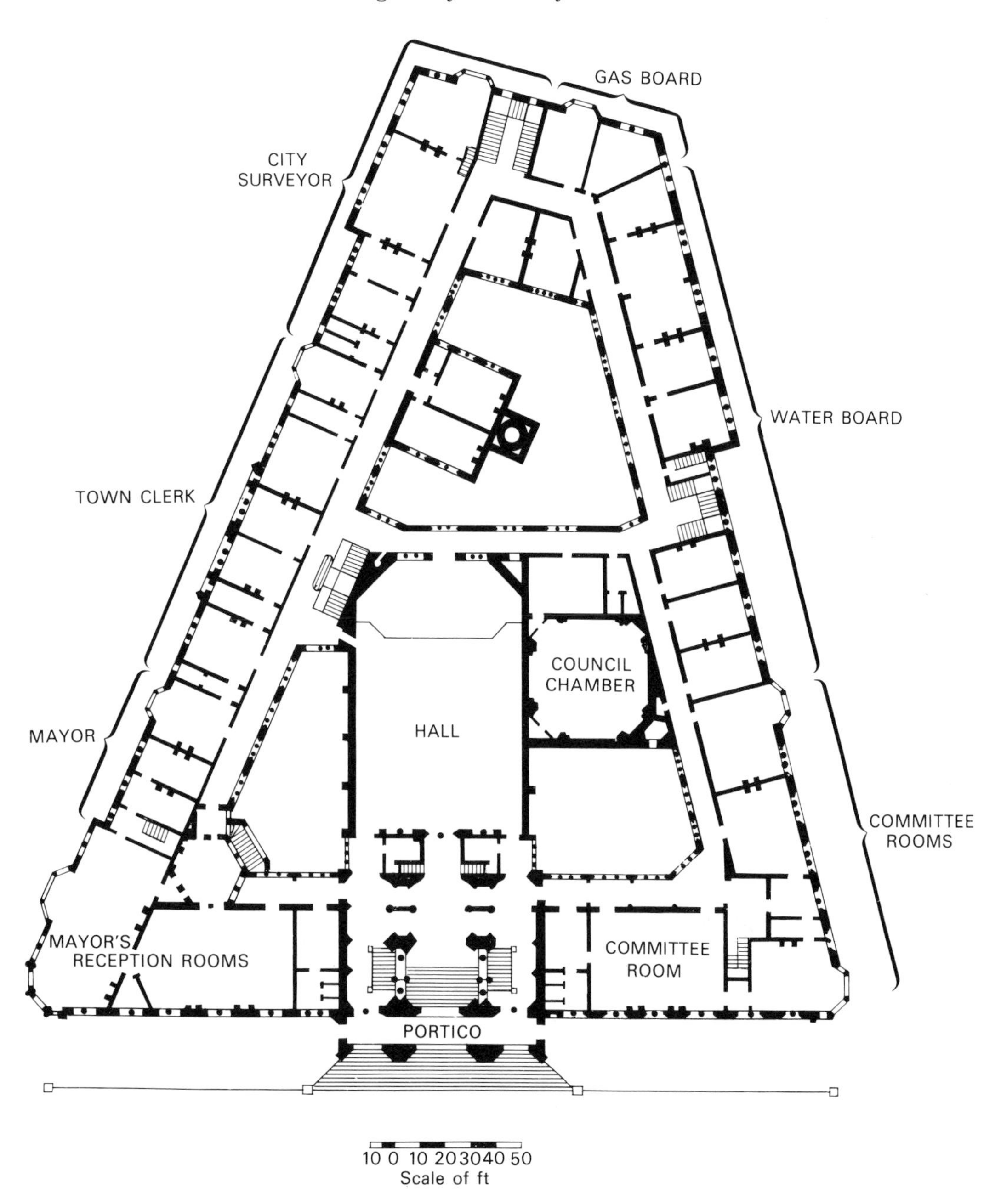

10 Manchester town hall, second stage competition plan, principal floor, Speakman & Charlesworth, 1868 (redrawn from *Builder*, vol. XXVI, 1868)

11 Liverpool municipal buildings, J. Weightman and E. R. Robson, 1861–9 (*Architect*, vol. I, 1869)

buildings (Fig. 11). The new block itself had provision for rearward extensions that were never in fact built; but their grandiose classical design clearly relates them to the other two municipal buildings, and their spire advertises their presence without detracting from the famous town hall dome. Again the later range of public buildings in William Brown Street makes a fitting backdrop for the St George's hall. Elsewhere even groups of quite modest buildings, such as those at Cheetham Hill in Manchester

(1853–5 by T. Bird and 1892 by Booth & Chadwick) by all accounts stood agreeably together.

Examples of extensions planned, built or merely allowed for are commonplace from the 1860s on. However, so long as a single façade was required the first comer would usually set the tone and only a bold hand would flatly contradict what was done. Aberdeen public buildings, with its solid Scottish baronial front by Peddie & Kinnear (1865–8) is not modified by the alterations and the new wing of 1895–1900. Reading and Chelsea provide further examples of extensions whose style is largely governed by the original block. Indeed once local democracy had established itself and built a town hall it was generally only by demolition that a former symbol could be superseded, as at Hull in 1906–14. It is interesting that there was usually strong opposition to the demolition of old town halls even when their functions were completely overtaken by the pace of legislation.[16]

Given the process of accretion and the wide range of functions to be found in different town halls it makes little sense to talk of town hall planning in a vacuum. The very restriction of cramped city centre sites, though an incentive to ingenuity, increased the variety of planning. There are several examples of town halls with a narrow frontage planned on a linear basis with reception rooms to the front, offices in the middle and courts or hall (or more frequently a market building) to the rear with a separate frontage to another street. At the other extreme are rarities planned vertically, like Colchester with the great hall on the second floor directly over the mayoral apartments, or like Wakefield with the mayor's parlour high up behind an overgrown dormer window. Though they are often the grandest there are relatively few examples of town halls on island sites such as Leeds or Bolton. In spite of the variety, however, there are certain common features in town hall planning that are specific to the new building type and which helped to shape its design. One can distinguish three main elements which are or may be present in a town hall and which involve special planning. The complete town hall would contain a public hall and mayoral suite, council chamber and courts, and offices. To these might be added various services such as a fire station or library. Each of these elements had its effect on the plan.

The grand hall was central to the display aspect of these buildings and crucial in determining the plan (Fig. 18). The very size of the hall (seating for upwards of 1,000 was by no means uncommon) allowed little scope for variety in placing. In a gothic composition the hall could be set separately to one side as at Middlesbrough, where it is effectively another building. Yet the most common position was in the centre of the building with a ring of offices around it. Leeds (Fig. 8), Bolton, Manchester (Fig. 9) and Cardiff are all examples of this type. In such a position the hall could be top lit as at Northampton or lit by windows at clerestory level. However the central position increased the problem of access. A grand entry for gala occasions, often with a foyer or waiting hall, was essential, and wide passages would be needed with several doors to allow easy access for the large numbers attending functions. If the hall was at first floor level, as at Rochdale or Manchester, a grand staircase was also necessary. This might afford a fine opportunity for show, but also required considerable space. Even the small town hall at Deptford has a huge and splendid central stair. The simplest solution was to place the stairs in a separate block, as at Rochdale, or in the tower, as at Halifax, but this was impossible on a cramped site or in a tightly knit composition, and an architect's skill in designing stairs might greatly affect the success or cost of the building. At Leeds a fine stair designed by Brodrick was abandoned to make way for the tower, and the four staircases that were built are far from matching up to the grandeur of the rest of the building.

The mayor's parlour and reception rooms can be considered jointly with the hall as parts of the celebratory element. Their status required properly grand access, and they were almost always designed to be reached via the main entrance and grand stairs. The reception room or rooms would be arranged en suite or at least connecting so that all or part of the rooms could be used depending on the occasion (Fig. 15). The mayor's parlour needed to be close to the reception suite and was often directly connected with it. Such a sequence of grand rooms required careful placing, and they were usually, though not always, a dominant feature of the façade. Most frequently they are set across the principal front at first floor level, and sometimes provided with a balcony for formal appearances (such as the announcing of election results) as at Leigh (Fig. 100) or Woolwich. At Leeds, however, the reception rooms were set to one side; and Bolton was specifically criticised for the fact that the mayor's parlour was only reached by a passage running past some of the offices. By raising these rooms to the level of the piano nobile their select occupants could if necessary be segregated from the throng in the public hall. This was rare before the 1890s, but in later buildings it was even possible to use the hall and reception rooms for quite different functions simultaneously. At Lancaster, Stockport and Woolwich, for instance, the hall is treated separately and given a lower status than the gala reception rooms by being placed to the side or rear with independent access from the street.

The second element was the housing of urban democracy, the core of which was the council chamber. This was usually closely connected with the mayor's apartments, but it needed also to be linked to the town clerk's offices and committee rooms. In smaller or poorer towns, such as Deptford, the hall might do double duty as a council chamber, but a specially furnished room, often semi-circular in shape, was more usual. The mayor, aldermen and councillors attended in state so the chamber would generally be accessible from, though not always close to, the grand entry. It was almost always on the same floor as the mayoral suite, but usually of double height since the public were admitted and generally accommodated in a gallery. The size of the room and its symbolic function often led to its being handled as a special feature of the façade, as at Cardiff; but access for the public was seldom by the grand entry and was generally a matter for some ingenuity. Barrow-in-Furness and Leigh afford typical examples of grand council chambers which the public reach by means of concealed spiral stairs or attic passages.[17]

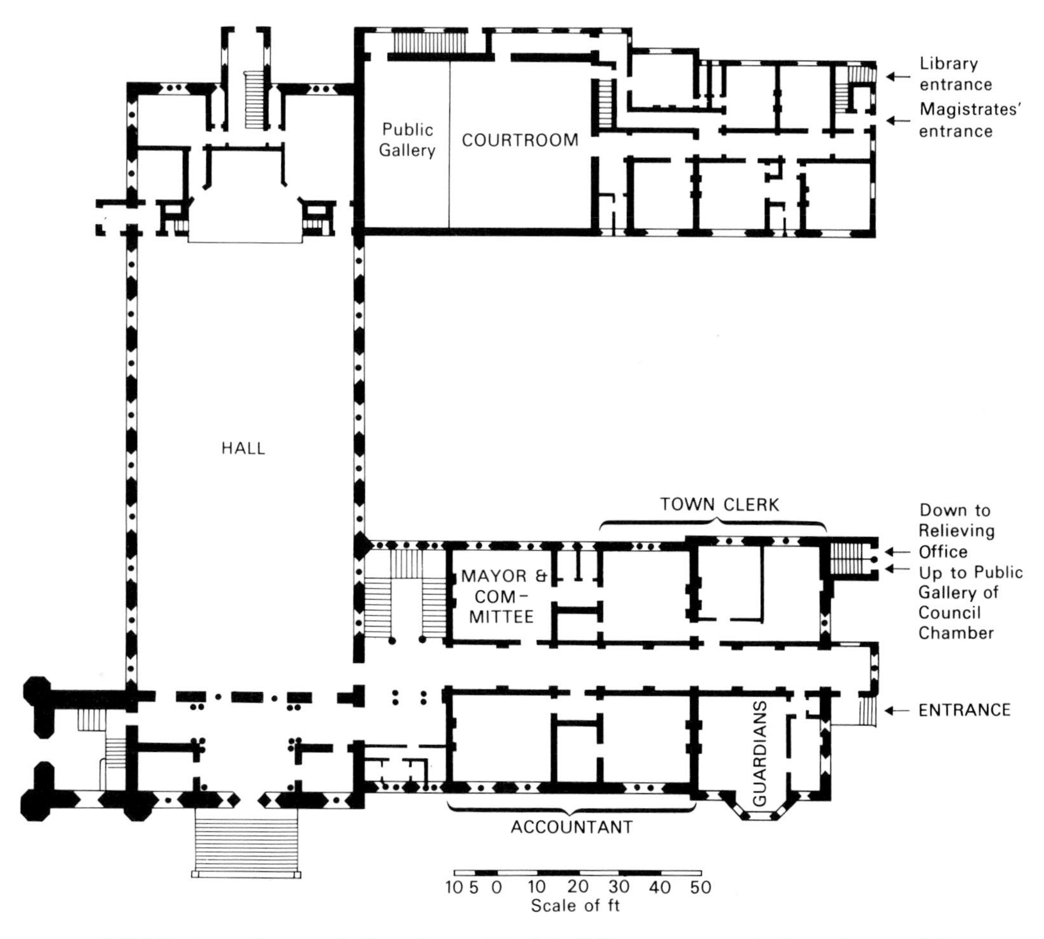

12 Middlesbrough town hall and municipal buildings, proposed plan of ground floor, Alfred Waterhouse, 1875 (redrawn from a lithograph in Cleveland County Archives)

Segregation of access was also crucial in the courts. Here again the hall or even the council chamber might be used as a magistrates' court; but the problems of planning proper courts were complicated. Magistrates, prisoners and witnesses at least needed different entries and waiting areas. This often led to great complexity as, for instance, in Waterhouse's design for Middlesbrough (Fig. 12), where separation of access is only maintained by unconnected passages running side by side. Frequently separate entries to the building were provided, and magistrates' and prisoners' doors are almost always on different sides of the building or at least at different levels. At Leeds the prisoners' door was in the podium and well away from all the other entrances. These arrangements meant that it was easier to set courtrooms at the corners of buildings, and often at first floor level, allowing space for a police station and cells with direct access to the dock beneath the court and magistrates' rooms. In some cases the police were then able to use the basement of the hall as a parade space, though this was more frequently provided in a yard within the building, as at Manchester, or to the rear from which there was discreet access for the villains and their usually disreputable visitors. Nowadays we seldom have to face the problems of having prison cells close to our gala centres, but the difficulties involved were not easy to overcome and failure certainly offended Victorian sensibilities. At Leeds there were problems both with the ventilation of the cells and with prisoners communicating with friends outside, since some of the cells had windows close to the grand entrance. These soon had to be enclosed in a yard with a monumental wall and barred gateway.

Local jurisdiction could be completely separated, as at Manchester, but local democracy required more than just a council chamber. We have seen that a single commissioners' meeting room was sufficient in Birmingham in 1832. Soon, however, a series of committee rooms was needed. They were often moderately grand and generally placed near the council chamber. The number and size varied enormously, and even in quite grand town halls, such as Lancaster, they might be designed to double as reception rooms. In addition there were the offices for the growing army of municipal servants. At first these were little distinguished; and at Leeds they were not even bespoken by their occupants until after the building was complete. They were, however, easily divided into departments such as town clerk's, borough surveyor's and so on. Each department needed an inner private office for the senior executive, and an outer office for the clerks. The difficulty again was in providing access. In larger buildings a separate entry was useful since the grand entry and stairs would not be suitable and might anyway be thronged with members of the public attending tea parties or lunchtime organ recitals. However many town halls such as Northampton and Colchester have only one main entrance. A narrow street frontage would almost

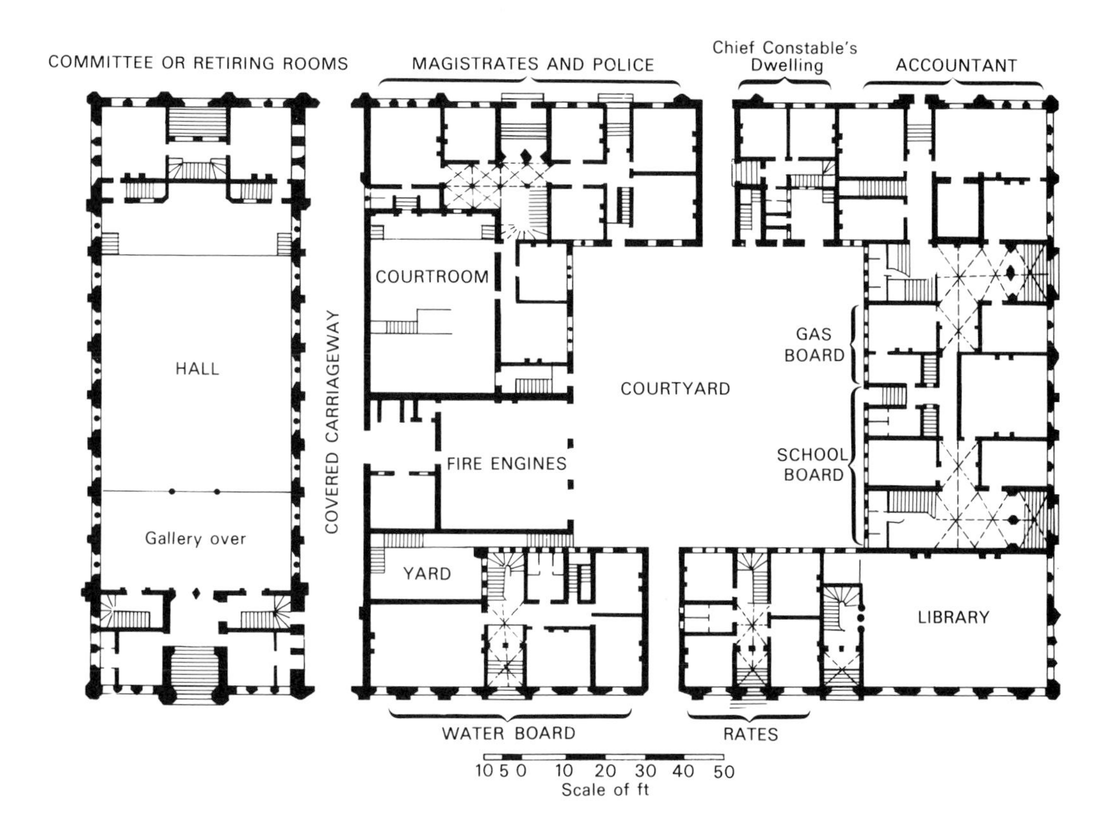

13 Middlesbrough town hall and municipal buildings, ground floor plan, G. G. Hoskins, 1883 (redrawn from an original in Cleveland County Archives)

certainly force such an arrangement. Sometimes separate entries were provided for almost every department, as at Middlesbrough (Fig. 13); but two or three office entries, as at Barrow or Rochdale, was more common. Internally there was a need for easy communication between departments by staff, and if possible this was kept separate from the public access to the offices. Usually the large clerks' offices were interconnecting; but the Sheffield firm of Flockton & Gibbs claimed a patent on the idea of separate passages (Fig. 14). The number and size of the departments, however, led to an almost infinite variety of arrangement. If the town hall contained offices dealing with an undesirable part of the public, such as applicants for relief under the poor law, they were usually provided with a quite separate entry. At Middlesbrough Waterhouse designed a spacious ground floor board room for the Guardians but the relieving office was reached by a narrow stair to the basement beside the equally unobtrusive stair to the public gallery of the council chamber.

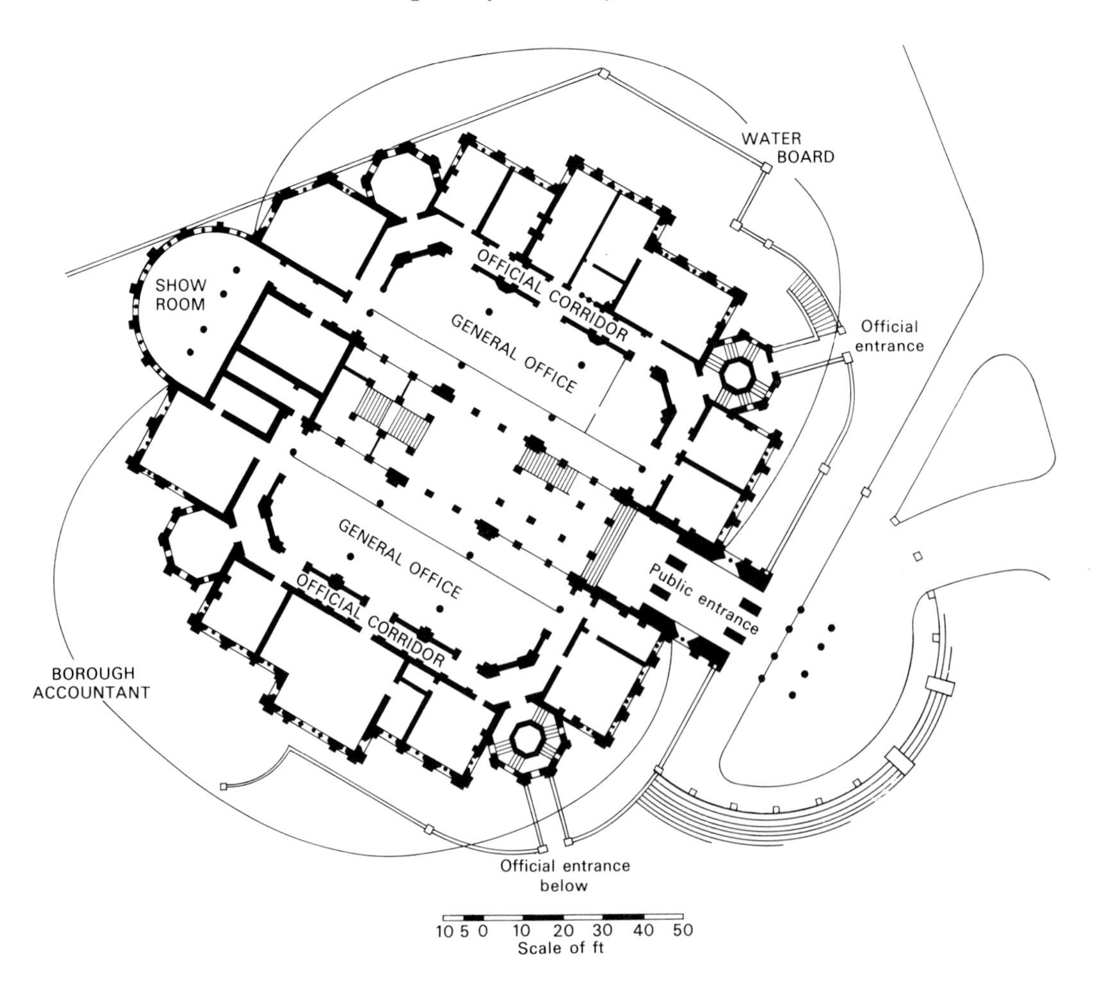

14 Sheffield town hall, premiated competition plan, ground floor, Flockton & Gibbs, 1890 (redrawn from *Builder*, vol. LIX, 1890)

The growing difficulty of finding convenient storage for records seems to have been little considered in an age devoted to statistics and reports. Town hall roof spaces and basements were used in this way from an early stage, and are still crowded with old files and documents. An attempt to use the tower at Leeds for storage had to be abandoned as the louvres were not weatherproof and the documents were soon ruined. However at Stourbridge (1887) and Sheffield (1891–7), for example, towers were designed for storage and special strong rooms constructed in them. In general,

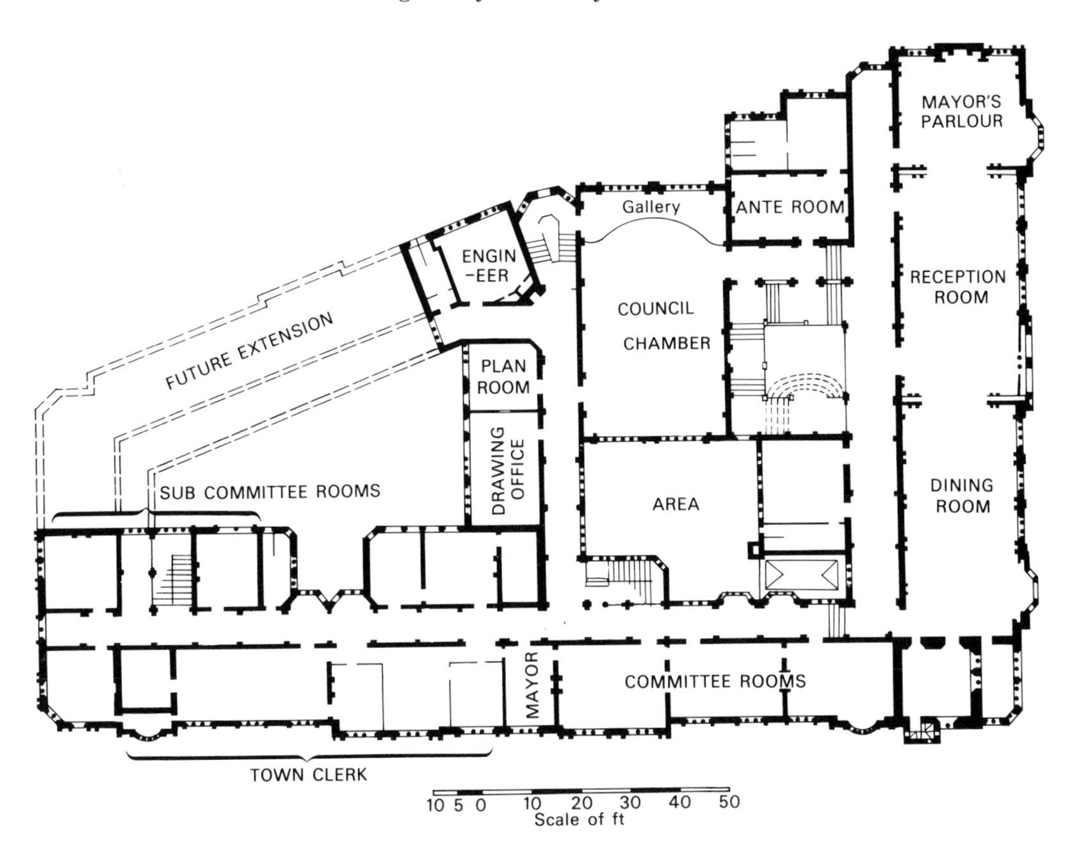

15 Sheffield town hall, principal floor plan, E. W. Mountford, 1890 (redrawn from *Builder*, vol. LVIII, 1890)

though, the example of the Houses of Parliament seems to have been ignored. The need for informal consultation areas was also largely left to chance. At Manchester they were provided for in the series of bow windows that break up the main passages, added to the original design at the suggestion of Donaldson and Street. They are still regularly used but appear to have been something of a rarity, and for the most part individual business had to be conducted publicly.

In addition to the three main elements of a town hall there were often, at least until around 1890, further services such as a fire station and stabling for corporation vehicles and horses. Most town halls had at least one yard that could accommodate these, though their layout was not always carefully considered. At Rochdale the fire station had to be turned through 90° at a fairly late stage so that engines could get in and out without having to make a 180° turn. At Hove Waterhouse put the fire station beneath the hall so that engines had to race out to emergencies up a steep ramp. There is no doubt that such extras had a low priority in planning and were fitted in on an ad hoc basis.

The last requirement was accommodation for staff. Where there was a large hall with a stage there was usually plenty of lost space beneath the platform for porters' rooms and kitchens, even allowing for performers' retiring rooms.[18] A formal porter's lodge was always associated with the grand entry. At Halifax it is conveniently tucked under the grand stairs, while at Manchester the door-keepers are provided with kiosks in the passages and the town hall keeper has an altogether grander office close to the main stairs but beneath the retiring room. More humble storage and space for essential maintenance workers could be relegated to any spare basement or internal open areas. Virtually all town halls also had to provide living accommodation for some of their staff. The grand and exciting mayor's flat on the upper floors of Manchester town hall is unique. It was more common for police and fire superintendents to live in the building, and their lodgings were usually quite substantial, running to two or three bedrooms and two living rooms. Rochdale provided a good example of a fire superintendent's flat in the upper floors of one wing.[19] The one regular occupant, however, was the town hall keeper, who was also usually the mace bearer. His flat might be in the basement or in the attics, and often with odd rooms at different levels. At Northampton access to his flat was through the unfurnished, undecorated first stage of the tower, lit only by narrow slit windows. The flat was usually quite spacious for a man of his standing, running to at least three or four good sized rooms (though less in smaller towns). The rooms, however, might be awkwardly shaped, to accommodate towers or flues, and the windows on the façade side were frequently ill placed. If the town hall keeper is to be regarded as roughly akin in status to the butler in a substantial household, it has to be admitted that he was generally housed in a more haphazard manner such as was more common for lower servants.

The problems of planning a town hall were complex and varied, and the needs of different elements often conflicted. The requirements could be ranked in order of status from the hall and mayoral apartments down to the keeper's flat. The biggest difficulty, however, was not in the provision and linking of types of room, for the total collection did after all divide quite easily. The real skill of the town hall designer lay in allowing for easy circulation; this problem was new and, in the provinces at least, most obvious in this new building type. Elmes and Brodrick were the first to work out a solution by providing a continuous corridor round their central hall with offices opening off it and stairs at intervals. This basic theme was adapted in many

16 Northampton town hall, central corridor ground floor, E. W. Godwin, 1861–4

subsequent town halls, but was really only suitable for island sites. On cramped sites, like Hull or Northampton (Fig. 16), or in linear compositions, like Rochdale, a spine corridor was most frequent running either from front to back or from side to side of the building.[20] The ring corridor occurs in most of the surviving competition entries for the Manchester town hall, but was most effectively refined by Waterhouse when he decided to add the three great spiral staircases in his entry for the second stage competition. Thereafter the pattern was firmly established and could be extended with cross passages and additional courts more or less ad infinitum as at Lancaster, Cardiff or in many of the designs for the London County Hall. The separation of the grand formal entry and circulation of clerks and ordinary members of the public became increasingly the key to a successful town hall as the range of functions expanded and the size of the buildings grew.

2

The growth of municipal patronage

Throughout the Victorian era municipal authorities were under constant pressure to provide accommodation for their growing services. Every decade brought the chance of new powers, which could be seen as an opportunity to build or extend. Given the excuse, a mayor or a significant part of the corporation might without difficulty find the opportunity to leave their mark on the town centre or even to shape its development for years to come. This is an entirely understandable desire and raises two questions: how far did the generations of councillors achieve their aim and why were such significant buildings not more frequently devised? The answers to both these questions lie partly in the problems of local pride and of finance. It was not always easy to ignore the claims of local architects or to fault their designs based on local expertise. Equally a grand town hall would certainly be expensive, and it would not always be easy to finance grandeur and remain in office at the same time. I shall show how these problems restricted the buildings in a later chapter. Here I want to look at the aspirations unrestricted, and to consider the corporations' growing power over, and delight in, commissioning works of art.

It would be easy to see Liverpool's St George's hall (Fig. 17) as the ultimate in civic patronage, and to list the few other major buildings as evidence that only the really great cities had the wit as well as the wealth to commission great works of art. Of course there is some truth in that, and the emergence of those buildings is central to this chapter. However, such a view does to a great extent miss the point that one can see the same spirit at work in several lesser town halls, and in some of the projects that were never realised. Indeed the sheer quantity of building, at least before the bureaucratic explosion of the 1860s, is in part evidence for the delight in commissioning what, it was hoped, would be works of art. A conservative estimate

17 Liverpool St George's hall, H. L. Elmes, 1841–56

gives 39 buildings planned or built in the 1840s, 60 in the 1850s and 58 in the 1860s; and this when only 178 municipal boroughs were recognised, and when only about two-thirds of those had their own commission of the peace.[1] The very expenditure contemplated,[2] bearing in mind the smallness of many mid-century boroughs, is also an indication. In the 1840s expenditure ranged from roughly £2,000 to £25,000 with an average of around £10,000 per town hall. This rose to an average of £13,000 in the 1850s (or over £30,000 if one includes the few really extravagant schemes) and reaches £17,000 in the 1860s (or £50,000 by including the now growing percentage of larger buildings).

A mere £10,000 to £17,000 may seem paltry but it should be remembered that we are talking here of towns for the most part with only between 10,000 and 15,000 inhabitants. A few examples can illustrate the extent of their commitment. Huddersfield numbered a mere 30,880 in the 1851 census, yet the eventual cost of the town hall that was proposed in that year (though not completed until 1876) was £76,000. A fairer example is the market town of Louth which, with a population of 10,467 in 1851 proposed to spend £4,000 on its town hall in 1852, or about 6*s*. 8*d*. for every soul in the borough. And the town hall was not the only public building of the 1850s in Louth. Sheer size is not, of course, necessarily an indication; and one needs to know what proportion of the population were ratepayers or men of substance, and in particular whether the town contained or had connections with any powerful or wealthy leader. Only such support can explain the commissioning in 1856–7 of E. B. Lamb's Byzantine extravaganza (Fig. 7) (which can never have been cheap[3]) in Eye, a town of under 2,500. Like most of E. B. Lamb's buildings it has considerable character, and it still dominates the town centre. Louth town hall, too, with its lush mid-century plasterwork has been rated one of Pearson Bellamy's best works, and he did a good deal of town hall building in Lincolnshire and East Anglia. The family of plump and pretentious town hall buildings (Fig. 51) of the mid-century are, I think, sufficient evidence that new town rulers did take a positive delight in commissioning fine buildings, and were determined to build something that was obviously more than strictly practical. The limit of their dreams can be seen in the short-lived proposal from Windsor, small even by the standards of 1851, to employ Philip Hardwick to spend £100,000 on a new town hall.[4]

If the joy in commissioning works of art was as widespread as the powers of the new corporations, it is none the less in the larger towns and larger buildings that the phenomenon is seen most clearly. There was never any real difficulty for the established cities in finding money for major undertakings, and it was comparatively easier to find larger sums. For instance, Louth's expenditure of 6*s.* 8*d.* per head of its population is not to be compared with Manchester's figure of nearer £2 10*s.* per head in 1867–77. Thus we do need to look at the larger buildings to get a full view of the developing power of patronage.

It was no accident that Liverpool was one of the first to commission a building, nor that its St George's hall forms one of the highest peaks of municipal building. However, it is worth noting how quick the corporation were to seize the opportunity of building something really significant. The original intention was to fund two buildings, a courthouse and a concert hall, both necessary and both requiring some degree of display. Elmes was not unique in winning the chance to build more than one of a corporation's buildings, but his is the only case where the corporation immediately decided to ask their architect to redesign the two as one. It is unlikely that there was any motive of economy in this. The final total of around £300,000 calculated in 1875 puts this building well up towards the head of the table; and despite the length of time taken in the building there is no record of the corporation trying to prevent the mammoth scheme going ahead. It is true that at least one of the contractors was incensed by the close scrutiny and querying of his accounts, but the delays seem to result more from the problems of the sheer size of the central hall and,

18 Liverpool St George's hall, great hall, H. L. Elmes and C. R. Cockerell 1841–56 (*Builder*, vol. XIII, 1855)

of course, from the death of the architect. The eventual building brought, and still brings, great credit to its town as one of the last great monuments of romantic classicism. It is also important that Elmes was able to sell the corporation a scheme that went well beyond what was in any real sense practical (Fig. 18). He planned a basilica in which it would be possible to see in one immense vista of open space from the back of the crown court down the length of the hall and on to the back of the borough court. Cockerell's treatment of the western end and the insertion of the organ (in its day the largest in the world) were certainly intrusive in the way they divided the one great space, even if they did make the building more usable. One could argue that the sculpture in the pediment represented an economy since it was originally designed by Cockerell for the custom house, but the very achievement of so massive a composition (it cost over £3,000 alone) indicates the value attached to the whole building as a work of art. We can see this again in the expenditure of £20,000 on the

19 Leeds town hall, competition design, Cuthbert Brodrick, 1852

decoration of the hall with its superb Minton tile floor to the designs of Grüner. Sculpture on the outside was always intended, though the carving of the panels is part of another story. A competition for the sculptured reliefs was held in 1882, but carved panels and figures between the columns of the north portico were intended from an early stage, as were free standing groups at the corners of the podium. In the event the sheer bulk of the structure was enough and outside decoration was for a long while restricted to the pediment and the four stone lions that were also carved by Nichols.

Leeds town hall (Figs 19–22) is the artistic successor to the St George's hall, and the saga of its building throws further light on the delight in commissioning architecture that should be a work of art. No one really doubted the necessity of having a building, nor was the efficiency of Brodrick's original plan ever seriously questioned; but the additions that were agreed and the excuses given for them are illuminating. The competition assessor, Sir Charles Barry, while warmly commending the design (Fig. 19), commented that a tower was really needed to complete the composition. The narrowness of the pro-palace majority meant that they could not achieve this until 1854, a year after the foundations had been laid (Fig. 20). But the designs and the tower that was eventually built show what store was set by making a mark. Indeed at the foundation laying the chairman of the town hall committee had claimed that 'the town council intend, in the first place to erect a building which will improve the public taste, and give an improved architectural appearance to the town of Leeds. . . . We are about to erect this town hall, first, as an ornamental building, and in order that the local or municipal business of the borough may be concentrated in one building, and thereby be done better and cheaper than it could be were it otherwise'.[5] The order is significant, and the theme was picked up by J. D. Heaton who lectured on town halls to the Leeds Literary and Philosophical Society as part of the campaign for a tower. He claimed that 'a necessity has long been felt for ampler accommodation and for architectural display more worthy of the wealth and importance of the town. . . . The municipal buildings . . . besides the primary object of furnishing convenient accommodation . . . are intended to present an appearance worthy of the wealth and prosperity of the town.'[6] Once the main point was gained,

20 Leeds town hall, alternative design for the tower, Cuthbert Brodrick, 1853 (*Builder*, vol. XI, 1853)

21 Leeds town hall, Cuthbert Brodrick, 1853–8

we see the striving for display in a whole series of extras that were gradually allowed. The arrival and multiplication of the vases on the balustrade, the elaborately carved ventilating shafts[7] and the modified entrance with its grand sculpture by John Thomas all attest the desire for quality of display. Then too the choice of J. G. Crace to decorate the hall, of Walter Macfarlane for the cast ironwork and of Osler of Birmingham for the chandeliers and Minton for the tiled vestibule shows that the corporation were out to get the best rather than to satisfy local trade, as became popular in later buildings such as the Birmingham council house. In this case the sheer number of extras leaves one amazed that the council ever agreed to press on.

22 Leeds town hall, Cuthbert Brodrick, 1853–8; lion by W. D. Keyworth, 1866

Brodrick's conception was essentially fluid, given the basic core, and he was happy to alter as things went ahead. He even had full-size mock-ups made to judge the size of the balustrades. The final touch is provided by the organ and the lions. The organ was not quite as big as that at Liverpool, but it was a five manual job so large that the builder had to dismantle his workshop to get it out; and the swell box was large enough to seat fourteen at dinner in a typical Victorian celebration. The four lions outside match those at Liverpool (Fig. 22), and at least a pair of lions later became *de rigueur*. Here they were not even commissioned until 1865, seven years after the building was opened.

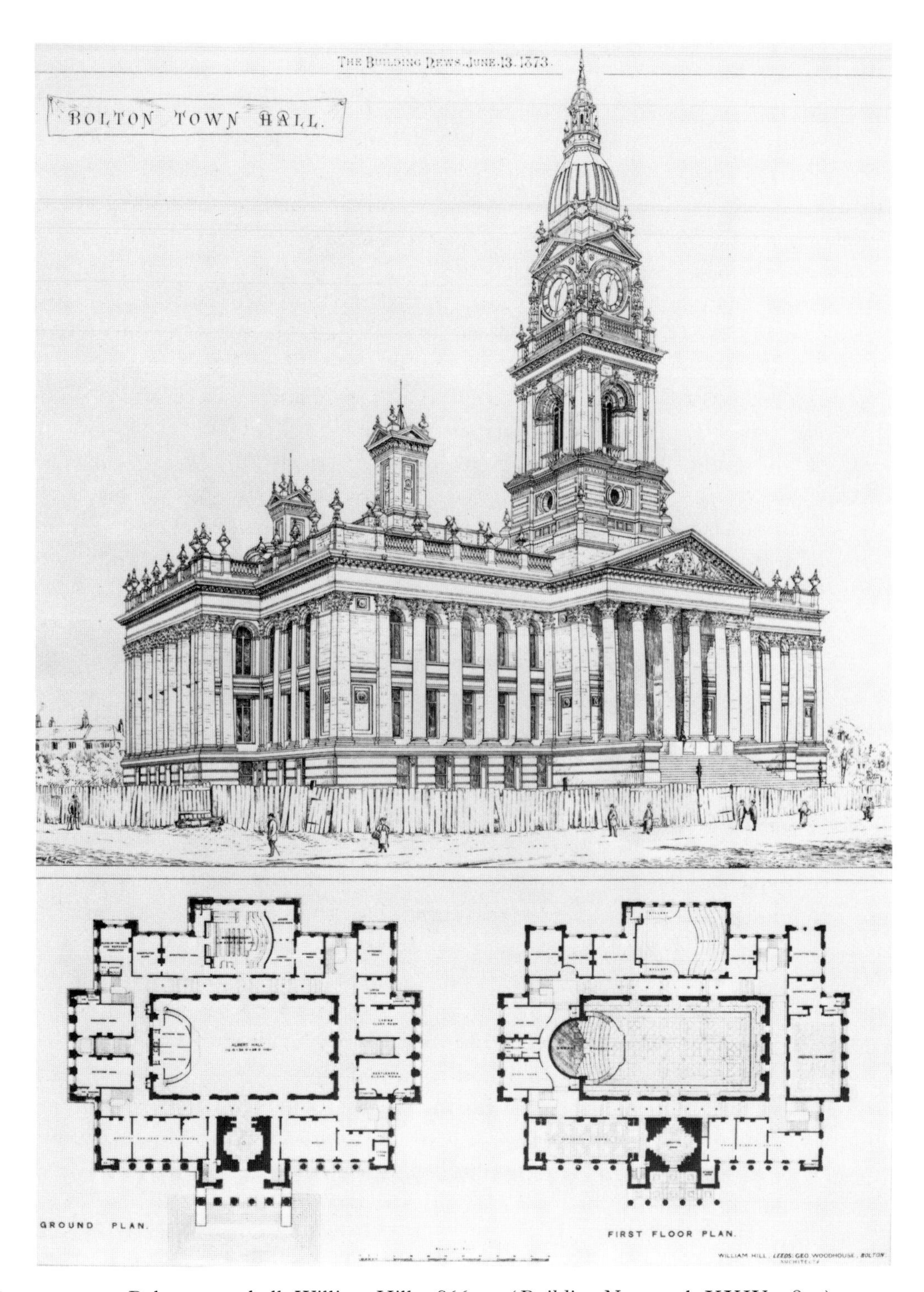

23 Bolton town hall, William Hill, 1866–73 (*Building News*, vol. XXIV, 1873)

One may wonder whether the final achievement was due more to Brodrick's determination or to the council's eagerness, but the success of the symbol is undeniable. There was always some tension between corporate accountability that required economy, and the way in which corporate funding could allow almost endless expense. The delight in patronage on the grand scale was inevitably the cause of estimates being grossly exceeded; but the fact that they so often were exceeded, and by such large margins, is more a comment on the determination of the patrons than on the incompetence of the architects or quantity surveyors. The success of the symbols when finally completed is shown by their ready exportability, and the way in which one town borrowed from another. We find the Leeds theme reworked at Bolton by Brodrick's pupil William Hill (Fig. 23), and again planned for Oldham by Potts who worked with Hill at Bolton. It was deliberately copied again by Portsmouth who, having seen and admired Bolton town hall, commissioned Hill to re-elaborate the scheme once again. Other echoes of the same theme are found at Birkenhead and Morley among others. Recognition of the power of the symbol comes from Wakefield, Leeds' former rival as an assize town, where the mayor admitted in 1877 that if the building they were about to erect had been put up ten years before, Wakefield might have won the privilege of holding the West Riding Assizes.[8] The most touching comment on the aims of the Leeds fathers is to be found in the many public aspirations. J. D. Heaton had said 'if a noble municipal palace that might fairly vie with some of the best town halls of the continent were to be erected in the middle of their hitherto squalid and unbeautiful town, it would become a practical admonition to the populus of the value of beauty and art, and in the course of time men would learn to live up to it.'[9] The same belief survived until the opening when the editor of one local paper commented, 'It is not, we think, anticipating too much to look forward to a greater appreciation of art among that portion of the inhabitants—the great bulk of the population—whose daily pursuits do not tend to encourage such a taste.'[10]

Such high-flown statements are not uncommon among town hall builders, but I think it has to be accepted that they were made generally in all earnestness. The genesis of two other buildings provides further proof of the earnestness that underlay such activity. Birmingham town hall and Bradford's St George's hall must count among town halls though they do not fulfil all the functions. They both originated in the same way. Though the Birmingham town hall was built by the town commissioners, the pressure for the building came from the musical society and their requirements conditioned the whole design. Many of the commissioners will have been involved in the musical society, but as such their prime purpose was to raise funds for the infirmary. That they did so by holding concerts, the famous triennial music festival for instance, really attests their belief in the necessity of cultivating 'taste' and thereby improving the lot of the masses! Of course the connection between a 3,000 seat hall and the lot of Birmingham's 150,000 inhabitants was tenuous in the extreme, but the charitable intentions of the musical society need to be taken as seriously as their commitment to high art. They got the commissioners to purchase a building that could advertise the prestige of art by its temple form and dominance of its surroundings. When the society then provided the huge organ that Mendelssohn found so exhausting to play, the whole end of the building had to be reconstructed to accommodate it.[11]

Lack of any such building in Bradford was also first mentioned at a meeting of the infirmary trustees, and the story is that Titus Salt was impressed with the poverty of such facilities in the newly incorporated town. Certainly he was one of nine directors of the subscription company formed to build the St George's hall, and was one of only four who subscribed the maximum of £500. His interest was undoubtedly vital. One has almost to consider the St George's hall as another facet of the urge for improvement that led to Saltaire. Yet one of the essential features of these buildings is that they reflect more than one man's desire to improve the artistic level of his town. The widespread support for the St George's hall in Bradford is evidenced by the speed with which the money was raised. The proposal was first made in 1850 and by August 1851 the building was up. The support was largely local too. Only eleven out of 138 subscribers came from outside the borough, and corporation backing is seen by the presence of three of the town's first mayors on the board of directors.

A good many of the earlier town halls were more obviously symbols, and may thus be regarded more as works of art than as functional edifices. Salford (Fig. 3) and Chorlton-on-Medlock are two that tuck some rather cramped accommodation behind imposing Grecian façades. Oldham town hall is another in this category and was built at precisely the time that the corporation's local jurisdiction was being put at risk by the threat to bring in county police to maintain law and order. Horace Jones' pillared town hall at Cardiff continued this style while Burslem town hall (Fig. 51) is another fine example of a showy building with rather little space for business inside. This might suggest that town halls could only be built as ornaments in the heady days of *laissez-faire* before the municipal bureaucracy grew. This is to a large extent true, and as the number of buildings increased in the 1860s, 1870s and 1880s so the proportion of really artistic creations declined. There are a number of reasons for this. In the first place, the corporations were fully established and accepted by the end of the 1850s. By then the first generation of urban industrialists had made their fortunes and were private patrons in their own right. Henry Bolckow at Middlesbrough, withdrawing from the town to his collection of rare books and pictures at Marton Hall, is typical. More and more of the corporations were run by managers rather than

24 Halifax town hall, Sir Charles and E. M. Barry, 1859–62 (*Builder*, vol. XVIII, 1860)

owners who, now that the new social order was accepted, seem not to have felt the need to express their status as corporations by purely symbolic buildings.

However, the need for corporations to commission buildings that would be principally works of art was decreasing at the same time as their need for more purely practical buildings was growing. Halifax (Fig. 24) is probably the last of those town halls where the artistic aspect of the design is more important than the function. The rare 'classical' spire[12] makes a splendid contribution to the townscape, but Barry's glass-roofed cortile, so suitable for a London club, is a poor substitute for the separate grand hall and is largely wasted as circulation space. For the future it would be more common to conceive works of art as additional features which, like carved ornament, could be spread as far as the purse allowed.

Pure art would never again feature to so great an extent as it had done at Liverpool, Leeds and Halifax. True, the commissioning of sculpture and paintings would continue, but seldom in the same proportions as before. Art had to take second place to practicality. It is significant that in 1868 Donaldson and Street should begin their report on the second Manchester competition, 'as to the comparative merits of the designs in an architectural point of view . . . we are of the opinion that the designs No. 6, No. 4, No. 7 and No. 5 are as works of art the finest . . . and with regard to relative merit . . . stand in the order in which we have here placed them.'[13] Their order was first Speakman Charlesworth, second John Oldrid Scott, third Thomas Worthington and fourth Alfred Waterhouse. It was Waterhouse's success in 'general arrangements and conveniences' and in his likelihood of being within the allowance of £250,000 that gave him first place. As the assessors explained when they were called upon to defend their choice, he was so far the best in these two areas that they felt his less handsome design should be given preference. The resulting building, though it is architecturally significant in the highest degree, owes its fame to its planning much more than to its quality as a total work of art; and many of its best architectural features were modifications of the original plan, some even suggested by Donaldson and Street. Indeed though Waterhouse modified and enriched his tower design, the Manchester tower is not as striking as his earlier simpler one at Darlington (Figs 75, 76). His façade (Fig. 25) was rightly criticised, too, for its cramped entrance. In a building of that size it was virtually impossible to design a grand entry that was both sufficiently large to tell and sufficiently small to fit beneath the reception suite without blocking its windows. The filigree gable is certainly a clever solution, but it does not compare with the elegance of the outside stairways proposed by Thomas Worthington or Speakman & Charlesworth. A firm hint in this direction had in fact been given by the ruling on the instructions for the second competition that steps might project fifteen feet from the building line.[14] It is true that the grand stair in

25 Manchester town hall, Alfred Waterhouse, 1867–77

Waterhouse's building (Fig. 49) is among the best of architectural experiences, but after that ascent the proportions of the great hall are disappointing and its rhythms less telling than those in Worthington's or Scott's designs (Figs 85, 86). Likewise Waterhouse's lovely sculpture hall has to be measured against Worthington's pair of double height ambulatories. That Waterhouse's design was preferred in spite of these weaknesses shows just how much weight was given to practicality.

From the point of view of the practical man who might actually have been involved in commissioning a town hall, the study of what might have been is largely a

26 Manchester town hall, second stage competition design, E. Salomons, 1868 (*Building News*, vol. XV, 1868)

waste of time. For architects (and architectural historians) the case is very different, and the designs dreamed of are often more informative than those actually built. In the case of Manchester the professional press ensured a good coverage of the competitive designs so that we, like the architects of the time, can judge the merits of the other schemes for ourselves (Figs 26–8). It was common practice for the competitive designs, or at least a large part of them, to be exhibited publicly; and detailed criticisms were published in both the local and the architectural press. In the case of Manchester it is important to remember that we are judging a finished building with all its extras, that cost nearly £1,000,000, against buildings designed to cost around £250,000. In the first place, Waterhouse was criticised for his façade; and the assessors recommended that he should alter the great entry to give it more dignity and modify the clock tower and Albert Square corners and should add architectural character to the interior courts. All this was done together with a large number of further additions which Waterhouse costed at £32,649 in 1873 when he reckoned the total of the whole as still £225,223.[15] It is hardly surprising that there was ill feeling at the time particularly from Speakman and Charlesworth who were placed second. The quality of Waterhouse's building was clearly recognised by the time it was completed, but it does not detract from the quality of the other designs. It is significant, too, that George Godwin, the assessor of the first competition, disagreed with the council in the selection of the designs for the second competition. He selected eleven designs by nine architects, but of those two had originally been rejected by the council and four had not even been short-listed. Clearly his criteria, as one of the architectural cognoscenti, were very different from the corporation's. His nine architects were reduced to eight by the exclusion of J. Robinson for a minor infringement of the instructions. Of the eight selected for the second competition E. Salomons might well have hoped to know precisely what the clients wanted, for he had been retained by the corporation to give evidence in arbitration cases during their piecemeal purchase of the site.[16] He offered a lush Renaissance style frothing with decorative sculpture and certainly distinctive (Fig. 26). Inside, his arrangements followed the same basic scheme as Waterhouse's, though not with the same finesse. In fact the site forced something of the same pattern on all the competitors so that Waterhouse's innovation was more in the details and the amount of space allotted to circulation than in the conception of the whole (Fig. 9). T. H. Wyatt's plan is particularly close to Waterhouse's except that his grander entry awkwardly breaks up the continuous run of reception rooms across the front at first floor level. However it is easier to see why his rather pedestrian classical façade failed to win a prize. Speakman & Charlesworth, on the other hand (Fig. 10), failed to achieve the same clarity in their use of an identical corridor pattern, and their stairs would have been a great disappointment after the grand entry. One who did give ample, perhaps too ample, space to the grander circulation areas was Thomas Worthington. His entrance, by means of free-standing stairs and a bridge, would have provided a romantic experience amply lived up to by the interior where the great hall was flanked by colonnaded ambulatories on two levels. Outside covered footways at both ends of the Albert Square façade would have provided a nice sense of involvement with the surrounding flow of people (Fig. 27); and the awkward junction between Princess Street and Albert Square was elegantly turned with a splendid jumble of oriels, loggias and turrets capped by a small tower. It is undoubtedly true that some of his offices could have been awkward, but his is the most effective romantic Gothic composition. Though his main façade is rather dull, it might well have complemented the delicacy of his Albert memorial more effectively; and one may well regret that his design was never built. Some measure of his popularity in Manchester is suggested by the unanimous decision, barely a month after the second town hall competition was begun, to employ him to build the police courts. These were originally to have been in the town hall, but were shunted to another site because of fears that the triangular site would be too small. In the event these fears were well justified, but this subsidiary scheme was not widely publicised. The design was the result of a competition limited by invitation to six Manchester architects. Waterhouse sensibly refused the invitation. One wonders what accusation of jobbery there might have been had Worthington won both competitions.[17]

The event has probably proved Manchester right in adopting the most practical plan and modifying it to enhance its grandeur. Still for many architects the chance to design a really grand exterior was a particularly compelling reason for trying this sort of work. Brodrick's fantastical design for Manchester town hall (Fig. 28) would have made even his building at Leeds seem dull. In fact by the 1870s when towns were considering the grand artwork less than the operational office block, architects were if anything more keen to design on an overambitious scale. As the town centres became more and more solidly developed, a town hall needed to be correspondingly larger and grander to stand out. Few town halls of the last quarter of the nineteenth century make the overwhelming impact on townscape that Birmingham town hall did. Another factor was the complete acceptance of the corporations as permanent features of the social scene with apparently bottomless pockets, at least compared to private patrons. Thus the extravagant 'artistic' design could become a thing to be resisted. We can see this at Leicester where a major municipal buildings scheme was launched in 1871. The appointment of Street as assessor indicated both the importance of the scheme and the likely type of design. It is true that only about forty designs were sent in, but that was a respectable number; and Street's first choice, E. W. Godwin, was by then an experienced town hall builder and could be expected to know what

27 Manchester town hall, premiated design from second stage competition, Thomas Worthington, 1868 (*Building News*, vol. XV, 1868)

28 Manchester town hall, second stage competition drawing, Cuthbert Brodrick, 1868

corporations wanted and how to deal with them. His design was not adopted, however, and he did not even collect a premium. Street was accused of merely choosing a pretty façade, and the corporation insisted on a different award. It was claimed that they didn't like London architects, but, though their first award was to a Leicester firm (Barnard & Smith), second prize went to a design with at least London influence by Goddard & Spiers, of Leicester and London. Most probably the corporation, besides any natural desire to promote local talent, were afraid of the sort of rocketing expense that might be involved in making a building whose dominant feature was a grand façade. It may be no accident that a change of site allowed them to hold another competition, with a different assessor. The design they finally chose (Fig. 58) was by a London architect and chiefly impressive for its façade, but none the less the style was not grand in the traditional way, and in any case the architect, F. J. Hames, was Leicester-born. It is difficult to know how far, if at all, the Queen Anne style was known in Leicester in 1872; but it is hard to resist the idea that this design, with its tower relegated to a side façade and stripped of gargoyles, columns and pediments seemed likely to be cheaper. Actually the cost rose from an original allowance of £25,000 (raised to £30,000 on Street's recommendation) to around £50,000, but even so the total remains modest for a major town hall of the 1870s, and the 100 per cent increase is less than many others.

After 1870 there are fewer really pompous buildings of any note, but the desire of architects to build on the grandest scale certainly didn't diminish. The possibility was kept alive by the few really big commissions, of which Sheffield (Fig. 52) is undoubtedly the outstanding example. At a cost of around £200,000 in 1897 this was clearly a major building. Significantly too, it was built in a town that previously had little public architecture to recommend it. There had been a proposal for a major public building to combine all the functions of the municipality and a large hall as early as 1847. A firm of Sheffield architects (Flockton, Lee & Flockton) had even drawn plans,[18] but the competition of 1890 was for what would be Sheffield's first chance to patronise the arts on a scale to match other comparable towns. The scale of the objective was amply matched by the publicity, and the 179 competitors produced a wide range of eclectic designs. Few of the designs were really original in their planning or façades, and the resulting building lacks the architectural élan of the very best town halls. However it does have a striking tower of a new design that will compare with any. Evidently the two pressures, for display and for functionalism, were beginning to pull apart; and though corporations could still want to act as patrons of the arts on the grandest scale, the possibilities were now more limited. A tower, however, remained indispensable as well as being an admirable vehicle for display. The grand entry and stairway were important too and both are features at Sheffield (Fig. 29). There is also ample sculptural decoration, but it is clear that the council rated function highly. They required architects to allow for office extensions as part of their design, and in their selection they passed over several designs that were more exciting and more dramatic than E. W. Mountford's which they chose. For sheer display, the designs by W. Henman, R. S. Wilkinson, H. T. Hare and Flockton & Gibbs all seem more exciting than the selected one. Even Heathcote Statham's extraordinary mélange (Fig. 65) is more original for the splendid tower of

29 Sheffield town hall, grand stair, E. W. Mountford, 1891–7

Mountford's design is largely prefigured in the Soane medallion design of 1885 by A. B. Mitchell, which he would most probably have seen.[19]

In spite of the pressures, however, town hall building as art patronage did not entirely die in the jungle of municipal bureaucracy. John Belcher's baroque extravaganza at Colchester (1897) (Fig. 71) is a vital contribution to the townscape. The composition of the main block is dominated by the great columns that flank the windows of the moot hall. Here the display element is emphatically to the fore, and the building succeeds because of that. The tighter limits on corporate extravagance do have their effect though, in that the tower, so essential to the whole design, was at first ruled out and was built in the end as a gift to the town by mayor Paxman.

There are many instances where corporations over-reached themselves in the desire for display. The functional needs in themselves were unlikely to prove too expensive to accommodate, for as the needs increased so too would the rateable value and thus the borrowing powers of the corporation. In the matter of display a town might be lucky enough to find wealthy supporters to help out, but otherwise fine features had of necessity to be cut. This can be seen throughout our period, as at Leeds where the gorgeous stair devised by Brodrick had to disappear in the face of escalating costs and the pressure for more seating in the hall. What is clear, though, throughout the century, is that corporations enjoyed and even felt it their duty to build more than merely functional buildings. This is not simply that Victorian architecture always involved layers of additive ornament. There seems to have been a need for corporate display as a means of advertising identity. The public patronage of sumptuous architecture met this need and was a fine way of showing off. It is easy to see how the newly established corporations felt this to be an important aspect of their work. The desire survives alongside the more serious need to house an efficient bureaucracy because that bureaucracy itself grew only with a developing town, which would need to advertise itself, or its power centre as a part of the development of its community consciousness.

3

Size and splendour

It might be assumed that there would be a high level of correlation between the size of towns and the phenomenon of display in public buildings. In so far as the largest town halls are found in the larger towns this is true; but in considering more than a very few examples the supposition is shown to be wide of the mark. A much closer connection would probably be revealed with the existence of individuals in the various boroughs with dreams of grandeur than between mere size and splendour. It is not simply that the raw population figures are uninformative, but that the chance to build depended so much on individual history and quality of the towns.

The concentration of population is only what distinguishes towns from rural areas. Without an extensive population reasonably concentrated within one area no town was likely to be granted a charter of incorporation. However there was certainly no firm distinction of size, at least to begin with. Bradford, with 23,233 inhabitants in 1831, was the smallest of the new boroughs mentioned in the 1835 Act, since only 1,500 lived within the borough boundary. Nevertheless Bradford was already important as a trading centre, and a much truer picture emerged when the outlying districts where the weaving was done were brought into the borough, making the 1851 population 103,778. Yet the contrast would have been very marked between Bradford, beginning to be a metropolis even in 1841, and Oldham, which was at that time substantially larger in numbers than Bradford. Such questions as the spread of wealth within the population are crucial, and in poorer boroughs, such as Oldham, the number of inhabitants who were ratepayers might be quite small and substantial ratepayers smaller still. The detailed interpretation of population figures is no part of my business in this book, and is, in any case, subject to argument. However sheer numbers could and did affect the sort of service provision that was required. And numbers might be used in the developing legislation as a means of ranking towns. For instance, towns of over 10,000 in 1845 could, if they wished, spend money on museums without special parliamentary sanction. The result was a number of town halls that included a museum. Under the 1888 Act 50,000 was the magic number allowing the status of county borough with all the attendant power. There had only been eight places of that size in 1835, but by 1891 there were fifty-four. This distinction immediately enhanced a borough's powers of building, for the larger boroughs controlled extra facilities; but it was clearly recognised that there was more to making a borough than mere size. The Royal Commission's thoughts on the prerequisites are interesting.[1] The population threshold is set at 10,000 for municipal boroughs and it is suggested that there needs to be some historic continuity of local control, civic cohesion and a good record of local administration. Given the importance of some Victorian new towns the historic continuity is perhaps a bit odd, but the rest is almost too obvious to need stating. Yet it is the historic continuity and the continuing history that distinguishes each town so that it is impossible to write about the typical municipality. All are different; but across this diversity cuts the desire to build and the need to provide services. All the Victorian boroughs were, or could be, involved in the provision of identical services, and barring other accidents of history, their success or failure would mark them out as good or bad prospects for investors. Building a town hall was a part of this common effort and a substantial town hall might go a long way towards establishing a town or determining its character.

It was obvious that some ancient towns were in the wrong place as far as nineteenth-century industrialisation went, and they were largely out of the running. Lancaster had been an important port so long as vessels remained small enough to navigate the Lune; but though it grew from 12,613 in 1831 to 31,038 in 1891 that was slow growth by the standards of most towns and Lancaster was never really in a position to compete with the newer ports. A similar relative decline is well documented at Bristol, a much larger city, which remained virtually outside the civic rat race until the close of the century. At Bristol there was a sufficient capital of civic consciousness and some hopes of development, and the guildhall (1843–6) by R. S. Pope was a product of this. However there is no civic architecture in Bristol to match its eighteenth-century glory. In terms of sheer numbers Bristol remained significant throughout the century, but the ensuing pressure for control of the city's amenities never led to any outstanding civic building. The assize courts of 1865–70 were certainly important buildings; but there was never any possible alternative seat for the assizes, and the demand for improved court accommodation, though often useful in providing an excuse for grand civic building, came from outside the local corporations. Even at the very end of the century, when the pressure for office space was becoming extreme, Bristol was unable to decide on a proper scheme. A competition for a building to cost £80,000 was proposed in 1891, but the matter was deferred. By 1893 they were talking about a building to house an art gallery, a hall for 1,000 people, a library and a banqueting hall as well as the municipal offices, but nothing came of the scheme. Action was delayed until 1898 when they finally agreed to build a temporary council chamber. This was to cost a mere £7,125, and the designs were by T. H. Yabbicom the borough engineer. The real new town hall was not in fact begun until shortly before the Second World War.

Nineteenth-century Bristol had no need to advertise for the city had a long past and was full of splendid buildings. The new towns of the Industrial Revolution were different, but even they do not form a single class. Places such as Ironbridge grew up around their raw materials and their transport, but they lay aside from the main lines of communication that developed later and so they too were by-passed. The most significant nineteenth-century building in Ironbridge is the Gothic warehouse on the river quay. The same is true for some of the early clothing towns such as Crompton or Belper which were hidden away either to avoid prying competitors or to secure a good water supply. Though their industries grew to quite sizeable proportions these towns did without grand civic buildings until the later years of the century. Even then their buildings are not particularly grand. Crompton mounted a competition for public offices in 1892 which drew fifty-two designs; and the competitors included Woodhouse & Willoughby of Manchester and John Johnson of London. The latter was frequently involved in municipal building and competitions and already had town halls at Staines and Bootle to his credit. In 1881 he had also built the public hall at Belper for their subscription company. By and large, though, these ragged industrial conglomerates, mostly in the edges of the Pennines, remained little but groups of factory villages throughout the period; and even when they did build, their horizons were generally provincial. Rawtenstall, Shaw and Haslingden are three typical examples that never achieved the urbanity to indulge in civic building. True, Haslingden had a public hall from 1852. Rawtenstall's public hall was built in 1868–9 by the Co-operative Society, a modest building costing a mere £7,000 by Maxwell & Tuke of Bury, who appear as competitors for a number of northern town halls. Rawtenstall town hall dates from the years after 1903 when they held a competition. Haslingden's municipal offices were not even worth a mention in the architectural press. Shaw, a little town with a group of immense mills, looked no further than Oldham for its architect, Harold Cheetham, who in 1894 designed a modest town hall in very red brick. He, incidentally, was also the winner of the Crompton competition in 1892.

Part of the failure of these towns is due to the fact that they were mostly dominated by a single employer and the mills are their real public buildings. But there is more to it than that. There are a number of cases where a single employer-patron provided what is recognisably a town hall for a borough inhabited mostly by his own workmen. That sort of patronage depended very much on the outlook of the individual employer and did not require the existence of a separate borough. One could contrast the industrial suburbs of Saltaire and Possilpark. Titus Salt provided the handsome institute (Lockwood & Mawson, 1867–71), the local equivalent of a town hall, sixteen years after he began to build Saltaire. At Possilpark in Glasgow, where Walter Macfarlane's foundry was actually producing the splendid cast iron ornaments that were fitted to so many town halls, there appears to have been virtually nothing beyond the foundry itself and the blocks of tenements.

Part of the reason for the failure to develop a municipal centre seems to lie in the fact that these towns were manufacturing rather than trading centres, and in most cases were producing only one stage and not the finished goods. Thus there was little reason for the town to appear attractive to outsiders who, if they came, would come to the mill. Essentially these places failed to become towns in the full sense. Their dependence on a market elsewhere robbed them of independence to an extent that they lacked the urge to claim it. Precise reasons for the failure of will in some of these nineteenth-century creations are still unclear. Personalities as well as finance are undoubtedly involved. However there are cases where completely new towns were created in the nineteenth century that did lay claim to, and achieve, the fullest urban character. Middlesbrough and Barrow-in-Furness provide good examples.

Middlesbrough, like many of the new towns, was away from the existing centres. It did not stand on any through route, and could claim no *raison d'être* as providing an urban centre or local market for surrounding industrial hamlets. The town was totally new, with a population of only 154 in 1831; and in its conception it was tied to the single unpromising process of coal trans-shipment. Perhaps for that very reason it was decided from the outset to design a properly urban centre so that the original town consisted of a central square with axial streets running north, south, east and west. The square was intended to contain a market and town hall, and, though the town had to wait until 1846 for these (Fig. 30), one should remember that the town was still very small (only 7,431 in 1851) and the real growth of the town postdates the first town hall. By the time the town hall and market were built the town had also acquired its second industry, ironfounding. However it was not the diversity that gave the confidence. Middlesbrough is a clear case of new town promoters setting out to create a real urban centre that would 'take the lead of the Tyne and Wear'. The Middlesbrough Owners were in fact a small group of Quaker businessmen of considerable vision led by Joseph Pease and Thomas Richardson. They always intended that the place

30 Middlesbrough old town hall, W. Lambie Moffat, 1846

should be a town in the fullest sense as well as housing their business interests. The iron kings, such as Henry Bolckow, Vaughan or Dorman, who provided the basis for Middlesbrough's later prosperity, merely followed their lead in giving the town extra luxuries such as a park or museum.

The first Middlesbrough town hall is important, then, in proclaiming the intention to be a town. It is a small, rather severe and functional building by William Lambie Moffat of Doncaster, built of white brick with stone mouldings[2] and containing a large room for town meetings, a commissioners' room, lock-up and police superintendent's house. Behind it lay the market. There was little about the building of display, though its isolated site gave it all the necessary prominence. The little tower was a later addition, and the only ornamentation was the domed cupola atop the octagonal market. A fountain was designed for the centre of the market, but it is unlikely that it was ever built. Such a building cannot by any stretch of the imagination be called splendid. Its significance was in providing a visible focus for the new town. Once that was established, and as urban consciousness began to grow, there were increasing demands for more suitable grandeur. Designs for a tower were drawn in 1857, but were never carried out. The precise date of the tower has yet to be established, but at any rate it was not earlier than 1863 and not later than 1871. There are good reasons for believing that it was designed by John Dunning, the town engineer and agent to the Middlesbrough Owners. It is even likely that the elegant wooden clock stage is a reuse of the clock turret he built on the corner of the new markets in 1863–6. This sort of parsimony might seem to belie the intentions of the original Middlesbrough Owners who still maintained a keen interest in the town. The fact was quite simply that the town was growing rapidly southwards away from the docks, and the exchange, the largest public building of the 1860s, was the best part of a mile from the original square. By the 1860s Middlesbrough was a rapidly expanding town of around 20,000 inhabitants and would need a new symbolic focus nearer to its actual centre if it was to continue to stand out as an urban centre. Although the new town hall did not in fact arrive until the 1880s, the movement for it began as early as 1866. In that year powers for a town hall were included in the Middlesbrough Improvement Act.[3] The corporation in the event delayed building, but when they purchased the site in 1873 the Middlesbrough Owners made it a condition of sale that the site be used for public buildings. Their interest is probably also to be seen in the Quaker involvement in the financing of the eventual building. Money was to be raised by an issue of corporation stock of £200,000 of which £175,000 was quickly purchased by the Quaker-controlled National Provincial Bank. The same connection, almost certainly through Joseph Pease, was probably responsible for the commissioning of Alfred Waterhouse to draw plans in 1875 (Fig. 12). A slump in the iron trade caused the abandonment of his building, but he later advised on the plans selected in 1882 (Fig. 31). I have already described (p. 19) how sheer size by then required the provision of a massive office block. Equally important though, is the tall tower and massive public hall which effectively established this building as the centre of Middlesbrough. It was a worth-while achievement and ultimately due to the vision of the individuals who formed the Middlesbrough Owners and whose interests were still important in the town.

At Barrow-in-Furness a similar paternal vision was lacking. The town was in many ways similar to Middlesbrough, a completely new creation owing its existence to the arrival of the Furness railway in the mid-1840s. Paternalistic control was exercised by William Cavendish, 6th Duke of Devonshire; and the town was largely run for him by his agent, James Ramsden, locomotive superintendent, secretary of the railway company and secretary to the harbour commissioners. There is no evidence that the Duke involved himself at all in the town except to receive the income;[4] and Ramsden was not appointed to create a town but to run a railway. Though he was involved, it is significant that he was not one of the promoters of the

31 Middlesbrough town hall and municipal buildings, G. G. Hoskins, 1883–8

town hall scheme, and in fact when the town hall finally arrived it was not a complete success. Ramsden did indeed have visions of a well-built and orderly town, and it is thanks to him that many of the terraced streets of Barrow are more spacious than any elsewhere. In 1856 he drew up a plan for the development of the new town round a series of four great squares along the Hindpool Road. One square was to have the market in it and the other three are labelled 'proposed site for church chapel or public building'. The terraces were built and the market, but the great squares never arrived. Barrow, in fact, was and still is short on public buildings, but its function as iron town, railhead and port meant that in the nineteenth century it existed as more than a mere factory suburb. Even in the severest slumps the diversity of industry was important enough and secure enough for the larger firms to help out some of the smaller industries.

Though there was obviously a growing community consciousness and the beginnings of an urban aristocracy, there was no symbol of township; and the council meetings were actually held in the board room of the railway company. The railway company owned the market, the first town hall and the police offices. The building of a grand town hall has to be seen as the result of a corporate desire to express the town's independent existence. It was planned together with the other vital element of

Barrow, the high level bridge linking the island to the town, and stands symbolically at the junction of the three parts of Barrow, the old village, the new town and the island. It was not the first step in corporate building; that again was functional—the market hall, to designs of Paley & Austin (1869–71), and the Ramsden baths are earlier than the town hall. Plans for the town hall began in 1874 and after a slump in 1875 work soon went ahead. There were some problems over the choice of architect, but in the end a competition of 1877 secured the commission for W. H. Lynn of Belfast. He erected a rather gaunt Gothic pile[5] with a dominating central tower which nearly collapsed during building and had to be drastically lowered. This building is still the most visible focus of Barrow, after the great Vickers crane, but it is an example of a town hall where splendour was materially affected by the state of the town. After 1875 the prosperity of the town had passed its peak and there was a slow decline in the 1880s and 1890s. In their attempt to erect a great symbolic building Barrow corporation over-reached themselves and Lynn's design had to be severely curtailed and was never completed. The banqueting hall, a fine room, was an addition to the original

32 Barrow-in-Furness town hall, entrance lobby, W. H. Lynn, 1882–7

scheme, but Lynn's suggestion of a great hall in the centre of the court was never adopted and the courtyard itself was only half built. The main problem was that a large part of the scheme required by the corporation was devoted to court space and police offices, but as the town was not growing at all fast the pressure for these was less. The original intention was to build the scheme in two parts, a fairly common practice, but indicating the council's awareness that the scheme as a whole was too costly. In the end the police station, courts and fire station were omitted and the main façade was shortened by two bays so that the tower appears too dominant. What saved the building from complete failure was Lynn's insistence that the whole façade to Duke Street be built. He did this by rearranging the office accommodation to fill the whole façade rather than just half of it as originally planned. He also saw to it that the finer spaces of the interiors were not abandoned.[6] The colonnaded halls at ground and first floor level linked by the main stair are a particularly fine spatial composition (Fig. 32); and the original grand council staircase was apparently transferred to serve the humbler office end of the building.

These two examples show that besides mere size and wealth there had to be a deliberate will on the part of individual town leaders before a successful town hall would be built. To some extent this desire might be born out of competition with neighbouring towns, but such feelings are not easy to substantiate, and are as likely to be the product of the local press. There was an element of competition between, for example, Leeds and Bradford. Bradford won the first round by the quick erection of the St George's hall, and it is interesting that the Leeds town hall echoes the pattern of its façade with heavy unfluted Corinthian columns rising from a rusticated podium. Yet the Leeds building (Fig. 21) so far outdid Bradford that the Bradford town hall when built had to be very different (Fig. 78). It is also assumed, and is at least likely, that the rivalry between Manchester and Liverpool was a factor in the choice of a Gothic rather than a classical design for Manchester. However, though there is no doubt that the possession of a grand town hall was recognised as a very desirable status symbol, there is little evidence to suggest that direct rivalry with other towns was often the prime cause of town hall building. The need to proclaim independence was, but that is not quite the same thing.

Town halls as symbols of separate existence are certainly important. The vestry halls of London have already been cited (p. 14) as examples, as have some of the smaller district office buildings such as Newtonheath town hall in Manchester. Lesser boroughs on the outskirts of great cities could never hope to compete and in any case relied on their larger neighbours for some of their services. Nevertheless a town hall was often necessary as a place of assembly, and certainly important for its effect. Wavertree on the edge of Liverpool is a good example. There in 1872 the outdated pattern of a grand hall with a few offices was still quite sufficient. The architect, John Eliot Reeve, arranged the offices behind a particularly elegant Italianate façade that distantly echoes the classical public buildings of the big city, but makes an important contribution to its own high street.

A more striking statement of independence by a minor borough is to be seen at Morley near Leeds. Morley was incorporated in 1885, and the town hall was the second major scheme of the new corporation (it followed the waterworks). A competition was held in 1891 and won by G. A. Fox (Holtom & Fox of Dewsbury) with a half-size version of Leeds town hall that is entirely delightful. The front with its great flight of steps and elaborately sculptured pediment proclaims the dignity of the borough, though the actual entrance is cramped. The tower with its easily recognisable silhouette advertises the message, and like Leeds the building contains a spacious assembly hall. The municipal offices were complete with a sumptuous double stair leading up to a suite of reception rooms furnished throughout by Christopher Pratt. This building is every inch a town hall even though never completely finished, and its repetition of a well-known type could only underline the civic message. The pride of the smaller boroughs in achieving corporate status often led to this sort of architectural advertisement and often to overstatement. Pendleton town hall (1865–8) is an earlier example, and the exaggerated baroque of Alfred Brumwell Thomas' Stockport town hall (1904–8) (Fig. 73) has to be seen in this light. It is a fine civic building, loaded with columns, dripping with swags and with a striking tower that was greatly enlarged in the course of building. Apart from the infirmary, which faces it, there were no other buildings of this grandeur in Stockport; and it can be seen as a symbol of independence aimed at a rapidly advancing Manchester which has now finally swallowed the town.

So far I have talked mainly of the Victorian new towns. Competition in building reached far wider than that. Some of the older market towns, like Chester (Fig. 33) Plymouth (Fig. 34) or Rochdale (Fig. 36), remained important or developed into major manufacturing or trading areas themselves; and their great civic palaces come as no surprise. Yet not all the old towns grew as rapidly as was hoped. Bradford-on-Avon had a long history as a woollen town and it is hardly surprising that the town built a grand town hall. Thomas Fuller's jolly Jacobethan pile of 1853 would hardly have disgraced the other Bradford when it was built; but Bradford-on-Avon never lived up to the aspiration, and the town hall still seems unnecessarily large. Equally oversize is the town hall at Todmorden (Fig. 38), but that was the result of private patronage. Obviously, though, in a century of urbanisation the economic progress of the towns could lead to a fairly precise ranking of towns which their efforts at civic splendour would generally echo.

33 Chester town hall, W. H. Lynn, 1865–9

34 Plymouth guildhall, A. Norman and G. Hine with E. W. Godwin as consultant, 1869–74

However there were a good many towns that remained aloof from competition throughout the century. These were the old market towns that remained predominantly agricultural market centres in spite of some industrialisation. Here town halls still appear as conscious symbols, and if anything come rather earlier on the scene. Yeovil produced a town hall as early as 1847–9, but as examples of grandeur Tiverton (1862–4) and Banbury (1854) are more telling. The open market space at Banbury provided a splendid site but the little Gothic town hall with its stubby tower by Bruton amply lives up to it. It is thoroughly distinctive and provides an excellent visual focus. Obviously in 1854 the scale was smaller than one might expect from the town of today, and the original accommodation was little more than a committee room and an assembly-hall-cum-courtroom. A decade later Tiverton's building by H. Lloyd of Bristol (Fig. 35) is altogether juicier and more eclectic. There the interest was such that the competition drew as many as sixty designs. It is almost as though some of these country towns, very urban in their day, were determined not to be outdone by their untidier manufacturing sisters. Mostly their civic pride ran parallel to private enterprise that built the plethora of assembly rooms and corn exchanges that one associates with towns like Newark or Boston. Worcester even put up two simultaneously around 1860 that ran in competition. These corn exchanges were usually simple rooms, only being more lavishly handled if they were intended to double as assembly rooms, though some were more lavish. Aylesbury produced one in 1864 (by D. Brandon) that housed market, exchange, reading room, town offices and assembly room in an Elizabethan style with a three arched front that spanned a new road. For town halls that were purely municipal offices these towns usually had to wait until the 1890s.

In the oldest towns civic pride was less obvious in the nineteenth century. Mostly like Exeter or Worcester they already had their guildhalls which were established and even beloved as symbols. A good deal of money and effort might be spent on restoring them. Exeter guildhall was extensively restored in 1885–9 and Worcester guildhall virtually rebuilt behind its façade in 1878–80. There was strong opposition to the proposal to replace the Worcester guildhall with a modern town hall; but it is likely that motives of economy also influenced the decision to reject the idea. In any case these old buildings could for the most part still be made to serve; and they could be handsomely extended if the need arose. Dover rebuilt its thirteenth-century Maison Dieu as a town hall in 1852–61, but the commissioning of William Burges to complete the town hall in 1880 was probably due to its continuing importance as a Channel port. Even York, a principal railway centre as well as a county town and ancient city, continued to use the buildings of the St Christopher's Guild as a town hall until 1889 when the city surveyor designed the rather pallid extension. Durham was unusual in acquiring a convincingly medieval town hall by P. C. Hardwick in 1851. It is a curiously humble façade, and was in any case attached to the guildhall which was of medieval origin. It was in fact little more than an assembly hall, and the fact that its hall is unusually large with a particularly handsome hammer-beam roof and fine stained glass is due to the generous support of the Marquess of Londonderry. Only the city of London was able to invest enough in its medieval guildhall to make it in the fullest sense a monument of civic pride. In that case the life of the city and the functional importance of the old building grew hand in hand. There were constant

35 Tiverton town hall, H. Lloyd, 1862–4 (*Builder*, vol. XXII, 1864)

and expensive restorations and extensions, first by J. B. Bunning and then by Horace Jones who succeeded him as city architect. All these modifications were thoroughly necessary to the civic life of the capital, and the extent of which is revealed by the record that £50,000 had been spent on ceremonials alone at the guildhall between 1856 and 1867.

In so far as the larger towns were more or less continuously involved in civic ceremonial there is an obvious correlation between the size of a town and the splendour of its town hall. However it is at least equally significant that town halls, often with a considerable element of display, sprang up wherever the independence or identity of a borough was sought. Deliberately planned magnificence was undoubtedly a feature in the growth of some of the new towns in the 1870s and 1880s, but a comfortable display of wealth was equally valuable a decade or so earlier in the established towns. The existence of public buildings that were more than merely functional was deeply felt to be a mark of urbanity and a necessary adjunct to any permanent concentration of population.

4

The workings of patronage: individuals

The idea of corporate patronage is not entirely new. There has, for instance, always been an element of corporate patronage in university or cathedral building. What makes the town halls a special case is the fact that the town councils were composed of men of the new rich manufacturing class, coupled with the fact that major decisions had to be at least approved by a majority of the whole council. There are therefore two aspects of corporate patronage that need to be considered: the place of the individual motivator, and the restrictive effects of the committee as a whole. These are not separate and distinct entities, but will be treated separately since they place entirely different constraints on the architects, and the man who could design the dream palace for an ambitious mayor was not always capable of convincing a committee.

The individual patron must come first since it is very often with him that the idea of a town hall originates. Indeed there are many cases where it is only the driving force of a single individual who sees the scheme through to completion. This is particularly clear in the case of Bolton (Fig. 23), where the town hall scheme had long lain dormant[1] until revived by the Liberals as answer to the splendid market buildings put up by the Conservatives (1850–5). In this case the scheme was raised by J. R. Wolfenden in 1859, within a year of his first being elected a councillor. He was unsuccessful then and in the next year; but by 1863, after two years as mayor, he managed to get unanimous support for a motion that 'a town hall be erected'. However the battle was far from over for in the following year the council, having held a competition, decided by twenty-six votes to six not to appoint an architect at all. Wolfenden was faced with an apparently massive swing of public opinion against the scheme because of fears of the likely cost. The fears were in fact fully justified, but Wolfenden produced a series of complicated financial arguments to prove that the town had assets in excess of liabilities amounting to some £76,000. The assessor had warned the corporation to expect a total outlay on the building of £70,000 to £80,000 (the actual total was £167,000!), and so Wolfenden's arguments were sufficient to re-establish confidence and the scheme went ahead. His personal drive certainly established the scheme, though opposition clearly didn't vanish. The worries about expense even led to a fierce squabble over who should officiate at the foundation stone laying and who should pay for the ceremony. Such was the feeling that the whole ceremony was abandoned. This was certainly most unusual and is, I think, unique in the history of town hall building. But then Wolfenden's case is not typical of the pattern of patronage by local magnates. It is very much as though he were concerned more with a personal political struggle than with a battle for the town hall as such; and it is interesting to note that he resigned from the council in 1870, three years before the building was opened. Yet it is undeniable that without his intervention the Bolton town hall would never have been built as and when it was. This is clearly acknowledged in the memorial booklet published at the opening.

Another pattern of patronage is shown by the exactly contemporary story of Rochdale town hall (Fig. 36). There the protagonist was G. L. Ashworth who, like Wolfenden, was chairman of the town hall committee but unlike him survived to open the building as mayor. In this case, though, it is clear that Ashworth was very much concerned to see the whole palace completed; yet at the start he was apparently unconvinced and opposed the scheme for some years. It may be that his original opposition was not entirely genuine (and his name does not appear at all in some of the crucial early voting lists), but I think there are good reasons for accepting that it was. The scheme was first raised by a relative, Thomas Ashworth, in 1858 a bare two months after the elected corporation in Rochdale had taken over power from the town commissioners. There is no record that G. L. Ashworth opposed this motion; indeed it is likely that he did not; but the immediate outcome was a wrangle over sites that lasted until 1863, and which undoubtedly concealed a variety of vested interests. However, since the site finally selected belonged to the ecclesiastical authorities, it is unlikely that G. L. Ashworth benefited in any way from the outcome. However, in 1858 and in 1859 there was strong opposition, not only to the site, but to the whole idea of spending £15,000 to £20,000 (the estimated amount) on a town hall. In December 1859 when borrowing powers were discussed by the council, the decision to build a town hall was taken by a majority of one. G. L. Ashworth was apparently not present, but, though Thomas Ashworth appears among the supporters, another relative, Edmund Ashworth, opposed the scheme. He proposed an amendment that the whole scheme should be delayed, though he added that if his amendment were lost he would heartily support the scheme. His amendment was lost by a majority of two.

36 Rochdale town hall, W. H. Crossland, 1866–71

Still the Ashworths did not wholly support the scheme, for three months later the same Edmund Ashworth, in response to a petition from the ratepayers, again proposed that the scheme be dropped until there was more unanimity on the council. This time the majority for the town hall was eight; but there was no strong supporter for the scheme, so that, as the church authorities were standing out for a high price for the site, the idea did in fact go into abeyance until 1863. By then the voting was twenty-six to three in favour of the building, and G. L. Ashworth took the lead of the sub-committee that was set up to visit other new town halls. However, he was still apparently unconvinced, for when his sub-committee reported the cost of some of the buildings they visited (or at least the published figures),[2] he joined those voting to restrict the outlay to £15,000. He pointed out that the site was such that 'it is only requisite that we should have a handsome frontage'.[3] The restriction, however, was defeated, but again by the margin of a single vote.

So far the council had not even considered possible designs, though they had visited Halifax, Leeds, Blackburn and Preston. It is impossible to say how far Ashworth's appetite was whetted by the visits, but from this point on, in spite of the narrow majority for the extra expenditure, he changed his allegiance and fought for all the extras that would eventually bring the total up to £155,000. There is a cautiousness in the way he tested opinion over several years before committing himself which is hardly surprising in a businessman and local politician. What is significant is that his opposition was almost all in the years before any actual designs were studied. Once he had seen what other towns had done, and once their own architect was chosen, he was completely consistent in backing the architect to the full.

From the architect's point of view this pattern of patronage might seem to be ideal, and it is certainly important that Ashworth did not seem so much concerned with the details of the design as with the achievement of all the architect wanted. However, it is unlikely that we can dismiss him as a self-made man without any taste of his own. For a start, the Rochdale competition was decided without an outside assessor, and we must assume that he took a leading part in the criticism of the various designs. The finished building is certainly acceptable functionally and very far from unsuccessful in formal visual terms (Fig. 37). Yet the architect, W. H. Crossland, was almost unknown at the time. Though he may have been recommended by Edward Ackroyd of Halifax for whom he had already built Copley village, he had no major buildings to his credit.[4] Thus we have to accept that G. L. Ashworth was able to decide for himself what was likely to be a fine building.

However, even G. L. Ashworth does not fully exemplify the pattern of local patronage. Perhaps the best known case is Halifax where the rival interests of the Crossleys and the Ackroyds led to a patronage struggle that links town hall building

37 Rochdale town hall, W. H. Crossland, 1866–71; replacement tower by Alfred Waterhouse, 1883

with the famous battle of the styles. At Rochdale they may have chosen Crossland's design because they wanted Gothic, and may have expected to get good Gothic from a former pupil of Scott. Yet we might notice that of the towns they visited, Halifax, Leeds, Blackburn and Preston, only one had a Gothic town hall, and there is no record that it particularly impressed them. At Halifax we see two major industrialists vying in their attempts to endow the town, and this rivalry naturally led them to prefer designs in rival styles. The fierceness of the rivalry led the protagonists to outbid each other in all areas so that Halifax benefited not only from expensive designs but also from expensive architects. Edward Ackroyd commissioned G. G. Scott, while Crossley commissioned Sir Charles Barry.

The rivalry goes back well before the town hall, however, and the two families competed in their munificence elsewhere. Ackroyd, for instance, built his workers the model villages of Ackroyden and Copley, and provided the £20,000 for Scott's All Souls' church. Crossley built the congregational church (costing £18,000), with an equally aggressive spire, and a public baths and also employed Paxton to lay out

Crossley park. The town hall battle finally decided who was the real power in Halifax, and marked the end of the reign of the Ackroyds.

The idea of a town hall originated in 1847 not from the corporation but, like many others of that date, as the work of a Town Hall and Public Buildings Company, with a capital of £10,000 of which £8,000 was earmarked for the building. The Ackroyd family were active in these proposals, but difficulties over the site delayed a decision until after the incorporation of the town in 1848. Then the matter was taken up in a very tentative way by the new council who suggested making a town hall by converting a warehouse at an estimated outlay of £200. We do not know who prevented them, but the Halifax Improvement Act of 1853 included powers to build a town hall costing up to £15,000. There does not, however, appear to have been any strong local feeling for the scheme; and the mayor was flatly opposed to building a town hall at that stage. Three years later, though, Alderman Crossley submitted plans for a building by the Bradford firm Lockwood & Mawson in the Palladian style. He also offered a site and undertook to pay for the tower himself. Ackroyd was clearly aware what was going on, for soon afterwards he submitted plans by G. G. Scott whose national reputation quite surpassed that of Crossley's architect. The town council, unable to decide which horse to back, asked the borough engineer to produce a third set of plans, and the three sets were displayed together in 1857. Ackroyd promised a munificent contribution towards the construction of his design, and with the support of the local paper forced Crossley to withdraw. A year later he was able to offer a new, more central site, and by then he had secured enough support on the council for his offer to be accepted. A large public meeting was organised to support his proposals, while the other side replied with memorials to the council complaining of the reckless waste of money his scheme would involve. Ackroyd produced a number of arguments against Crossley, who was now supporting a Grecian-Italian design by the borough engineer. At this point Scott withdrew his plans which had been prepared for the other and much larger site, and the way was open for Crossley's schemes. The borough engineer's Grecian-Italian design does not survive, but there is little to recommend his first Gothic one. Quite possibly Crossley was well aware of this, but now that the field was clear we find that the plans were submitted to Barry who saw little merit in them. I find it difficult to believe that Crossley did not fully expect this. At any rate Barry was immediately commissioned to draw designs himself. This he did and offered an estimate of £20,000 which was soon revised upwards to £33,000 including the site and architect's commission. The final cost was in the region of £50,000, and the building, Barry's last (Fig. 24), was completed after his death by his son who may have been responsible for the curious and delightful spire.

The story of Halifax town hall is unusual, but not without parallel. There are a number of features too which indicate the lengths to which Crossley was prepared to go. For instance, the work for the foundations was put out to tender in January 1859 before the borough surveyor had been appointed architect, several months before Scott withdrew his design and long before Barry was formally approached. Crossley was rumoured to have given in the region of £100,000 towards the whole scheme, and this probably covers the redevelopment of the streets around the town hall which he certainly financed. For this he employed Lockwood & Mawson, and one wonders instantly what was the connection between this scheme and their suppressed design for the original town hall. For architects this jungle was unpleasant and could even be dangerous, and the patronage of such protagonists in competition could be cramping and restrictive, though the rewards were sweet. The result in this case was a fine building, and we can conclude that where patronage involved outbidding a rival the townspeople were likely to end up with something substantially more grandiose than they had originally planned.

At Halifax the rivalry may have given the corporation more say in their town hall

38 Todmorden town hall, J. Gibson, 1870–5

since it was ostensibly being built to their order and at their expense. However there are cases where a town hall was commissioned by a single patron almost without rivalry. The power of such all-embracing paternalism often led to imposing buildings; but they are often too grand for their towns. Todmorden town hall (Fig. 38) is an example where the building of 1870–5 would do credit to a town at least twice the size. The patronage in this case was that of the Fielden family who provided most of the local employment. Their handsome stone temple by Gibson totally dominates the centre of the little town that numbered only 11,000 inhabitants in 1871. It is true that the town doubled in size in the decade up to 1881, but even now the town hall is the only building of heroic scale in the town centre. It was certainly a complete town hall with its borough offices, magistrates' court and public hall all under one roof, but the paternalism of the patronage is underlined by the fact that Fielden not only footed the construction bill of £40,000 but also provided an endowment to run the building. Yet even so this building must be seen as an example of civic pride for it was in fact the completion of a scheme projected more than ten years earlier. The original intention had been to form a subscription company to finance the building. However the company went bankrupt when only the foundations were built and the architect even had to sue for payment.

Total patronage on the scale of Halifax or Todmorden was relatively rare, but it was not unknown. One of the grandest examples was the gift to Lancaster of a town hall by E. W. Mountford. Though built in 1906–9 it was the answer to a proposal of 1892. As at Todmorden, the council, who already possessed a handsome, though much extended, eighteenth-century town hall, wanted to build offices under one roof and provide a large public hall. They hesitated to build because of the burden on the rates; but they were fortunate that the town's largest employer was the immensely wealthy and megalomaniac Lord Ashton. Even so it was twelve years before he offered to help; but significantly when he made his offer in 1904 he spoke only of a minimum cost of £50,000.[5] Previously the corporation had estimated £70,000. The final total is thought to be nearer £155,000, but the intention was obviously to provide a handsome building. It is not surprise that the commission was given to E. W. Mountford at the height of his fame with Sheffield and Battersea town halls behind him. This was his last major building and is proudly baroque and rich with coloured marble inside, but it is none the less rather too large for Lancaster and feels a little aloof. The more obviously necessary fire station beside it (Fig. 39), designed as part of the scheme by Mountford's assistant F. D. Clapham, feels more friendly. Oddly enough the cupola of the eighteenth-century town hall makes a greater contribution to the townscape from a distance, though the new town hall fills the whole of one side of a grand square.

Another example of individual patronage of this kind occurred at Alloa, where J. Thompson Paton made the town a gift of a £30,000 town hall in 1887–8. Again, since this was to be a monument to his munificence, the quality was important even though the building was not large, and so the commission was given to Alfred Waterhouse. He produced a modest Gothic building in local sandstone containing a hall, library, reading rooms, billiard and smoking rooms and art school. Unlike Lancaster town hall, this building did not contain any provision for the town managers and, though a celebrated architect was chosen, it appears that extravagant display was kept to a minimum. The decoration ran to Burmantofts faience tiles on the pillars, but that might be no grander than the average bank or library. In fact with an overall size of 165 ft × 87 ft and a great hall of 95 ft × 49 ft the expenditure would not have allowed anything lavish. Paisley town hall is only slightly different. This was the gift to the town of the Clark family who owned the large Anchor thread works. The original donation of £20,000 came in George Clark's will, but the town was left to manage the competition for designs. It was won in 1875 by the local firm of Rennison & Scott, but the architect appointed in 1878 was W. H. Lynn of Belfast which might suggest intervention by the family. Lynn's design had been ruled out of the competition on the grounds of cost, but Mrs Clark provided an extra £30,000 when the estimates were presented. For this the town got a large concert hall (it is also known as the Clark Hall) in dull but monumental classical dress, and Mrs Clark promised an organ and a statue of her late husband.

In direct commissions like these the donors clearly had plenty of scope for directing or controlling the design. However, it is interesting that, in the case of both Paisley and Lancaster at least, the actual management of the competition[6] and supervision of the building really was left to the council. There is no evidence that they felt inhibited by the presence of donors in the background; on the contrary there is the same overspending that we see in other towns such as Leeds or Rochdale.

There were other celebrated benefactors who indulged in town hall giving along with their better known munificence. John Rylands, for instance, provided a town hall for Stretford in 1879; but that was only the work of a local architect, W. A. Lofthouse, and was in plain debased Gothic. Most of these buildings consisted solely of the public hall or of hall, library and club rooms, since the gift of a place of assembly and acceptable entertainment was more widely felt than the gift of offices. However, the Todmorden town hall is complete with borough court and offices, and the Lancaster town hall gives greater emphasis to the local government section. Govanhill municipal buildings, given to the town in 1879, appears to be another such example. Nor was such philanthropy confined to the latter part of the century. The market house and public hall at Chippenham was a £12,000 gift from the local MP in

39 Lancaster town hall, fire station (town hall behind), E. W. Mountford and F. D. Clapham, 1906–9

1850, and the Duke of Bedford paid for the Tavistock guildhall in 1848. Paisley and Lancaster were important towns, but the patronage spread right down the scale too. Guiseley near Leeds was given a £3,000 town hall by the MP for Bradford in 1866, that contained hall, library, reading room, school and town offices and was held in trust by the Local Board. At Saffron Walden in 1879 one of the town's own aldermen provided the town hall.

More often though, the patronage of individuals was confined to particular parts of the building, especially the ornament, as such huge gifts were only for the richest to afford. It was more likely that an individual patron would merely start a town hall scheme and contribute towards the cost. Thus although J. Guest, the new MP for Merthyr Tydfil, proposed to give a town hall in 1847, we find three years later that a public subscription was being raised for the building. At Dumbarton Lord Overton made a gift of the site in 1898, and Lord Mostyn did the same at Llandudno in 1894, but it was for the corporations to carry the scheme through. Throughout the period, too, there are innumerable gifts to complete the ornamentation of a building. The

Anglesey marble for Birmingham town hall in 1831 was a gift to the town, while the spread of trade resulted in a similar gift of all the marble for the council house from the city of Milan. At Manchester a group of citizens presented a magnificent silver gilt table service designed by Elkingtons to go with Waterhouse's building.[7] The Colchester tower has already been mentioned, and other common gifts were clocks, stained glass, organs, furniture, paintings and sculpture. The clock at Worksop public rooms and town hall was the gift of the Duke of Newcastle who owned the land. Joseph Pease gave the clock in the Darlington municipal buildings in 1864. The Duke of Portland gave £20 for furnishing Mansfield town hall in 1836. James Ramsden gave the stained glass windows in the lobby of Barrow-in-Furness town hall and also a bust of the queen. The list is endless and, as one would expect, the local landlords and the local industrialists are about equally represented. A few smaller towns were lucky enough to be able to draw on wider historical connections to elicit handsome gifts. Lerwick was particularly lucky in the gift of a fine set of stained glass windows from various Netherlands trading cities including Amsterdam. However, this sort of generosity came only after a scheme had got off the ground, and is less significant than the total patronage of individuals.

Yet, as I have suggested, even where a single donor was responsible for the whole, the towns often seem to have been responsible for the arrangements of the plan if not for the choice of style or architect. In fact the close involvement of the towns was really essential as without it the gift might appear unwanted and patronising. The great importance of the private donors was closely akin to the role played by the ambitious local magnates such as G. L. Ashworth. In the same way there is relatively little evidence of any local magnate significantly affecting the design of a town hall once the scheme was started. Individual patronage may have extended to the selection of an architect, but seldom further; and the main contribution of these powerful individuals was less in the design of the town halls than in the event of their being built. What is important is that there were individuals who saw a town hall scheme as worth staking their reputation on. Once such people had committed themselves to a scheme their determination to see it through was often a vital part in the achievement of a grandiose building.

5

The workings of patronage: committees

Commissioning by committee must have placed an unusual strain on the architects. It was not only that the scope for manipulation in winning a commission was enormous. It is no surprise that a considerable number of town hall commissions were awarded to local architects either directly or as the result of competitions. There are even quite a few cases of local architects being appointed after others had won the competition. The number of local contractors involved is even higher, and the majority of these will have had some connections on the council. Indeed one is tempted to connect the rarer occasions when councils looked beyond their own confines for craftsmen with the desire for real quality. Yet the problems of jobbery were not by any means the most serious for an architect who received a commission at the hands of a committee of twelve or more who would supervise his work. There was no single client whose wishes and needs could be identified and satisfied. Each design change would need to be agreed by at least a majority, and changes on the committee could lead to constant modifications. In the face of these problems it is not surprising that many architects were tempted to design an appealing façade behind which could be fitted whatever became necessary at any stage in the building. In the greater town halls the architects learnt to manage their disparate masters, and we shall trace their success in the following chapter; but first we need to look at the difficulties.

In the first place, committees can be notoriously indecisive; and there might be great delays in settling who should build a town hall or whether it should be built at all. Such battles were often long-drawn-out and might precede any design by a matter of years. What concerns us here is the effect of such delays on the designers. I want to ignore the indecisiveness that was so often seen in the awarding of premiums for a competition. Even when an architect had finally landed a commission his difficulties were seldom over. In the first place the decision to build a town hall was seldom unanimous, and the opposition might well be able to stop the scheme even after the designs were drawn. This was especially likely since there were now firm estimates for the first time and these might very well, indeed generally did, not correspond with the figures named as the original allowance. The allowance was seldom based on an accurate estimate of the likely cost of what was wanted, but more often simply named a desirable limit to the cost, at best related to the known cost of earlier buildings. Besides, especially in the years before 1860, a town hall was a complex yet nebulous type of building so that it was difficult even to predict with any certainty what accommodation would be wanted in the form of offices, let alone what it would cost. Corporations might be quite genuinely in doubt about sensible requirements for some of the lesser facilities such as police parade grounds or witness accommodation. Also if the early opposition was at all sustained, or the choice of site delayed, the progress of municipal legislation might necessitate substantial expansion of the accommodation required. Most designs allowed for some extra office space, but the scope for expansion was seldom sufficient if the scheme took more than a very few years from conception to realisation. The inevitable result was that some of the early estimates were hopelessly wide of the mark, and yet had to be used as guidelines in the early discussions. Quite often they remained as targets even when they were no longer appropriate. The case of Rochdale has already been described. At Leeds too, where the ultimate cost reached around £125,000, the first agreed allowance was only £20,000. The same story recurs in almost every town hall building venture. And inadequate funding was only part of the problem, for in the vast majority of cases the winning design needed modification even before the work began. Some modifications could save money, and were intended to do so, but there were often a host of minor changes, each of which meant a slight increase, so that the final total sometimes bore little relation even to the original architect's estimate.

This sort of vacillation did not always work against the architect, but it might well involve a considerable amount of work in redesigning that would be wasted. The case of William Hill's design for Preston town hall is one of the worst. He won the competition in 1854, but the council were already alarmed at their own estimate of £30,000 and so asked him to design a building costing only £16,000. They then decided to build only £9,500 worth of his scheme; then a fortnight later asked for additional buildings bringing the value up to £12,000. The building committee then asked for a number of improvements, such as fireproof floors, which brought the estimate back up to £16,151. At this point the council declined to proceed with the building at all, and the whole matter was left in abeyance until 1862. In that year G. G. Scott was commissioned to build a town hall that cost in the region of £70,000

(Fig. 40). Hill's miserable story is preserved in a letter to the *Builder*[1] where he claims that he was not even paid in full for the work he did, and was unable to sue for payment since he had no contract under seal of the council and had only acted on the instructions of the town clerk. The experience does not seem to have deterred him from competing elsewhere, and his success at Bolton will certainly have recouped any loss.

Hill's case was not unique, and even when buildings were erected, major changes were not uncommon. The classical Birkenhead town hall which stands so appropriately in the centre of the upper side of Hamilton Square is a case in point. The competition was for a site at the corner of the square, and, though Ellison's designs for that site have not been traced, they must have been very different from what was appropriate for the freestanding building that he eventually put up. Changes in the direction of piecemeal construction were more common, particularly in smaller towns, and must generally have frustrated good design. At Aston, Alexander & Henman produced a unified design for public offices, baths and library in 1879. When the tenders appeared it was decided, on the grounds that there was a trade depression, that only the public offices should be built. Though the library was in fact added in the following year, one major element in the composition never arrived. An ensuing frustration for succeeding architects was the request to design extensions where the original building restricted the choice of style. Where a partnership survived, this might not be a great problem. For instance, the Hampstead vestry hall of 1876 by Kendall & Mew was extended by F. Mew in 1886. At Rotherham, by contrast, R. J. Lovell, the architect of the extensions, which are admittedly of little merit, was blamed by the professional press for the nastiness of the building he was commissioned to extend. Reading provides one of the saddest cases of extension. The municipal buildings were opened in 1877, a highly competent design by Waterhouse; but the town still lacked a new public hall, library and museum. These make up the second block, begun in 1878 and completed in 1882. Unfortunately the town was unwilling to re-employ Waterhouse, and, after several months of indecision, pruning of the estimates and an abortive competition, T. Lainson,[2] a much less competent designer, was given the task of producing something to fit with the Waterhouse block. Such a process could not but lead to an ensemble that tails off badly, and it must be admitted that, although the total cost of the two buildings was kept to around £50,000 (of which the corporation provided less than half) Reading missed a major opportunity. Waterhouse's larger block at Hove cost only about £40,000 and was a great asset to the town until its recent destruction by fire.

Even in major towns this indecision caused considerable problems. Yeoville

40 Preston town hall, selected design, G. G. Scott, 1862; the tower was heightened in building

Thomason had suspiciously good connections with the Birmingham city council, yet he was forced to design his council house (Fig. 2) piecemeal. The first stage with the offices was built from 1874 to 1879 and provided a unified frontage, but the whole block containing the remaining offices, museum and art gallery was not begun until 1884. The result was that Thomason was deprived of a major opportunity for civic grandeur. There was little scope for designing a processional route into a building that was effectively a single row of offices backed by a corridor. His staircase was set baldly against the back wall, and, though its dome composes adequately from the front and the actual stair gives a grand entry to the banqueting hall, that was clearly not all that Thomason wanted. Seen from the rear, the stair and dome still look improperly integrated into the design and a plan of the 1880s shows what Thomason intended. He planned a grand bridge running across the middle of the courtyard above an arcade. The earlier plans too (published in 1878) clearly show a similar intention. The bridge was to link the main block to the art gallery and is an imaginative conception that would have provided a welcome second axis to the interior. However, since the art gallery was not added until several years after the completion of the council house, the bridge could only be achieved by adding L-shaped passages outside the stair well so that after mounting the stairs and turning about at the half-landing one had instantly to make another complete about-turn to seek for the extension. This was such an awkward progression that it was in fact never built, but it could easily have been avoided had the building been designed as a whole. Now the courtyard is left as a single space, unnecessarily large even with the more recent extensions into it; and interior access to the art gallery was confined to a glazed iron walkway propped high against the side of the building on long cast iron pillars.

There are cases, though, where an architect did manage to achieve a major building in spite of indecision. At Hull the competition of 1861 was decided in dubious circumstances.[3] The town was not unanimously in favour of building at all, and the pro-town hall party was itself divided over the choice of site. However Brodrick managed to emerge the eventual winner, and his fruity Italianate building (1862–6) became a landmark in the town. It was, incidentally, tacked on to an existing building at the rear, but visually took no account of that. He produced a block whose façade was completely self-sufficient and a unified design. This sort of good fortune was, however, rare, and many architects who were even better connected with their prospective employers than Brodrick failed to get their own way.

The most obvious scope for indecision and restrictions was at the time of the commission. A detailed examination of some of the buildings, however, makes it quite obvious that committees could and did exercise a troublesome and minute control over the whole building. I have already described the building of Barrow-in-Furness town hall where the council's attitude resulted in an incomplete building (p. 63). Some aspects of that story are relevant here. In the first place there is evidence of continuing economy on the part of the council. The original allowance for the whole scheme had been £70,000, and, though only part was to be built, the estimated cost was still £50,000 (as against the architect's estimate of £20,000) since a library, museum and banqueting hall were added, and it was decided not to leave the mayor's parlour until later as originally intended. It is hard to be sure of the final cost, but the figure was between £69,000 and £79,000, which is closer to the original estimate than any other town hall of comparable size. If that represents a triumph for the economy party, it certainly made things difficult for the architect, W. H. Lynn. The constant scrutiny and paring of estimates made it difficult for him to insist on the best quality material from his suppliers. The most dramatic result of this was the failure of the tower. The soft red sandstone was inadequate as it was not cut from the very hardest beds, and the tower began to subside. Blame was never fully apportioned, though J. P. Seddon was called in to arbitrate, but one factor was undoubtedly the contractor's difficulty in making any profit on the job. They changed quarries in their search for good stone, but it was evident that they wanted to 'cut ashlar out of rubble'.[4] In spite of the architect's fears the committee refused to authorise better quality stone, and even ordered the work to proceed after the first reports of settlement. At this point Lynn produced an alternative design for the upper stages of the tower in wood, but it was not adopted. This was unfortunate for a month later, as the town hall keeper recorded, 'a serious defect [was] found in the tower. . . . The men stopped at once . . . men commenced to take down the tower, they had only about three foot more to do before it should have been finished'.[5] The tower had to be partially dismantled, and when re-erected was shorter by 13 ft and lighter by some 200 tons.

The council's close supervision and economy can be seen at all stages. They frequently delayed paying their bills, and their squabbles with the main contractor dragged on for two years. They tried to abandon a number of small essentials, such as enclosing the weights of the clock, and even allowed the architect to make the attic windows non-opening. They queried the architect's purchase of a pitch-pine flagstaff when a Norway spruce had been specified, though the difference in cost can only have been a matter of a few pounds and the pitch-pine pole was ready to hand in the docks. More damaging from the design point of view was the diminution and even abandonment of some of the carving. The loss of the intended allegorical panels beneath the council chamber windows materially detracts from the success of the façade. Lynn's patience and persistence obviously helped in the retention of the grand elements of his interior, but the cumulative effect of the restrictions was not a happy one.

The abandonment of individual features, particularly in the decoration, is, however, more common than overall parsimony. Towers were a frequent target for the economists, and Lynn's other great town hall, at Chester (Fig. 33), had to begin without its tower. Blackburn never built the two low towers planned, and there are other similar economies. Certainly a town council could save money by choosing its materials carefully from the start. However, if they were to be really successful in their economy they would be bound to end up with a simple building that would do no particular credit to the town. Pendleton town hall is a case in point. The town was about the size of Bolton when it began its town hall, yet the intention was to spend no more than £9,000. The cost was slightly more than this, but there was no question of a building to advertise the town. The town hall is of stock brick with Yorkshire stone dressings, and, though the Franco-Italian motifs are handled as adequately as in most contemporary office buildings, it lacks any outstanding feature such as a tower. The lush doorway in Caen stone with columns of polished Aberdeen granite is no substitute. As the town was even then little more than a well-to-do suburb on the fringes of Manchester, the advertisement of independent existence will have been unnecessary, and the more substantial residents anyway looked to Manchester itself. In fact it required exceptional circumstances and ability to produce an effective town symbol on the cheap. Waterhouse was about the only one to achieve it in his market and public offices at Darlington, which cost only £14,000 in 1864.[6] These are striking because the whole dramatic effect is concentrated in one of his best towers (Fig. 75). Yet the materials are cheap, stock brick again with simple stone bands and carved mouldings only on the clock stage. The offices come in two small blocks, one adjoining the tower, that are no more than utilitarian, while the bulk of the building is a simple glass and iron market hall. In fact it is little more than a market building, and barely counts as a town hall. The council never met in the offices, but in a little regency building nearby. However it deserves a place for its contribution to civic dignity and it remains a most effective urban symbol even today.

Clearly, though, elected councils were doing little more than manage their households well when they made real attempts to economise. The architects needed to be able to adjust their plans so that any modifications could be made without the main features (and especially the façade) being materially affected.[7] T. E. Collcutt narrowly avoided that at Wakefield, where his unusual town hall with its Queen Anne windows and its gothicky tower (Fig. 79) makes a delightful and complete composition. Behind the façade the plan is clearly workaday, but the main rooms are handsomely fitted up. However the council balked at the rising cost of the carved ornament, and ordered the work stopped, so that the panels on the rear of the building remain uncut to this day. The same economy can be seen in the much less ambitious town hall at Oswaldtwistle which still has along its façade a row of uncarved stones that should have been Corinthian capitals.

Perhaps, however, these minor economies were to be preferred to the difficulties caused by a committee that could not always persuade the whole council to do what they wanted. At Oldham the architects Potts & Woodhouse get no credit at all for a building that might have made its mark by sheer size. It is true their design was derivative, but too little was built for us to form a fair judgment. They were asked to produce designs for extensions to an older building, but the extensions were incomplete and the architects undoubtedly had a clear idea of how they would ultimately grow into a whole building. These ideas must have been developed to please the committee, but they failed to win the support of the full council. It was later admitted: 'how the new building came to be part of a large and comprehensive scheme instead of simply an "extension" as it is still rather incongruously styled, is not one of the most creditable episodes in our municipal history.'[8] Once the secret was out the council refused to proceed and the whole scheme fell to the ground. Potts & Woodhouse had achieved the equivalent of only the central section of one side of Leeds or Bolton town hall, though their plans were for a whole building of that type that would have been around 240 ft square and larger than either of its predecessors. The only façade of these extensions is in a narrow side street and has no opportunity to contribute to the townscape.

It would seem, however, that the influence of committees was detrimental mainly in the imposition of detailed restrictions and small excisions that were the result of close scrutiny of the expenditure. In that these came from a whole group of people, each with a different interest in the building, their potential difficulty should have been immense. Yet it seems that these committees were generally reluctant to interfere in the more important aspects of design so that the architects were mostly able to achieve almost all that they had intended. Indeed I know of no parallel to Oldham where a scheme was completely abandoned halfway through. The normal situation was that once a council had committed itself to building, the nature of corporate finance and the fear of corporate loss of face encouraged a bull-doggish determination to achieve what they had set out to do.

6

The strong architect and the corporation

In determining to achieve their goal rather than suffer the loss of prestige involved in abandoning a half-built town hall, town councils were putting themselves very much in the hands of their architects. A lucky architect could persuade his clients of the desirability of any number of extras, and, provided the corporation maintained the will to finish a building, the money could generally be found somewhere. Bankruptcy of the client at least was an impossibility. This aspect of the relations between architect and client had a generally beneficial effect on the buildings produced. And in the case of town halls, the smaller scale and the smaller circle of people concerned meant that architects were not subject to the same extremes of pressure that we find in the great national public commissions. Yet because the clients were public bodies, financing the building as part of a very much larger budget than could be supplemented by issues of stock or government loans, architects could generally be sure of achieving everything that was politically acceptable at the time. It was accepted that 'the tendency of all corporations is to go in for some degree of dignity'[1] with the supposition that today's extravagance should be appropriate for tomorrow's town. It was for the architect to provide the visible grandeur that was wanted, and provided it could be suggested that it was necessary or a good investment the corporation would be likely to accept.

Sir Charles Barry in 1859 summed up a feeling that survived right through the period and beyond. 'A town hall should in my opinion be the most dominant and important of the municipal buildings of the city in which it is placed. It should be the means of giving due expression to public feeling upon all national and municipal events of importance. [It should serve] as it were as the exponent of the life and soul of the city.'[2] His choice of the word city rather than town simply underlines the tendency to aim high, excusing it as building for the future. That events often justified these aims is a matter of history, but it also meant that over-grand town halls could become perfectly acceptable working symbols. They seldom remained mere window dressing. An anonymous pamphleteer in Blackburn provides a retrospective appreciation of his town's extravagance. 'I could not but think of the debt we owed to the prophetic and courageous spirit possessed by the fathers of many of the gentlemen on the platform. . . . what did they do? They bought a green field and put the town hall and market on the growing grass. That was the measure of their courage and faith in the future of Blackburn, and we of this generation . . . are enjoying the reward.'[3] He was arguing in the 1880s for the replacement of Patterson's building of 1852 by an even grander Gothic fabric.

Leeds town hall which now seems such an appropriate symbol, and which has long proved too small, must have appeared hopelessly oversize when it was first built in what was largely a residential area. The story of its building illustrates particularly well the relations between architect and client. There was undoubtedly a sufficient need to make the clients accept the functional necessity of a hall. Dissatisfaction with court and council accommodation went back at least to 1830, and the only big public hall in Leeds dated from 1792. A move for a Peel memorial hall and rivalry with Bradford led ultimately, and in spite of some opposition, to the competition of 1852. There were only sixteen designs (unpromisingly few when compared to sixty-eight at Birmingham in 1830), but Sir Charles Barry, in selecting the young and inexperienced Brodrick, recommended him warmly. 'After what he had seen of the drawings [Fig. 19] he felt sure that there was sufficient talent and genius in the architect to carry out anything which an architect could be required to do.'[4] He also opened the door to modification and enrichment by declaring that none of the prizewinning designs 'would be altogether worthy of being adopted without undergoing a considerable amount of modification'.[5]

In the early stages Brodrick produced a number of alternative plans to meet Barry's suggestions. He offered single and double rows of offices along the side of his great hall, but his most creative suggestions relate to the grand entry and stairs. He had toyed with the idea of a pediment (which was later taken up at Bolton by his pupil Hill) and rounded colonnaded corners. One design (Fig. 8) shows an entry via a huge octastyle portico to a transverse colonnaded hall some 125 ft by 25 ft with stairs rising in straight flights on either side of the doors to a colonnaded first floor with a semi-circular council chamber, apparently divided from the hall only by a glass screen. Unfortunately this was not built; neither was the other grand stair he designed which must also date from the early period before the tower was agreed on. All the new plans, however, increased the depth of the building by two bays, and this extra accommodation was never queried. Barry's principal criticism had been the lack of a tower, and the whole front and gallery of the hall were rearranged to allow for this. The portico was widened to ten columns and the doorway set farther back, while the vestibule became roughly cruciform in shape beneath a dome. The other increase was the adoption of the double instead of the single row of offices which allowed Brodrick to create a more or less solid block instead of a grand hall with courtrooms in pavilions loosely attached at the corners. This was a sensible addition, but a substantial increase in the cost, and in May 1853 an application for an extra £10,000 was submitted to the council bringing the estimate up to £45,000. This was already more than double the first working figure, so £6,000 was refused and the tower cut out. Brodrick's contract drawings survive, and make no provision for the tower, though the gable end of the hall is suspiciously plainer than his competition sketch. Even so with prices rising rapidly the main contract in 1853 was for £41,835.

The corporation minutes and the log book of the clerk of the works between them preserve a minute account of the steady accumulation of extras that brought the final total to around £125,000. Brodrick was determined to have good quality and kept an eagle eye on the work. He gave instructions 'to put plenty of hoop iron in the walls and through the openings [of the foundations] and never to mind if the quantity should exceed the contract'.[6] The contractors were driven to complain of 'the dressing of so much of the face of the rubble walling generally and the expensive manner in which they were required to execute the work generally'.[7] On one occasion Brodrick 'was so dissatisfied with the . . . stone being used for cornice in the small intablature that he took a hammer and destroyed a cornice stone to prevent it being used in the building'.[8] When the clerk of the works tried a similar tack he was 'threatened to be knocked off the scaffold by the bricklayer'.[9] Then Brodrick frequently made alterations, trying out ornaments and altering the outline of the cornice. He even delayed work on the base of the tower as 'he thought he might alter the outline a little'.[10] He will have needed council support for each item of extra expenditure and it is significant that there were few occasions when his requests were turned down. It was hard even to keep track of the extras, and when the contractor sued the council for the recovery of £20,000 that was owing to him he claimed that £13,800 of that was for extra work. The council estimated only £3,598 worth of extras.

In the end the only major alteration to the building that was refused was the making of the construction fireproof. The biggest single advance was the decision to allow a tower after all. As early as February 1854 £1,500 extra was allowed for alterations 'in order that a tower may be erected on the building if it should at any time hereafter be thought desireable to do so'.[11] This must have involved the complete redesigning of the vestibule and new foundations, but the tower was not designed until 1856. Then Brodrick produced two designs (Figs 20, 21), one, that was built, rather cheaper with a domed cap and one for a much taller fantastic spire. Even the cheaper design was estimated at £6,500 extra; but once again Brodrick got what he wanted, and when all the tenders turned out over that figure the council added a further £500 to the later application for £5,000 extra for the organ, apparently without demur. Brodrick was also allowed, apparently without comment, to roof the great hall with a new and daring system of laminated ribs.[12] The worries and expense of the hollow tile vault of the St George's hall at Liverpool must have been well known, but there is no record of any questioning when Brodrick decided to change his design from a well tried girder system to a method that had only twice been used in the country and never in conjunction with a plaster ceiling. The transept of the Great Exhibition building and King's Cross station were both covered by roofs supported on lightweight ribs of laminated wood held by wrought iron bolts, and were the only accessible precedents. We do not know precisely why or when Brodrick adopted the new design but it evidently caused some interest in professional circles. Donaldson records that Sir Charles Barry and his son visited the site in 1855 to see the plans for the proposed alterations and improvements to the roof.[13] A week later he also notes that Brodrick ordered the number of laminated ribs to be doubled, so it may well be that Brodrick was acting on Barry's advice.

In fact the only serious disagreement between Brodrick and the Leeds city council was over the four large ventilating towers which began to sprout from the roof without any warning. Brodrick clearly had definite ideas of the form his heating and ventilating system would take, and apparently anticipated the council. He probably wanted to avoid the sort of problems that Dr Reid was causing Barry at the Houses of Parliament, a squabble of which he must have been well aware. In fact Dr Reid had also done the heating of the St George's hall at Liverpool, which the council had visited when preparing their brief; and the building press had already reported how the building had been 'cut and hacked and altered by Dr. Reid with his tinkering'.[14] The lesson was not lost on Brodrick who was determined to find a scheme that would work and a contractor who would co-operate. He chose Hadens of Trowbridge;[15] and they visited the site in 1854, presumably at his invitation.[16] No other heating contractor is recorded as visiting the building, but their visit was two years before the council even considered methods of warming and ventilating the building. None the less, when the ventilating towers began to be built, Brodrick had neglected to submit plans of them and the committee had the work stopped. Brodrick eventually persuaded them that the towers, though visible, could be ornamental, and six months later the work went on. The surviving drawings of different alternatives show how much care Brodrick gave to their outline. They are an important feature of the whole design, though they were not part of the original scheme, and they are closely copied in the derivative building at Bolton.

The continuous changes and rising costs must have been a problem for the corporation, but it is significant that throughout the period of construction the town hall question never became an issue of confidence in the council or at the municipal elections. However the council could not be seen to be indulging in wilful extravagance and thus were unhelpful when the contractor's cash flow problems brought him into difficulties. Brodrick refused to certify extra sums for payment, and the council accordingly forced the contractor into bankruptcy. It may well be that he had seriously underestimated the costs (it was a period of rapid price rises anyway), but it was not uncommon for councils elsewhere to allow for adjustments in prices. It is unlikely that in this instance they saved any money, but the contractor, Samuel Atack,[17] proved a useful scapegoat. His successors got on better with the architect, or at least were more successful in anticipating his intentions, and subsequently built Hull town hall for him. The bankruptcy added a good deal of drama to the story of the building, but it did not change the situation over the provision of extras. Brodrick's modifications and additions continued until the opening of the building in 1858, and even after. The organ has already been mentioned; it also required an ornamental case which Brodrick designed. Then there was the clock for the tower. Brodrick even had difficulty in persuading the committee to accept his design of a face only 10 ft 6 in. in diameter instead of 15 ft, and he eventually compromised on 13 ft. The redesigned entrance was capped by a splendid and expensive sculpture by John Thomas (Fig. 83), and carved panels were needed beside the doors. Even the £1,600 asked by J. G. Crace was not in the original estimates. The surroundings had to be laid out too, and supplied with handsome cast iron lamps, not to mention Marochetti's bronze statue of Wellington. The final embellishment suggested by Brodrick was the provision of four Portland stone lions in 1866 (Fig. 22). These were carved by William Keyworth who had worked for Brodrick at Hull, and necessitated the buildings of plinths and the low wall that conceals the entries to the basement. They are important aesthetically and do not look like an afterthought, so Brodrick may well have intended them as replacements for the four groups of statues he originally intended.[18]

The final achievement is masterly, and ranks among the most impressive buildings of the mid-Victorian period. It is as though Brodrick was intent on making his name with the building, as indeed he did. He was later one of six architects invited to produce designs for the National Gallery in London as well as being selected for the second competition for Manchester town hall. It is also interesting that, though the corporation did not accept his offer to design further municipal buildings on the adjoining site, he was also responsible for three other outstanding public buildings in the city—the corn exchange, the Mechanics' Institute (now the Civic Theatre) and the Calverly Street baths. He clearly established excellent relations with his clients and remained firmly in their favour. Outside Leeds, though, the story is rather different, for the tale of soaring costs became the bogey of other corporations, and in spite of similar experiences elsewhere the Leeds town hall became a by-word for costliness. It was only in his native Hull that Brodrick was able to secure another town hall commission, and his competition entries for both Manchester and Bolton were turned down.

Experience of course was important, and future corporations and architects could learn from the situation at Leeds. None the less it remained difficult to ensure that estimates were anything like accurate or even made on a proper basis; and it was still only where an architect was lucky enough to serve a council really determined to achieve a complete art work that he was likely to succeed. Early in the period neither architect nor client can have been quite clear how things would work out or how effective a building could be; there were after all few precedents. Birmingham (Fig. 1) became a *cause célèbre* for the way the commissioners forced the architects into bankruptcy. The architect's rashness is a feature in the story, but the commissioners are often blamed for the way in which they held the architects to a fixed price. There must be an element of sharp practice in the way the experienced businessmen on the board calmly accepted the young architect's optimistic estimates and held him to them. However they can be excused some caution in 1832 when such corporate magnificence was so completely new. They were careful in requiring the plans to be submitted to Soane for advice, and subsequently to Foster of Liverpool. Modifications suggested by both of them were adopted. Unwisely, however, Hansom did not stand out for specific payment for the extras, but in this he acted no differently from Barry at the Houses of Parliament in the 1840s. Soane's suggestions actually meant a slight saving so Hansom proposed to use Corinthian rather than Ionic columns for the interior which brought the estimate back up. This elaboration was not at the request of the committee, but they did retain the Corinthian columns when they also took up Foster's suggestion of reverting to the original expensive colonnade instead of the cheaper version suggested by Soane. Then there was no extra allowance when it was decided to build the west wall in stone instead of brick and plaster. Since the architects and their friends had undertaken to act as sureties for the cost, any great increase would obviously result in their bankruptcy, and in spite of every ingenuity on Hansom's part[19] the extra work meant that costs inevitably exceeded the estimate and Hansom and Welch were made bankrupt in 1834. The brief relationship with the

Birmingham masters was not a happy one, and was almost certainly hampered by Hansom's warm support for trade unionism and his involvement in the Operative Builders' Union in Birmingham for whom he designed a guildhall in 1833. Financial problems in a building of this size, however, should have been expected and Hansom was unique in being held to blame. Other architects were held responsible for architectural failings (Burrell who was blamed for the unsafe state of Longton town hall in 1872 is a case in point), but it was possible to escape even this. The architects of Winchester guildhall, Jeffery & Skiller, escaped a censure motion of the council by a handsome margin after the rear wall had begun to collapse; and Pearce, whose town hall on the river bank at Yarmouth subsided a whole foot, was not even criticised. Bellamy and Hardy escaped censure, too, when a decayed cornice block fell from their town hall at Ipswich and killed a man. The building had been up ten years and it was pointed out that it was the building committee who authorised the particular materials (in this case Bath stone), though presumably the architect also accepted them.

Still, the bankruptcy of Hansom was hardly a victory for the street commissioners who were left with a half-finished building. One wonders whether Foster of Liverpool, who took over and offered his services free, felt any twinge of conscience. At any rate the building was not finally completed until 1850, by which time the orchestra wall had been completely reconstructed and the total bill was about £50,000 instead of the intended £17,000.

If they wanted their building there was no way a corporation could avoid footing the bill eventually, and Liverpool's treatment of Elmes was in marked contrast (Fig. 17). What had happened in Birmingham must have been known in detail by the time of the Liverpool competition, for Foster was the borough surveyor of Liverpool. Again the winner of the competition was a youngish man, H. L. Elmes, but once selected he was given every opportunity. Presumably the corporation even paid for his visit to Berlin to study Schinkel's work after they had asked him to combine his law courts and concert hall in one, and there may even have been another visit to Munich to study the hollow tile roof of the Jesuit church there.[20] Construction was admittedly slow, but there is no record that the corporation were particularly impatient with their architect and his increasing ill health. When he died in 1849 the hollow tile vault was barely completed and no work had been done on the interior. The corporation were prepared, too, to provide the very best assistance, and Cockerell's connection with the building goes back as far as 1846 when his design for the sculptured pediment was adopted in spite of some local opposition. In the event this was as well for no other architect could have finished the building as effectively. It is good to note also that Liverpool's interest in Elmes extended to financial support for his widow, which was doubly honest for his commission was now being paid to others. And though the cost rose to £300,000, over three times the originally intended sum, Liverpool can hardly be said to be the loser. Even the parsimony or prudery that defeated the sculptural programme did not materially affect a building that could not have been conceived, let alone achieved, except on a generous scale.

Waterhouse was probably the master at managing relations with his council clients, for he had no difficulty in persuading the Manchester corporation to spend nearly four times their original estimate of £250,000. So far from any recriminations, the cost of nearly £1,000,000 became a matter for boasting and proved that Manchester had the wealth to spend that on its town hall. Such advertisement was worth much more to trade than any improvements along the banks of the Irwell. By and large the big cities did not boast of having spent large sums on their town halls. They wanted the grandest possible building, but preferred to preserve the myth that estimates had not been greatly exceeded. Actually Waterhouse's relationship with Manchester corporation was a long one, and is nearly typical of town hall architects, for he was a Manchester man and had only moved his office to London shortly before the town hall competition. He was well connected locally, and the name Waterhouse appears regularly in the lists of council members. Also he had done good work locally before he won the town hall competition. His first public commission was for education offices, later council offices, at Droylsden in 1858, which were substantial but cheap. In the next year he won the major competition for the assize courts which were justly praised. It may have been an error of judgment in artistic terms to opt for banded brickwork which would easily succumb to the dirty atmosphere. The justices complained that the pattern was obscured within a year of opening, and their doubts may have been a factor in deciding the council to insist on stone for their building. Waterhouse was quite undeterred, for when he was approached to design the royal exchange in 1865 he drew a building, again in striped brick, that included an open promenade at first floor level for the merchants to do their business al fresco. Needless to say this was never built, but the fact that he was approached rather than competing indicates the status he had achieved with the Manchester burghers. As I have already said, he was one of six local architects invited to compete for the police courts; and there is Owen's College to consider too, though he was not appointed architect there until 1869.

He was clearly well established with many members of the corporation by the time he won the town hall competition. J. Neild, then one of the younger members of the corporation, was sufficiently impressed with Waterhouse's approachability to recall years later his satisfaction at the way the tower design was changed. The committee had expressed some doubts about the rather dull tower, but were nervous of pointing out so major a fault when they had after all selected the design. Waterhouse disarmed them by frankly agreeing that his design was mean but had been made so to enable him to stay within the estimates. Could he design a proper tower? The committee, of course, accepted and he built a far more elaborate version (Fig. 76). In fact Waterhouse managed to include a good many other extras, as well as those suggested by the assessors. An interesting list is preserved in the corporation proceedings for 1873–4.[21] He divides the extra work into six groups. First, extras to make the building more monumental, which included terracotta walling and groins in the main passages, stone vaults instead of plaster for the Albert Square block, stone doorways in the reception rooms, stone groining instead of girders in the mayor's hexagon, stone panels for paintings in the reception room and ornamental slating for the roof. The long passages were broken by side bays with seating, a most imaginative and useful touch, and even the upper passages had their length relieved by the insertion of pointed arches in brick. So much of this is essential to the final building that one wonders whether his design would have been at all successful had he been forced to work more nearly to his original designs. His second category was extra work to improve the light, which carries an implied criticism of his fine planning. This involved the provision of ceramic tiles or white glazed bricks in the areas, and white glazed bricks in the cross passage where they are functional but contrast oddly with the main corridor. Then there was unspecified extra work on the three circular staircases and the grand stair. Perhaps this included the polishing of the risers to bring out the colour of the three different marbles. The fifth category was extra work that should have been in the finishing contract, but was better done early to avoid damage by later scaffolding. Finally there was a good deal of extra work for strength. Only one part had to be rebuilt, when an old well was discovered under the foundations; but a number of relieving arches were added and brick piers and vaulting replaced cement, and window mullions were cut from solid stone instead of stone and brick. He slips into this category the substitution of Forest of Dean stone for Robin Hood stone in the groining on account of its better colour. There were also extra iron beams and girders, extra chain bands in the towers, and finally lead roof ridges instead of tiles. Stone parapets instead of eaves in the courts were excused as being a better fire risk. This was an enormous list of extras and does not cover the last years of building when there must have been further increases connected with Waterhouse's plans for the decoration. It says a great deal for Waterhouse's relations with the council that no trace of serious disagreement has been preserved. He was certainly able to convince them that it would be well worth while.

We look back at completed buildings, but it cannot have been easy to maintain the confidence of a corporation when there was little to show and the money was draining away. This group of four major town halls, however, does not provide the only instance of corporations being more or less willing accomplices in their own fleecing. The prices in Appendix III show very clearly how estimates were exceeded with monotonous regularity, and yet the buildings were completed. Of course once the building began to rise there would be something to show, and Manchester was only one place where strict rules had to be enforced to stop the flow of visitors that was impeding the work. Rochdale (Fig. 37) provides another good example of corporate stubbornness. Crossland's design was supposed to be for a town hall within the allowance of £20,000. There were some modifications to his design before work began, but the first tender of over £5,000 for the foundations alone must have seemed an alarmingly high proportion of the total. Admittedly these involved huge cellars in fifteen feet of made ground on the marshy river bank, but they were essential and one wonders whether Crossland and the other competitors had been fully informed on the site or had allowed for this when they made their designs. At any rate Rochdale had G. L. Ashworth to fight the scheme through, and Crossland was fortunate in a patron who maintained his confidence in him. This was in spite of some difficulty, for letters preserved in the Rochdale reference library reveal serious trouble with the clerk of the works. He questioned some of Crossland's instructions and fell out with the workmen; and Crossland wrote sternly that he was to stop spreading rumours of trouble with the contractors 'for that is now over'. He was also to refrain from comparing the workmanship here with his previous job for 'the report now going through Lancashire is simply ruinous to me'.[22] The clerk of works may have been justified for only a dozen years after the opening the spire was found to be so badly affected with dry rot that it had to be demolished (Fig. 36);[23] but that was the only structural failure. More important was the ease with which Crossland appears to have been able to modify and extend his scheme. His designs for the tower went through several stages of improvement and elaboration, as did the fenestration of the front. He was able to enlarge the hall by cutting out the only through passage at first floor level. And there are very few instances of omissions except in the latter stages of the sculptural programme. The only alteration that was purely functional was the realignment of the fire station to give the horse pumps easy access, but that would hardly have increased the cost. Still the total list of extras is some tribute to his vision, and the final result was a fine romantic ensemble that displays its unselfconscious irregularity along the promenade that was created as its stage. The land behind and to the west was bought and laid out as a park, a new street was constructed along the river bank and planted with Canadian elms, and a handsome balustrade and new bridge were constructed shortly after the town hall was completed. The whole makes an extremely impressive composition, and taken altogether was the second most expensive undertaking of the corporation in the years up to 1886.[24]

The underlying theme of the successful town hall schemes almost throughout this period was a fierce determination to see the scheme through to completion whatever the consequences. Cases where town hall expenditure can be specifically blamed for a shift of power on the council, as at Bolton, are remarkably rare. Thus an architect who secured a town hall commission could have good hopes of his whole dream being realised, even, with luck, expanded. It is questionable whether the virtual removal of the normal cost constraints led to any improvement in design standards or whether the clients as a type were any more appealing to a creative architect. As the century progressed we find many of the more creative architects unwilling to look to the corporations, especially as the line between creative eclecticism and mere copyism became harder to draw. Among the key architects it is significant that Norman Shaw was only once involved in town hall building (at Bradford) and that distantly in the last ten years of his life. Belcher, Brumwell Thomas and E. W. Mountford contributed some of their best buildings but one would not necessarily count them as important figures in the field of architectural progress. There were certainly some good commissions in the years up to 1914, and the best of the Edwardian town halls have a generous fruitiness that suggests the same attraction to display that we see in Rochdale. Increasingly, though, the new town halls were office blocks and there was less scope and less incentive for extravagance. In the 1860s and 1870s the theatrical façadism of designers like E. W. Godwin could be easily adapted to buildings of widely varying status. The estimates could be raised for buildings such as Bristol assize courts or Northampton town hall or the ornament pared right down for smaller structures such as East Retford town hall. Full blown baroque revival was generally only effective on the largest scale and with the developing social conscience and the ebbing of the economic tide in the early years of the twentieth century it became more difficult for other than established figures to persuade corporations to indulge themselves. The young E. A. Rickards who designed the Cardiff city hall and law courts was a fortunate exception and in any case gifted enough to make even quite small buildings look grand. For the most part after about 1906 there were no more really successful display pieces among town halls and municipal buildings.

7

Competitions

'I should be glad to think the day not far distant when competitions would be rarely, if ever, resorted to, except for works of the greatest national importance', wrote Alfred Waterhouse in 1890.[1] Though he himself owed his rise to fame largely to his success in the great competition for the Manchester town hall, his weariness with the system can be taken as perfectly genuine for by 1890 he had seen more of it than most as both competitor and assessor. Dislike of the competition system was general among architects, and the evils of the various bodies who commissioned them was a by-word. The very first volume of the *Builder* contained an article on bad competitions,[2] bewailing the prejudice and ignorance of committees. Yet throughout the nineteenth century the competition continued to be the normal means of selection employed by corporations who wanted to look outside their own employees for an architect. And, despite repeated pleas for professional solidarity, there was seldom any lack of candidates for the competitions. It was of course to be expected that the big corporations with a great deal of money to spend would attract large numbers of entries offering, as they did, the prospect of celebrity and a handsome commission. Waterhouse, for instance, was paid over £25,000 commission on the Manchester town hall over a period of fourteen years; and with the usual rate of commission at 5 per cent on cost it is easy to calculate approximate figures for most town halls. So it is no surprise that the Manchester competition attracted 136 entries. Sheffield in 1890 drew 179 entries while Glasgow drew 98 entries in 1880 and, only a year later, when the first results had been set aside, still drew 125 entries.[3] In general though, something between 20 and 30 architects would be likely to submit a design, perhaps 40 or 50 in a larger town or for one of the London buildings; and there is certainly no indication of a fall in the number of entrants as the century progressed. Yet this was in spite of the obviously heavy odds not only against winning, but even against covering the costs involved. In fact Augustus Frere had published a general analysis of competition odds and premiums in 1863.[4] He reckoned the odds against winning as 20 to 1, and calculated that in a total of forty-five competitions the grand profit to the profession, including the commission gained by the winners, was £5,508 on a total outlay of £291,388. This represents a premium of about 2 per cent to the winners where 5 per cent was normal on public buildings, and takes no account of the labours of the losers which Frere reckoned at £15 each. Though obviously not accurate in detail, this picture will have remained true in substance throughout the period. Indeed, since the opportunities in civic building did not expand greatly after the 1870s while the number of architects in practice did, the odds will, if anything, have worsened.

It may seem odd that so many architects were keen to risk so much time and money. E. W. Godwin entered at least nine competitions for civic buildings, H. T. Hare entered thirteen and Harry Cheers nine, while Brightwen Binyon (six), J. M. Brydon (eight), William Hill (six), and Malcolm Stark (six) are only some of the inveterate competers. It is true that the really established architects often held aloof or at any rate only competed for the biggest prizes, but this simply underlies the compulsion felt by the architects who had yet to make the grade. Mostly these civic competitions offered the chance to direct the construction of large and elaborate buildings which could be expected to make any architect's name. Waterhouse was only the most famous of those who rose in this way. Cuthbert Brodrick owed his success almost entirely to winning the Leeds competition, and the Sheffield competition certainly established E. W. Mountford. However the chance of a premium and even extensive commission was not the only attraction of these competitions. There was a good chance that the designs would be exhibited publicly (though supposedly anonymously) and better still a selection might be published in the architectural press. Men like Daniel Brade of Kendal (Fig. 41), who entered several but never won a civic competition, will certainly have benefited from such publicity.

The chance of lasting fame is surely what drove Joseph Hansom to take such risks at Birmingham. The story has been cited already, but the architect's rashness needs some explanation. On Hansom's own admission there was a mere £357 between the accepted tender and the allowance of £17,000 yet that would have to cover any contingencies as well as commission and expenses. Add the fact that the accepted tender was some £6,000 lower than any other and that it was submitted by a firm that had previously worked for the partnership, and the scale of Hansom's optimism is apparent. That he still allowed himself and his partner to be held to the

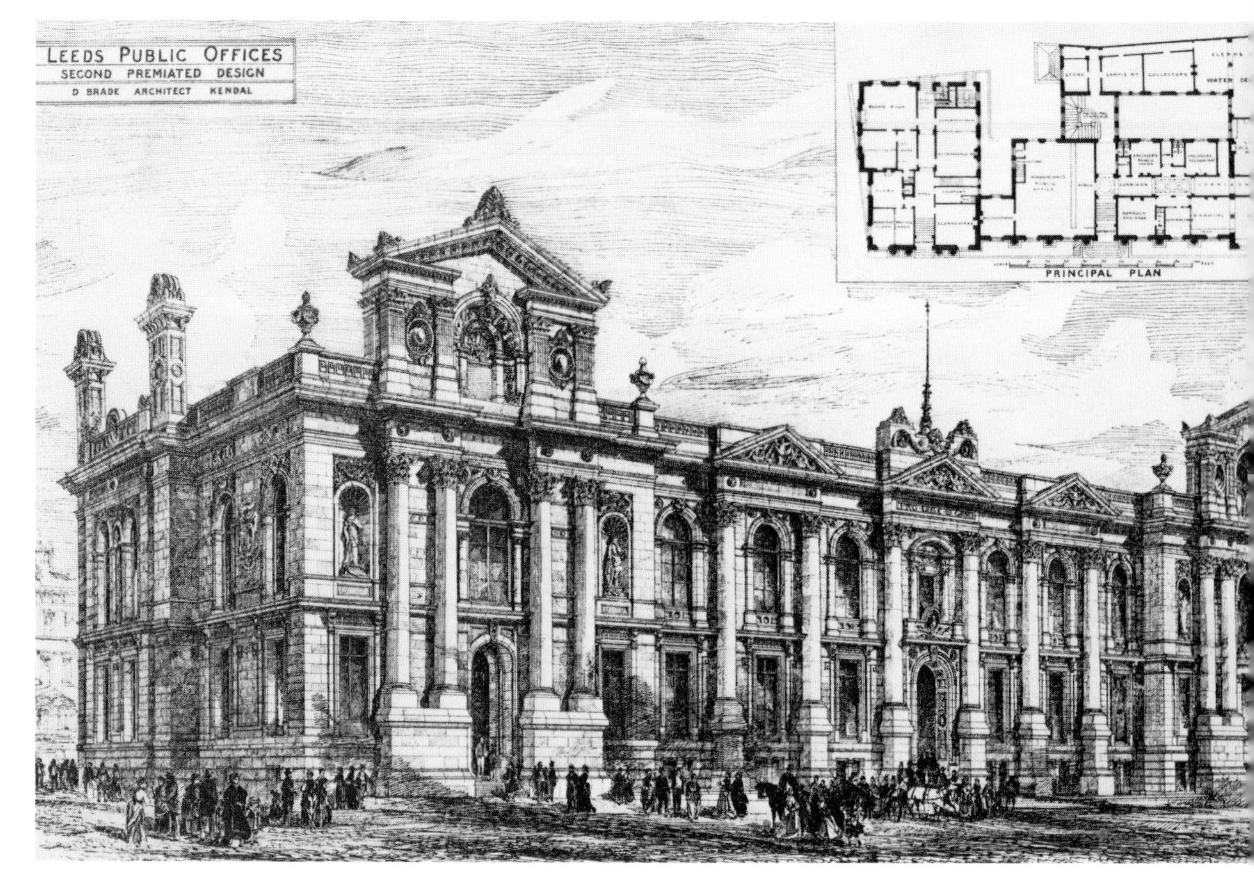

41 Leeds municipal buildings, second premiated design, Daniel Brade, 1876 (*Building News*, vol. XXXII, 1877)

original sum and to stand surety for the cost, in spite of the addition of extra work at the request of the commissioners, is as much a comment on his eagerness for the job as it is a reflection on the sharp practice of the townsmen. Hansom's ensuing bankruptcy can hardly have been a surprise to the businessmen of Birmingham. However his rash overconfidence is equally to be explained when he could see himself at the age of twenty-seven having defeated Charles Barry, Beazely, Rickman and Goodwin in open competition. There had even been designs from the offices of Soane and Nash!

If the attractions of the competition system for the architects are obvious enough, its employment by the corporations needs some explanation. Often enough there were architects on the corporation who could be expected to know the local requirements very precisely. G. G. Hoskins is a case in point; he was a long-standing member of the Darlington corporation and even mayor of the town, but he was only placed third in the competition for the Darlington municipal buildings in 1894. He did, however, build the exchange at nearby Hartlepool and the town hall at Middlesbrough. At Birkenhead there were at least two architects on the council when their town hall was being built, yet even there an outsider was preferred. There are in fact very few cases indeed where a serving member of the local council was commissioned even though he could if necessary resign to take the job. Winning commissions in nearby towns was less rare, and Norman (of Norman & Hine) who won the competition for Plymouth guildhall in 1869 was in fact mayor of Devonport in 1874, the year in which the building was opened (Fig. 34). However, in that case the design was clearly that of the consulting architect, E. W. Godwin. In the few cases where a member of the local executive was employed their resignation from the board is usually clearly announced. G. Elkington is a case in point when he was commissioned to build the Penge vestry hall in 1874. The employment of J. Loxton, a member of the local board, to build Wednesbury town hall is one of very few cases where the architect's resignation from the board is not attested.

It goes without saying that members of any council should draw on their own expertise to help in the provision of local amenities, but they couldn't or shouldn't be paid for their pains. Even more objectionable was to see them do so as the result of a supposedly open competition. The frequency of the accusations of unfair treatment might almost be expected to have led corporations to refrain from competitions and employ their own staff as is most frequently done today. Yet they didn't, and, with the exception of the few towns looking for a nationally known name, they must surely have expected some benefit from the outlay of the premiums and the acrimony that was likely to ensue. One answer would be that only a competition could sort out the claims of rival factions within the corporation each pushing its own architect. This might be true of the number of cases where all the prizewinners were local and the corporation acted as their own assessor, but it is impossible to substantiate any such general supposition. Too much local interest always led to suspicion and the Bradford competition is the prime example. It attracted liberal criticism in the professional press. However the Wednesbury competition with twenty-five entries drew two winners from Wednesbury and the third from neighbourng West Bromwich, and there are many other similar cases. The whole problem of covert influence is much wider than that, and pervades nearly all the competitions, not to mention other aspects of town hall building. Such difficulties did not really affect the decision to indulge in competitions, and there was another and more practical reason for doing so. A town hall was difficult to define in purely practical terms, and I have already argued that the show element was equally essential. The variety of possible solutions to the design problem was thus infinite, and more often than not corporations would not have a fixed idea of what they required. By setting up a competition they could expect to have twenty or thirty different solutions to choose from. It might even be possible to combine features of different plans. This was frequently attempted, but generally led to ill feeling, and was only really successful when the designers responsible were appointed jointly. This was the case at Bolton; but at Birmingham the attempt to buy in W. H. Lynn's plans, that had been placed first by the assessor, so that their more imaginative features could be grafted on to the local architect's design, predictably came to nothing. Another use of competitions was simply to help corporations to decide what course to take. The best example of this type is the double competition at Worcester in 1872, one for the restoration of the guildhall and another for its complete rebuilding. Neither winner was employed, but the building was restored, or rather reconstructed, by the city architect with G. G. Scott as consultant.

Sometimes queries from competing architects would awaken the corporation to possibilities they had not foreseen, and they could even be persuaded to change the conditions in the middle of the competition, much to the frustration of the competitors. At Bradford, we are told, 'the rules and requirements were found to be so unsatisfactory in many respects that letters of enquiry and explanation passed in great numbers, until at last the different points of the instructions were so modified that the competitors were virtually told they might do just as they liked.'[5] The same is true of Wakefield where Gothic designs, having been excluded, were suddenly allowed only a few weeks before the closing date (Fig. 42). At Edinburgh in 1886 alterations to the site after the competition was announced meant that several competitors were involved in substantially reworking their designs. Even more ill feeling was caused by the finding of unexpected solutions. At Godalming (1898) the unusual solution to the problem of carriage access to the rear of the building proposed by Lanchester, Stewart & Rickards appeared to break the essential condition of the competition and their award of first place was fiercely criticised. A similar case is found at Burnley where most of the competitors ignored one instruction but the anger was such that the Society of Architects announced that it would take legal action. It didn't.

A common source of ill feeling was the detailed interpretation of the building line, since some encroachment could clearly result in a better building yet might be ruled out by the letter of the instructions to architects. Hansom's design for Birmingham town hall produced the required accommodation because he dared to build right to the road line so that the pavement actually runs through the podium. There is no record of complaints at this, but the instructions for Birmingham's council house were more strictly interpreted. W. H. Lynn's design was especially

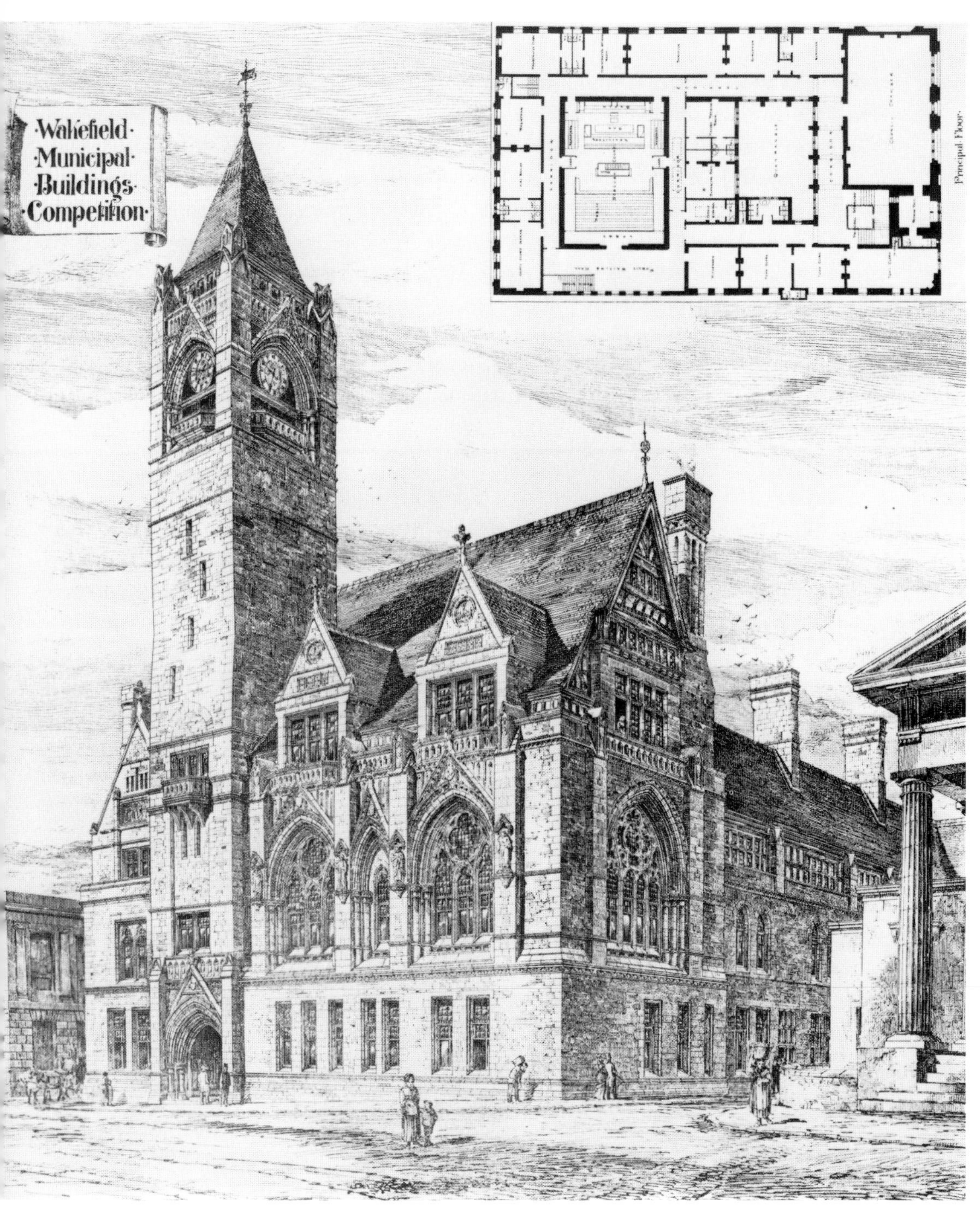

42 Wakefield town hall, alternative design, T. E. Collcutt, 1877 (*Building News*, vol. XXXII, 1877)

commended but eventually ruled out because it provided direct access between the mayor's apartments and the town hall by a bridge and thus infringed the building line. The attempt to buy the plan and incorporate parts of it in Yeoville Thomason's design shows, however, that the corporation were aware of its merits. Generally speaking there was nothing to stop the corporations drawing on any of the ideas presented to modify or enlarge the designs of the winner. This must have been a frequent occurrence but difficult to prove so that complaints are less common, though there was understandable ill feeling in the two-stage competitions when the rejected designs and even sometimes the selected ones were exhibited before the second designs were completed. Messrs Flockton & Gibbs were particularly incensed that a planning arrangement, that they claimed to have patented and had incorporated in their sketch design, was made a condition of the second competition for the Sheffield town hall which they didn't win.

Certainly the system was open to abuse in the vagueness of the instructions, in the conditions of the premiums and the subsequent decisions of the councils. The presence of jobbery could very seldom be proved but was always suspected. It could, however, never be ruled out as a possibility, and it may not have looked quite so iniquitous to its perpetrators who were after all elected to look after the interests of their own citizens. It was the architectural press and the losers who made the fuss. The most famous case of jobbery is provided by Bradford town council whose competition was entirely won by local men—1st, Lockwood & Mawson (Fig. 78); 2nd, Milnes & France; and 3rd, Samuel Jackson, all of Bradford. There was a great deal of righteous indignation, and even the picturesque story that the winners had had their 'anonymous' design carried framed but unwrapped through the streets of Bradford from their office to the place where the competition was to be judged. Criticisms of the competition made it clear that the winning designs were uninspired, and that if Lockwood & Mawson's plan was the best of the bunch it was a pretty poor bunch and the design was cribbed in any case.[6] 'What a "happy family" must this one be when all the plums are given to its own children irrespective of good behaviour.'[7] Yet only nine years later the editor of the *Builder* was to recall that he had 'had the pleasure to illustrate the fine Gothic town hall of Bradford, interesting as showing what may be called romantic architecture in a town of very unromantic manufacturing associations'.[8] Later in 1890 the *Building News* listed Bradford with a dozen others as having erected a building worthy of its importance.[9] Horrified reports of 400 applicants being reduced to thirty (and those poor fools being trapped in numbers increasing 'according to the inverse ratio of their proximity to Bradford'[10]) are not entirely borne out by recently discovered correspondence at Bradford. Only 282 applications are preserved, though it is likely that there were a few more. True only about twenty-nine architects actually submitted designs;[11] but that compares well enough with places like East Retford where 108 applications produced eighteen designs. The main burden of complaint in the surviving correspondence at Bradford centres on the shortness of time for completing the drawings. J. P. Seddon complained of this along with twelve others, and C. O. Adkinson, at least, failed to submit for the same reason. Thomas Jeckyll certainly had his suspicions when he wrote that he would not compete 'understanding it to be useless'; but the surviving letters of complaint after the result are aimed particularly at the award of the third premium to Samuel Jackson whose estimate at £45,000 was £5,000 above the allowance though the instructions were clear that any such excess would be ruled out.

There is, however, no doubt that the ill feeling engendered by this competition was widespread and the fact that no evidence survives cannot exculpate the corporation. They reached their decision with remarkable rapidity and without the aid of a professional assessor, and must be suspected on both counts. The success of Lockwood & Mawson within Bradford was also too good to be true. In 1851, only two years after setting up practice in the town, they were commissioned to build the St George's hall. In 1864 they were placed first in the competition for the Bradford exchange, and in 1869 they came first in the two competitions for the town hall and the Kirkgate markets. They were certainly not the only architects with friends on the council, but they clearly chose their friends with care. None the less it is abundantly clear that any influence at work in this competition was not greatly different from that normally to be expected. It must be rembered that even with carefully prepared instructions and the help of three famous assessors the Manchester competition saw three Manchester men among the prizewinners,[12] yet there was no accusation of jobbery. Bradford's mistake was in failing to comply with what by 1869 was recognised as good practice. Indeed Bradford was not by any means the only example of bad practice in the period and certainly not the worst. The Eastbourne town hall competition of 1880 provoked a furious storm when the result was set aside and the borough surveyor instructed to do the building. The competitors wrote angry, even libellous, letters to the press; and it was not until 1884 that the deadlock was broken and the winner W. Tadman Foulkes, appointed subject to the supervision of Henry Currey, the architect of the Duke of Devonshire who owned the land. Another south coast town, Hastings, found even more trouble when they decided to shelve the results of their competition in 1874. The disgruntled competitors got as far as taking legal advice as to whether they might sue the council. However, once again the problems were solved and the original winners appointed. In both cases the difficulties had arisen from the wide discrepancy between the council's intended cost and the architects' estimates. At Hastings the allowance was £10,000 but the estimates were £20,000. It was small wonder there was trouble. Yet it was all too often the case that the competition instructions called for a building that could never be built within the cost allowance. Sometimes this led to the abandonment of a competition, though seldom to the saving of money. The accusations of jobbery that were freely bandied about were no doubt exaggerated, but in the case of both Eastbourne and Hastings it is at least likely that there was a solid foundation in fact. The trouble was that even at the time it was virtually impossible to substantiate such fears. Whatever the truth of the Bradford affair it was remarkable how Lockwood & Mawson managed to secure almost all the major corporate commissions. In smaller towns there was probably even more scope for influence of that sort, and even established architects could be entangled. The town hall extensions competition at Leek (1887) is a prime example. Alfred Waterhouse, for whatever reason, was induced to make a design and was placed first in the competition. A local architect came second and another local firm, Sugden & Son, third. However the competition results were set aside after organised opposition to the application for a loan from the Local Government Board whose inspector was led to recommend the Sugdens' design as being more practical and economical. Without further explanation the commission was given to the Sugdens who between them built virtually every major building in the town from the 1870s to the 1890s. Such outrageous treatment might well have given rise to comment, but the fact that Waterhouse made no complaint suggests that he accepted these chances as a part of business life, which may be just how the councillors saw them.[13]

This was by no means the only case where a competition was set aside, and among the major commissions Glasgow provided a similar disappointment for George Corson. He was selected by Charles Barry in 1880 and then ruled out on the grounds of cost. Yet when Barry and the city architect assessed the new competition in 1881 the allowance had been raised from £150,000 to £250,000, which was £30,000 more than even Barry's estimate of the likely cost of Corson's design. Probably a complete failure of will caused less ill feeling since at least the competitors all suffered equally. Yet cases were comparatively rare where a corporation having held a competition refused to build anything. There might well be a postponement of a few years. G. Bidlake of Wolverhampton, for instance, had to wait twenty years from 1852 to 1872 before he could begin work on the Bilston town hall, but that was exceptional. It was Edinburgh that provided the biggest disappointment of all by arranging a competition (1886) for a really major building that could be expected to carry enormous prestige, and then totally shelving the plan. Fifty-five competitors submitted designs ranging in cost from £66,000 to £280,000 for a building with a handsome frontage to the High Street, mostly with a good forecourt, and a superbly romantic north front tumbling some eight storeys down behind Princes Street Gardens (Fig. 43). None of the designs was really outstanding, it is true, but several would have been a credit to the city. However, there was opposition from the ratepayers and in 1887 a plebiscite was held to decide. The majority against building was 13,426 and the scheme was accordingly dropped.

The actual management of competitions was haphazard to begin with, but that was an area that could be, and was, improved as the period progressed. To start with, instructions were meagre and corporations were reluctant to commit themselves to employing the winning architect. Later it was more common to offer a first premium that would merge with the commission if the winner was appointed, and many corporations specifically stated that they would employ the winner. None the less they were not actually bound to do so, and even in the late 1890s we find cases such as Surbiton where an excellent design, by Wimperis & East, was placed first in the competition and rejected in favour of a much less satisfactory affair by Forsyth & Maule that had won the second prize. It was, however, less common for unpremiated designs to be built. The premiums themselves were barely more than honoraria to begin with, but they did increase substantially during the period. Among the early competitions premiums of between £5 and £20 were not uncommon. Burslem in 1846 offered only two prizes of £50 and £20 and yet attracted thirty-four designs, while Yeovil, still important in 1847, offered only £15 and Islington as late as 1857 offered only £50 and £20 for its vestry hall competition. Prizes as large as the £100 for Leeds in 1850 were very much the exception. However by 1860 a range of three prizes at £100, £75 and £50 was the norm. Later larger competitions offered a good deal more. Sheffield (1890) and Nottingham (1883) with prizes totalling £600 were not unusual, and by then smaller prizes clearly indicated much more modest competitions such as those at Motherwell or Ormskirk.

Even so the actual prize money was a small thing. The careful preparation of instructions was much more important. Architects needed to be allowed reasonable creative freedom, yet accusations of jobbery could not be avoided if the instructions were not precise. Leeds was regarded as a very fair competition though the instructions only dealt with the main hall and courtrooms. By the time of the Manchester competition (1866) detailed lists were sent out specifying the number and area of the offices required for each department. Frequently the number of floors and the disposition of the rooms was specified too. The scale and type of the drawings needed to be laid down also, since it was early apparent that a beautifully finished and coloured perspective could entice an unqualified council. At Manchester, for instance, the use of perspectives was completely ruled out for the first competition, and in the second competition, the point from which the perspective drawing was to

43 Edinburgh municipal buildings, unsuccessful

M. Brydon, 1886 (*Builder*, vol. LII, 1887)

be taken was actually specified, though not in the event adhered to. These developments had two advantages. They helped to ensure a greater degree of fair play, or at least that all competitors designed within the same constraints. Probably more important, however, the corporations were forced to think in greater detail about what was required, and, though rising costs and the addition of extras meant that estimates were still frequently exceeded, it was possible to ensure that the competition allowance was at least realistic for a structure of the size and type required. These moves were very much fostered by the profession, in particular the RIBA which by the 1890s had a permanent competitions committee with the younger Charles Barry as its chairman. It was a common cry that the Institute or the assessor should be allowed to vet competition instructions before the competition, but the RIBA never had any power for all their increasing authority among architects. The Belfast corporation sought their opinion in 1896 on the instructions for the Belfast city hall competition, but then declined to take the Institute's advice, and the RIBA was blamed for the inclusion of various obnoxious clauses.

If detailed instructions were one advance, the adoption of two-stage competitions was another. It was clearly impossible in the larger competitions to reach a decision on a hundred or so detailed designs in a few days. At Bradford it was supposed to have been done in a couple of hours! Manchester (1866) was the first city to offer a sketch competition from which a small number of winners would be selected to compete again with more detailed drawings and perspective view. The instructions for the Manchester competition were recognised as very fair and clear and formed the basis of the instructions for the Glasgow competition. The existence of a copy of the Manchester competition instructions with the Bradford town hall papers suggests that they were consulted there too. The publicly expressed fears of jobbery at Birkenhead seem to have been largely allayed by the knowledge that the arrangements for that competition were to be based on those adopted at Glasgow. There was certainly a good deal of borrowing and gradual improvement which clearly benefited both corporations and competitors. However, the development of the sketch competition immediately allowed for a ready appreciation of a large number of designs which could be prepared at relatively little cost to the competing architects. There might be ill feeling at the choice of competitors for the second stage, but that was probably to be expected. Manchester was, rightly, accused of unfairness in choosing four Manchester men out of eight for the second competition and refusing to increase the number though the instructions had promised a second competition for between six and twelve. Two-stage competitions were not universal, but were subsequently used in Glasgow (1881), Sheffield (1890), Nottingham (1883) and Oxford (1892) where the profession seems generally to have been satisfied with the procedures and the results.

44 Aberdeen municipal buildings, Peddie & Kinnear, 1865–7 (*Building News*, vol. XV, 1868)

There was another way in which the corporations could limit their difficulties, namely by inviting specific architects to compete. In this way not only could the scale of the judging problem be better predicted, but by selective invitations even the general style and quality could be settled in advance. Unwilling architects could, and often did, refuse to compete, but the whole level of argument was instantly reduced. It was usual to allow free entry to local architects while inviting a few famous men or to confine the whole competition to men from the locality. Colchester (1897) provides a good example of the former method, with invitations going to John Belcher, E. W. Mountford, Brightwen Binyon, H. T. Hare, J. M. Brydon and Beresford Pite. Two Colchester firms competed, and it must have been obvious that the corporation expected to get a building of high quality in the baroque style, as in fact they did. Competitions limited to local architects were relatively rare in England, and mostly for humbler buildings. Local competitions were more common in Scotland, and the splendid pile built by Peddie & Kinnear in Aberdeen (Fig. 44) was the result of just such a competition which had only three entries. Drogheda in 1864 was similarly parochial, though the five competitors included Sir Thomas Deane and W. H. Lynn. Gloucester (1889), Bodmin (1891), Stourbridge (1887), Richmond (1889) and Rhyl (1874) are some further examples of limited competitions. Some of the London boroughs, too, restricted their competitions, but that seems to be because they intended a modest building and feared the pressure of the massed architects in London. This sort of limitation was attractive from the corporations' point of view and one might wonder why it was not more frequently adopted. However, the range of local talent was often too limited for the extravagant dreams of the town hall promoters and the attraction of a nationwide competition with the possible prestige accruing was too much to resist. At Chelsea, for example, we find a limited competition of 1884 followed in the next year with an open one that led to the actual building by J. M. Brydon (Fig. 45). His elegant Renaissance revival pile is undoubtedly more assured than anything likely to have come from the three original little known architects.

The final element in the successful competition was of course the assessor. A professional with no interest in the affair was essential for fair play, and a number of successful architects were in demand for this. Sir Charles Barry assessed the Leeds competition, and his prestige will have gone a long way to forestall any criticism. His son Charles subsequently acted as assessor in eight major competitions, and established teachers such as Professor T. L. Donaldson were often called upon. J. MacIvar Anderson, E. W. Mountford and William Young were frequently employed as, of course, was Alfred Waterhouse. George Godwin, Sir William Tite and G. E. Street are other names that occur, as one might expect. Even so these men were often accused of unfairness and frequently hampered in their choice by unsatisfactory instructions. Barry, for instance, was roundly slated for his choice in the first Glasgow competition, which, it was said, didn't comply with the instructions. Though he was retained for the second competition he had to assess that jointly with the city surveyor. There were occasions, too, when their choice was questioned by the clients or even rejected outright. Waterhouse's first choice in the Birmingham council house competition was twice rejected in favour of the local man placed second on each occasion. Barry's choice of a winner for Llanelli in 1892 was set aside in favour of a local firm.

The actual choice of an assessor was of importance too, not so much because his taste might dictate the choice of design (Waterhouse, for example, was remarkably catholic in the designs he selected), but for his standing and integrity. There are

45 Chelsea vestry hall, J. M. Brydon, 1885–7

innumerable letters of concern throughout the period that this or that competition seemed likely to be decided without the aid of a professional assessor. The bigger the name the more reassuring for the competitors, but it was the assessor's professional status that was of most concern. When Yarmouth looked no further than Norwich for an assessor, and incidentally accepted his choice of a Norwich architect as winner, there were no serious complaints. Assessors from within the borough were, however subject to the same sort of pressures as the councillors. At Inverness (Fig. 46) where one D. Bryce was assessor we find the selected architect was the same man as was employed to check the quantities of all the competing entries. Or at Slough where

46 Inverness town hall, A. Lawrie, 1875–8

F. W. Albany assessed the first competition and T. R. Richards was placed second, we find a second competition with T. R. Richards as assessor and F. W. Albany placed first. The employment of T. H. Lainson, the eventual designer, as a sort of assessor in the competition for the additions to Reading municipal buildings caused a good deal of discontent.

High premiums, detailed instructions and assessor's fees (sometimes as high as £300) meant that the smaller towns were less and less likely to want or be able to mount a proper competition. In 1895 the Woking Public Hall Company could only offer a prize of 2 per cent commission, and part of that was to be in shares in the building. Not surprisingly they attracted only two designs. By the turn of the century it was generally fairly clear from the start whether a particular competition was likely to be satisfactory or not. Besides, from about 1900 on, the RIBA and other organisations were much readier to advise against entering doubtful competitions, publishing the names and even on occasions requiring their members not to enter.[14] In short, the competition problem was largely solved by the turn of the century, and the obvious disadvantages of bad practice made it virtually self-solving. There were still bound to be disagreements and misunderstandings, especially as both architects and corporations might change their minds as a particular scheme progressed. However, the continuing number of competitions and general level of entries proves not only that the corporations felt they were valuable but that architects in large numbers were willing to take the risks and spend the time involved. That a gradual improvement in the terms and conditions was not matched by any diminution in the number of complaints can be partly dismissed as the inevitable sour grapes when a commission of thousands of pounds was at stake. Also pressure could still be put on councillors to support a particular selection; and it has to be remembered that the supposedly anonymous entries were seldom as unrecognisable as was promised in a world where assessors and even clients were likely to know the competitors quite well and be able to recognise their drawing styles. One result of the system, however, was that with the designs generally being exhibited and frequently criticised in the professional press the spread of ideas was greatly enhanced, and of course the competitors gained valuable publicity.

8

Developing styles

We have spent a great deal of time considering the reasons for building town halls and the political machinations involved in financing them. These buildings cannot be understood apart from that context, and only in their context can they be properly appreciated and their contribution to the development of urban and corporate life be fully realised. The buildings themselves, whatever their quality, mostly make significant contributions to the streetscape, and it is that and the developing styles of the buildings themselves which we must now examine. The buildings can then be seen as they should be, as the culmination of a process of aspiration, argument and persuasion in which the architect's ideas as to style are only an element, and not always the most important one.

In tracing the stylistic development of town hall types I have consciously avoided a strictly chronological description of a succession of styles. For about the first twenty years the accommodation requirements meant that the type itself was particularly fluid. There was the gradual development from the regency mansion to full-blooded Roman magnificence. In the late 1850s and 1860s there was a search for a new style which resulted in such buildings as Halifax and Hull town halls or the early Gothic buildings. Gothic finally came into its own in the mid-1860s when the pressure for an increasing variety of office space made the planning of formal classical buildings increasingly problematical. Gothic in fact survived in a fashion almost to the end of the nineteenth century; but the real story of town hall styles in the years from 1870 to 1890 is of continuing eclecticism in which features of one style fuelled the development of others. The planning problems centred round the business of fitting an increasing number of disparate offices, halls and committee rooms into a single block. The Roman grandeur continued, but its development into Italian and French

Renaissance styles was easier to handle and more common as it was generally less exciting. Queen Anne and Jacobean added variety and lightness to the decoration in the same way that continuing Gothic could offer an extendable froth of carved or moulded ornament to suit any pocket. Yet it was out of the segregation of different departments that these free façades allowed that there came the development of a formal frontage almost as a separate unit. This could be conveniently clothed in the grandeur of the baroque which brings the period to a triumphant close.

All these buildings are by definition symbolic, and since their symbolic language needed to be readily understood, they tend to use an established architectural vocabulary. There were few senses in which the buildings as a type were totally innnovatory, and so they tend to follow the established patterns of style. The very bulk of some of the buildings, particularly the later ones, was a new element, but did not of itself lead to any new architectural forms. Wings and pavilions could be added more or less indefinitely, and the standard decorative motifs, classical or Gothic, added accordingly. One feature that belongs especially to the town hall is the tower. This was not universal, but generally desirable, and towers are by no means unique to

47 Oldham town hall extensions, council chamber, G. Woodhouse and E. Potts, 1879–80

town halls. However, in these buildings they did find some of their most lavish and exciting appearances; yet even so the tower was seen more as an ornamental appendage to be clothed in the same decorative dress as the rest of the building. Even structural iron and steel, the newest and most exciting of the materials of the period, were never displayed in a town hall tower, though they were frequently used. The other new features, large halls and suites of banqueting rooms, had so many precedents in earlier palatial architecture that there was little likelihood that they would lead to new departures. Even the council chamber (Figs 47, 48), very much the mark of these buildings, made no new demands on space; and the special arrangement of the seating, usually semi-circular, was hardly ever made the basis for the formal expression of the room as a part of the whole conception.[1] The scope for exciting spatial effects arising from the need to provide public galleries in both courts and council chamber seems hardly to have been realised. This leaves the final element of circulation where the problems were unique, but where in the nature of things the solutions however novel would not necessarily govern the external form of the whole. There are a number of town halls where the solution of these problems did lead to a creative design for the whole, and more where the grand stair affords the most exciting architectural experience of the whole scheme (Fig. 49). The most general tendency was towards a looser articulation of the constituent parts, a move which was greatly accelerated by the adoption of the various versions of the Gothic style. This freedom was also fostered by the Queen Anne style, rare in town halls, and the later eclectic mixtures of French and Italian Renaissance themes that appealed to so many corporations. Only with the sudden appearance of Edwardian baroque, and more especially of 'Wrenaissance' strains within it, did the trend towards fluid composition get reversed, though even so a good many buildings avoided strict symmetry in linking large halls and municipal offices. In the last years before the Great War it was the influence of the French Beaux Arts training that finally restored the straitjacket. However, by then the town hall as a building type was a well-known creature, and attempts to train it into a suitably rigid layout were less likely to be upset by the development of a new need.

This might suggest that in terms of formal architectural history there was little to recommend any of these buildings, since they would not in any case reveal significant progress and few are key monuments. Their importance lies, I think, in the increasing variety of ways in which the traditional vocabulary was reinterpreted to create an expression of each town's individual personality. It is also possible to trace the development of the type itself, though the different pace of development in the different towns makes the progress particularly uneven. In the period up to about 1840 the town hall and corporate offices formed a relatively new type of structure and

48 Manchester town hall, council chamber, Alfred Waterhouse, 1867–77

there was no established architectural type to which they would naturally look back. Their distance from the town halls of the previous century was marked by the increasing growth of urban consciousness and the freedom from the old restrictive corporations; while any reliance on the old market hall forms was made difficult by the need to incorporate new offices. Town halls of the late eighteenth century, such as James Wyatt's building at Ripon (1798) or even John Carr's earlier one at Newark

49 Manchester town hall, grand stair and landing, Alfred Waterhouse, 1867–77

(1773), aped the grand town house or palazzo in typical English Neoclassical or Palladian. There was often nothing to distinguish them from the houses of rich merchants except possibly their size. These roots did continue to inspire the designers of town halls in the early years of Victoria's reign, though, oddly, the best examples are less grand than Newark or Ripon. Middlesbrough old town hall (1846) has already been cited and is a late example of the type, but it occurs also at Mansfield (1835–6) and at Little Bolton (1826).

Outwardly there is little to distinguish Mansfield town hall (Fig. 50) from any number of small Regency mansions. It has a symmetrical front of three bays with a rusticated ground floor that is in no way out of the ordinary. However various details mark this out as a public building. In the first place it fronts the market, exactly like the old town hall at Middlesbrough; but that is not what gives the building its character. The town hall is all of ashlar masonry and divides into a formal front block backed by a police station, town offices and shambles forming the tail of a stubby T. All the main formal rooms are in the front block, though there is internal access to the offices at the rear. This treatment of the façade or façade block as a separate entity is typical. In this case it is only one bay deep and the 'service' wings are distinguished by

50 Mansfield town hall, James and W. A. Nicholson, 1835–6

the absence of the slender string course at first floor level and by the plainer first floor windows. The formality of the front is enhanced by setting the triple ground floor windows of the side slightly forward as though they formed shallow bows. But it is the grand entrance which really marks the building out. The centre of the front is set slightly forward in the usual fashion, but is capped by a small false attic which contains a public clock; while the actual entrance is through a heavy tetrastyle portico of four unfluted Doric columns beneath a correct straight entablature. This is heavy for the façade, and further interesting in that there is a pair of columns *in antis* forming a second row and the actual entry to the building is thus well behind the line of the front wall. This space was designed for use as an exchange, and has no real parallel in domestic or palatial architecture. From it there is access to a double height hall at the back of the formal block. The two main offices lead out of this hall while the stair rises round three sides of the well. The whole of the first floor of the front is taken up with the large assembly room.

This gives us the basic pattern of committee rooms beneath an assembly hall forming the main front with a service wing of offices to the rear if necessary. There is a precedent of sorts in the arrangement of some of the earlier town halls such as the Worcester guildhall (1721); but the actual detailing of the Mansfield building with its spare simple classical motifs is entirely regency. At Little Bolton there was an even humbler version. It stood on a corner and its two façades were decorated with vaguely Soanian pilasters and a series of labels above the upper windows. A simple porch had paired Tuscan columns while the side door was set in a rusticated surround. Only the borough arms in the pediment and the situation in any way mark the building out from dozens of similar small mansions. Yet if many of these early town halls are only a little different from so many houses of the period, their site at least marked them out. At first town halls were freestanding at the head of a market place, and this remained common in a number of smaller towns. However, as the development of town centres became more concentrated difficulties of finding a site that was sufficiently large for all the offices and public rooms required increased enormously. In the larger towns from the 1860s on it was possible to fill a whole city block with the town hall as Leeds and Liverpool had done earlier. However town halls were in general rarely designed as freestanding buildings like churches, and it was increasingly common to find them designed to fill a space in a street. L-shaped town halls with only two street façades are quite common, and there are even a few that run through from one street to another while being entirely built up on both sides. This means that there is a great deal of variety in planning and it is hardly possible to talk of a development in town hall plans. There are a few basic arrangements that reoccur frequently. The Leeds type of central hall ringed by offices (Fig. 8) was obviously most suited to buildings occupying a whole block. This type remains more or less constant throughout the period. It was adapted to a triangular site at Manchester by Waterhouse (Fig. 9), but the principle is the same; and it reached a triumphant climax in Cardiff city hall. A ring of buildings round a courtyard, often with the hall to one side, is a rarer variety of this type that developed in the 1880s when the need for office space was important. Middlesbrough (Fig. 13) is probably the best example of the type and Birmingham council house is similar, while Sheffield (Fig. 15) and Lancaster town halls are modified versions. The Mansfield type with its assembly hall at the front was superseded by a long-lasting type with suites of formal rooms across the front, usually at first floor level. A hall could be added at the rear or to one side. Stockport is a fine late example of this type and Hereford and Leigh are two others of similar date that are typical. This is in fact the arrangement at Manchester too, but it was particularly suitable in cases where the frontage was flanked by other buildings. Congleton (Fig. 77) and Northampton (Fig. 54) are only two versions of this pattern by E. W. Godwin, but it could be adapted for almost any style and shape of site. H. T. Hare's design for Oxford town hall (1893) is no more than a variation on this theme. In smaller towns the ground floor could even be let off as shops to assist with the cost.

On a long frontage it was often sensible to allow the different units or blocks of offices to be only loosely articulated and arranged as convenience directed. This layout was particularly suited to the Gothic style, and is best seen at Rochdale (Fig. 37) or Plymouth (Fig. 34). However the clear articulation of parts could be organised symmetrically, and the same basic idea of different departments laid out along a long frontage could be adapted to the classical and other styles. There are, too, a number of town halls in Gothic styles whose planning owes its main features to classical precedents. Leicester town hall (Fig. 58) is something of a breakaway in stylistic terms, being the first and only major town hall built in the Queen Anne style, making full use of the freedom of layout but without Gothic dressing. Several subsequent eclectic buildings followed the pattern of free layout with the new freedom in decorative dress with Jacobean revival as one of the most popular modes. In the 1880s there was also a tendency towards more logically ordered façades, and J. M. Brydon's Chelsea vestry hall (Fig. 45) is probably the best example of the marriage between the system of loosely articulated blocks and a strictly classical façade. However the same basic arrangement was also well suited to designs derived from French Renaissance sources with a symmetrical arrangement of pavilions that was infinitely extendable. Only with the new century was there any real sign of a development in planning with a return to freely articulated asymmetrical or even separate blocks. This arrangement probably developed from the plans used in the various Free Renaissance buildings of the early 1890s, but was admirably suited to the high Edwardian baroque of 1895–1910. Some of the designs for Walsall municipal buildings, especially those by W. A. Pite, provide good examples. This type of layout can be seen as the prototype of the grouped buildings of the civic centres of the late 1920s and 1930s.

In short the variety of accommodation required and the variety of sites available means that it is difficult to compare plans of different town halls. The effect of this variety, however, is that the façade becomes more important, particularly in cases where the site is cramped. There was a genuine functional need to advertise these buildings by an impressive, sometimes even an aggressive, façade. The need to compete with warehouses, banks and insurance companies only increased the need for display; and in fact the town halls remained distinctive and usually larger than their competitors for most of the period. Only in the last decades of the nineteenth century, and then mostly in the larger cities, did the surrounding buildings and offices of the vast corporate companies begin to be as grand as their contemporary town halls. Quite possibly this was a factor in the rapid development of the really extravagant municipal baroque in the late 1890s.

However, from the start it was recognised that the façade was important, and that could be easily stressed. Indeed it is in the provision of a pillared front that we see the next stage in the development of grandeur away from the regency mansion type. Three Lancashire town halls provide excellent examples. Salford (1825–7) (Fig. 3) and Chorlton-on-Medlock (1830–1) are both by Richard Lane, while Oldham (1841) by Joseph Butterworth continues the tradition. In these the basic arrangement is the same as at Mansfield, but the portico is enlarged to cover the whole height of the façade, and topped with a full pediment. There was scope for considerable variety here and for a fair variation in size. Reconstruction at Chorlton has destroyed all trace of the original interior, but the façade is of nine bays, the wings lightly stressed, with its centre formed by a projecting tetrastyle Doric temple front. The frieze is decorated with four wreaths instead of metopes and triglyphs. This slight departure from accurate classicism offsets the severity of the building, and is a motif that Lane had earlier used at Salford. There the building is smaller, of five bays only, and the temple front is made up from two columns *in antis* and is not fully projecting. This building is much closer in arrangement (and in overall size) to the Mansfield town hall, but with the vital difference that its stairs were set to one side to allow direct access to the market at the rear. Here, too, we see the typical feature, not found at Mansfield, of a fine stone façade backed by a brick building. The tradition is continued at Oldham in a building that is both slightly more grand and slightly less elegant. The façade is of seven bays with a projecting tetrastyle portico of Ionic columns. The plan is very similar to Mansfield, but the stairs are grander with a central flight that divides and returns.

There is added grandeur too in the steps to the portico necessitated by the slope of the ground. However, this is a less competently handled classicism and the attic is too heavy and the columns of the portico are cramped. The design is more firmly rooted in eighteenth-century precedent and even has municipal ancestors such as Lancaster's old town hall (1781). The basic arrangement of all these three buildings and the Mansfield town hall is, however, no different from the many eighteenth-century assembly rooms, and only the Oldham town hall was in fact built for an elected corporation of the new type. The basic arrangement of this sort of building was not sufficiently flexible to allow for the needs of the larger towns and the grander concert hall was in any case beginning to replace the assembly hall.

In the wake of the Greek revival it is no surprise to find the Roman temple form used for concert halls such as Birmingham town hall. Barry's entry for that competition was in fact in the form of a Greek style Doric temple, though with the addition of a Roman podium. Roman classicism offered more richness and more scope for the variety of towns, and Francis Goodwin's original Manchester town hall[2] is a good example of the eagerness with which the imperial Roman mode was adopted. This time the nine bay façade consisted of three elements all tied together by the same strong horizontal cornice with an attic above. The two wing bays recede slightly while the recessed centre is concealed behind a portico of four huge Ionic columns *in antis*. The size of the order and the provision of an attic allowed for a further floor of offices at the rear while the main reception room with its dome and columnar screen was far larger and more sophisticated than the assembly rooms of Oldham or Salford. This building in fact represents a new type, and its ancestors are really metropolitan buildings such as the royal exchange or the mansion house. The exchange at Bristol or the town hall at Liverpool, both by John Wood of Bath, are rare examples of municipal buildings outside London that are on a similar scale, and the development of the style into the municipal monsters of the nineteenth century really belonged to the 1840s and 1850s. For the most part the early town halls were on the scale of Mansfield, and only avoided domesticity by the aid of similarly overgrown porticoes and pilasters. At Upton on Severn, for example, a small town hall was built in 1832 that barely broke the roof-line of the street, but which is made massive by the addition of a couple of giant attached columns. At Stalybridge the assembly rooms and town hall of the same year is built in a straightforward way against the slope, and only avoids being mistaken for a mill by the provision of a careful Doric portico at the level of the lower ground floor and a pedimented gable two floors above. Generally the tradition of the classical court house was adhered to, as in the new façade at Beverley guildhall. Classical ornament from almost any source could be added to even the plainest building in stone or stucco to achieve the requisite splendour; and throughout the years up to about 1860 we find examples such as Kidderminster corn exchange and public rooms (Fig. 4) where the brick façade of a very simple building is splendidly dressed in rustication and composite pilasters. The result is not at all unpleasing and is typical of the mid-century display building. The slightly earlier Stourport town hall showed the other end of the scale with only a small balcony on scroll supports and plain stone door surrounds.

However, problems of size such as faced Manchester in the 1850s were not unique and there was increasing pressure for an enlarged type of building. Two solutions were found. The monumental Roman approach sketched out at Manchester found its climax in buildings such as the St George's hall at Liverpool (Fig. 17) and Leeds town hall. The Liverpool building is unique and dominates by its sheer bulk with its gigantic north portico of sixteen columns and three floors of offices filling only the podium and lower half of the order on the south side. Such a design could hardly be followed, though its decorative rhythm provided the basis for the St George's hall at Bradford and for the Leeds town hall where it was transformed by the addition of a tower. It was in fact the Leeds type which provided the most fruitful solution and most effective urban symbol. The planning there is more developed with the hall in the centre flanked by a continuous double ring of courts and offices. This was a satisfactory and economical arrangement that could be easily adapted, and which survived to the end of the period. The direct successors are Bolton (Fig. 23) (where the axis of the hall was swung through 90°), Portsmouth and Oldham; but the similar plan at Cardiff, also with the axis of the hall parallel to the façade, allows for a particularly lavish stair and colonnaded sculpture hall. A similar type appears in a Royal Academy competition design of 1902 of a town hall for a London borough in a heavy Vanburghian mode.[3] The great advance of Leeds, though, was in the provision of a tower. This actually spoils the internal arrangements, but its contribution to the townscape is vital and we shall return to it again.

One offshoot of the fully classical type was important though examples are rare. At Burslem (Fig. 51) and Todmorden (Fig. 38) are adaptations of the temple type of Birmingham. They have another precedent in Nash's town hall at Newport, IOW (1816),[4] which is a particularly elegant version of the small assembly room with town offices. The full requirements of borough court, offices and reading room could all be packed into the basement while the upper floor was given over to the hall. At Todmorden the hall stairs are elegantly fitted into an apsidal end, but the ingenuity required to stay within the simple temple shape rendered this type of building unsuitable, and the Todmorden example of 1870 is a very late survival. The overall form of these buildings would have contributed to the townscape in much the same way as the typical eighteenth-century market and town hall had done, and it seems to

51 Burslem town hall, G. T. Robinson, 1852–7

me significant that in spite of the existence of these few fine examples the type was not more widely imitated. Not only were they functionally problematical, but the very continuity of overall form may have seemed unsatisfactory as a symbol of the new type of urban entity.

There was, however, a real need for more flexibility, and this was found in various adaptations and revivals of a Renaissance or palazzo style. Newcastle was one of the first of these with its free use of classical motifs to clothe what was effectively a block of offices on a wedge-shaped site. The addition of a small tower, almost a forerunner of that at Leeds, effectively signalised its importance. The free classical dress certainly allowed more flexibility, but without the tower Green's building would be in no way different from any other office block, bank or shop. At Blackburn a similar but more restrained style was applied to a town hall that in the event got no tower, but the size of that palazzo makes it significant even today. Even Halifax town hall (Fig. 24), created by the acknowledged master of the palazzo style, Sir Charles Barry, is significant far less because of its main block than because of its tower, which is simply superimposed on one corner of the building. None the less it was relatively easy to spread a veneer of Italianate or French Renaissance motifs over a façade, and if the building was big enough the necessary grandeur would be achieved. The elegant little town hall at Wavertree represents one end of this scale, while the Accrington town hall, built as the Peel Institute, provides a more solid and splendid example. The ground floor is rusticated with round headed windows beneath exaggerated voussoirs while the entry is stressed by a fine porte cochère beneath a pillared and pedimented loggia.

The development of the classical type from the regency pseudo-mansion to the palazzo of Accrington parallels a more or less continuous development of the building type. By about the mid-1850s both the corporations and the type of building they would need was sufficiently well established. What was not so clear was which style of dress was suitable. The classical mode was, as I have suggested, capable of a fairly wide range; but the opportunities for real classical grandeur on the scale of Leeds were rare, and on a smaller scale any pure classicism was likely to lack the aggressive dominance and opulence that would make the town hall significant in a rapidly developing town. Thus it is not surprising that most of the classical town halls from the 1840s to the 1860s were in one or other of the many varieties of Renaissance styles. The range is so wide that it hardly deserves the name of a style, but it is worth noting how widely even the best buildings ranged in their inspiration. Hull and Burslem display all the richness of ornament, inside and out, that could be afforded and amply epitomise the grosser aspect of the mid-Victorian delight in the sumptuous. These two are fine buildings, but it was rarely that this mode was handled with the sureness and elegance displayed by Barry at Halifax. Generally a more or less extreme variety (according to the money available) of motley classicism, such as was used at Kidderminster, was the rule. On a symmetrical façade the recipe could be varied and repeated without undue danger as the late example of Pendleton town hall shows.

Tiverton in Devon, of about the same date, applies the method to an irregular façade with prodigious enthusiasm that achieves only a very uncertain success. It is not really that there are so many different sources, but that the individual motifs really require a grander and more regular scale than was possible on small but complex buildings of this sort. The strong French influence was to persist, particularly in the use of mansard roofs, which, as we shall see, could be enlisted to serve either Gothic or classical styles. However, the free Renaissance buildings of the late 1860s and after are materially different from those of the mid-century and can be more conveniently studied as part of the move towards eclecticism that began in the 1870s. I have used the term eclecticism to describe buildings of the Sheffield type, but we should remember that the mid-century classical styles were just as freely eclectic. What changed was the acceptance of eclecticism in its own right and not as the perpetuation of architectural solecisms. Once it became acceptable it was immediately found to be suitable for the largest and grandest buildings, and particularly valuable in that by the

52 Sheffield town hall, E. W. Mountford, 1890–7

1880s, along with flatter façades, the various parts of the buildings were more loosely articulated and their various forms were not concealed (Fig. 52). This was the lesson learned from the adoption of the Gothic style, and in fact Gothic town halls outnumbered classical from the 1860s on. Classicism undoubtedly survived, often as an alternative by the same designer for the same building, as with Lockwood & Mawson at Bradford. However, its importance declined, and, in spite of such grandiose designs as Daniel Brade's for Leeds municipal buildings (Fig. 41), little more was achieved in a properly classical style until such piles as the Glasgow municipal buildings opened the way for the revival of baroque.

Returning to the mid-century, we find that the end of the 1850s saw the beginning of the erosion of classical or Renaissance dress in favour of Gothic (Fig. 66). There are several reasons for the emergence of this style, not least the increasing study of Gothic architecture by leading architects and the writings of John Ruskin from the publication of *The Stones of Venice* in 1853 onwards. Of course there were the growing romantic associations with 'olde England' and more particularly with the world of the medieval guilds and continental town halls, which were evinced as exemplars in the battle for the Leeds tower. And one should not ignore the prestige of the growing Houses of Parliament. Then there was the ease with which a Gothic design could support a tower. It was never easy to plant a single tower on the corner of a classical building as Barry did at Halifax, and his spire there is a masterpiece of compromise (Fig. 24; cf Figs 28, 40).[5] Finally, and most important for the long term, there was the flexibility of Gothic which allowed complete freedom from the axial symmetry needed for most successful classical designs. I have already indicated that few town halls could be built on open sites. Few could even be easily seen from in front and the acceptance of Gothic allowed much greater scope for designing town halls that could be seen effectively along a street.

However, this was not immediately apparent. E. W. Godwin's Northampton town hall (1861–4) (Fig. 54) was one of the early Gothic town halls and the first properly Ruskinian one, yet it was as obstinately classical in underlying form as the Houses of Parliament. A seven bay façade of two storeys is surmounted by a central tower giving a completely symmetrical arrangement. Behind the façade the actual building was fitted into an irregular narrow site as conveniently as possible. The Gothic dress, though, was for the first time convincingly and extravagantly Gothic.[6] Bands of coloured stone proclaimed the Ruskinian precepts about constructional polychromy, and the capitals are richly decorated with foliage and whimsical figure sculpture. The traceried windows of the first floor are flanked by canopies sheltering figures on pillars that represent kings of England.[7] Above these the parapet makes no attempt to conceal the steep roof, made handsome with its patterned slates; and the

53 Dewsbury town hall, Holtom & Fox, 1888–9

composition is capped by the short tower with its steep pyramid roof. The whole was an extremely effective piece of window dressing and the play of light on its richly carved polychrome surface is a real pleasure. Still one has to admit that another reason for its original success, as one can see from the contemporary engravings, was its considerable bulk in relation to its neighbours. The recipe was so successful that Godwin repeated it at Congleton (1864–6) (Fig. 77) where it can still be seen in relation to its original neighbours. There in a smaller façade he made the tower even more dominant. The same theme reappears in his competition design for East Retford town hall, where it reveals even more clearly its probable source in the Casa del Orologio at Venice. The pattern could be easily elaborated as far as funds allowed, and Godwin produced several further versions, one in a published design for an unidentified town and one in a sketch that is probably for Reading town hall. His

54 Northampton town hall, E. W. Godwin, 1861–4; extensions (extreme left) by M. W. Holding, 1889–92

attachment to symmetrical Gothic seems almost a denial of a freedom that might have been welcome.[8] In essence these façades are all identical to the façade Brodrick designed for Hull town hall. This is something of a surprise in a romantic Gothicist like E. W. Godwin, but is easily explained by reference to some of the old medieval town halls of the Low Countries and of Germany. These were increasingly studied and a good many were illustrated in the architectural press from the mid-1860s on. They not infrequently had symmetrical façades. Ypres was, of course, the prime example, and the tradition continued on the continent in such buildings as Erfurt town hall (Sommer, 1876) and of course Gilbert Scott's design for Hamburg town hall (1854). In this country it was taken up for a number of designs. Lynn's designs for Chester (Fig. 33) and Barrow town halls are both basically symmetrical (that for Chester exactly symmetrical) with a central tower as is the Gothic design for Wakefield town hall by R. Knill Freeman (1877). Even Manchester town hall has a nearly symmetrical façade, and Scott's design for Halifax town hall was for a symmetrical building with a projecting central tower. In fact the pattern could be successfully adpated for almost any dress or none at all, and Hartlepool market and town hall (Fig. 74) by C. J. Adams is a particularly effective but plain example. There are a great many other simple more or less symmetrical blocks tricked out with Gothic windows and carved ornaments. Even Bradford town hall is more or less symmetrical and, as we have seen, might easily have been clothed in classical dress. However by the mid-1860s Gothicists, and Godwin among them, were making use of the added freedom of the style to design loose agglomerations of buildings. Godwin's design for Leicester town hall clearly shows this as does an alternative preparatory sketch for the same competition.[9] At Leicester Godwin broke up a long range of miscellaneous offices, courts and halls by frankly expressing each separately behind a varied façade of gable end, turrets, hall roof with traceried windows, tall tower, tiered hipped roof and finally another plain gable with a second tower to the rear. The design was criticised at the time for being merely a pretty façade, but it would undoubtedly have produced a varied streetscape even if it did not gain from being seen as a whole. Godwin was also consultant for another major Gothic town hall at Plymouth (1869–74) (Fig. 34). There again Norman and Hine had produced a design for a free composition of blocks with gables, towers and turrets. The building was suitably decorated with statues on the towers and over each gable, and was a more delicate alternative to the weighty Gothic of Manchester that came to be the norm. There are, of course, dozens of other designs, built and unbuilt, for loose groupings in the Gothic style. T. E. Collcutt's Gothic design for Wakefield town hall (1877–80) (Fig. 42) and his earlier competitive entry for Chorley town hall make similar though less extensive use of variety. In each of these the main hall block is expressed and separated from the humbler offices by a large tower. All these buildings, though, are different in type from the town halls of the Leeds period. They house not only the public hall and courts but a much larger bureaucracy that might not fit so easily behind a symmetrical classical façade of the same extent. Rochdale (Fig. 37) was one of the first of these pantechnicon buildings to be built in the Gothic style, and there one department is simply added to another with a particularly refreshing insouciance. The rear view is revealing, but significantly the façade, though not symmetrical, is carefully balanced and set off by its corner tower with the great hall clearly expressed externally. The free

55 Rochdale town hall, grand stair, W. H. Crossland, 1866–71

composition allowed the architect to assemble all his effects without any hindrance and the processional route through the building is among the finest in any town hall. The large vaulted porte cochère[10] leads into a dark aisled exchange with a rich heraldic floor of Minton tiles (Fig. 91). From the back of this a wide stair (Fig. 55) rises up into a blaze of light from nine huge windows filled with heraldic stained glass. The vault hangs high overhead on tall slender columns round which the stairs return to bring you in at the centre of the great hall, darker with its immense hammer beam roof but glowing with stained glass. This showy progress has, not surprisingly, nothing to do with the mechanics of municipal government and the council chamber (Fig. 56) and offices are tucked away to the side. This architectural promenade is essentially for display and reveals the essence of civic pride.

Showy frontages like this one at Rochdale were naturally popular; and even at Preston (Fig. 40), where G. G. Scott built his only English town hall, we see a return to the arrangement of Salford or Mansfield with the grand rooms set along the front and a service wing of offices running back along a side street. The arrangement of the parts is, however, much freer and the two main elements are divided by a grand corner tower that gives emphasis to the whole. However, it is really only the main façade that is worth looking at, though in this case the formal parts of the interior were richly appointed too.

If the choice of a Gothic style allowed freer grouping and a ready expression of the constituent parts, it also made it easier to build higher, for offices could be fitted into the roof behind dormer windows in a way that was not possible with classical architecture. The immense height of Manchester's town hall (Fig. 25) is not readily apparent, and is in any case relieved by the exciting silhouette of gables, chimneys and finials. As city centre streets developed into canyons this sort of effect was increasingly desirable, whereas town halls of the Leeds variety needed to be seen across a great square. There were, of course, difficulties in planning offices in the garrets, and some

56 Rochdale town hall, council chamber, W. H. Crossland, 1866–71

of those at Bradford are eccentric in shape to say the least. However, the criticism made there that they would be dark because the dormer windows were so small is quite unfounded since they are also lit by extensive skylights and are in fact a good deal lighter than the formal rooms of the principal floor. Similar arrangements under a classical dress would have required a succession of heavy attics and balustrades or a pile of superimposed orders which, in the case of Bradford, would most probably have been less satisfactory on the long but rather shallow site. Besides, it was less easy with a classical design to provide the sort of dynamic roof-line that is so important a part of the Manchester town hall. Halifax on a rectangular site makes two tiers of orders into a lucid and impressive block, but there there is always the tower and the small turrets on top of the balustrade are of considerable importance visually. Blackburn with an extra storey and less decoration remains distinctive by its bulk; but Burnley town hall (1884) shows the weakness that results from the free application of a succession of different orders to a cramped town hall façade that must be seen along a street (in this case a steeply sloping street). The design is merely competent and suffers badly from its oblique viewpoint while the dome is too small to tell as it should on the sloping site. Corson's municipal offices in Leeds suffer in the same way, though the effect is less damaging there for he was building two separate blocks in any case, School Board offices and library, museum and art gallery. He topped the School Board offices with a pair of hipped roofs over low turrets that make an effective skyline feature on the corner block.[11] Besides, he was able to apply his decoration (it is in fact rather flat) so as to distinguish the two blocks while echoing in both the pattern of Brodrick's town hall opposite, and thus his buildings benefit from borrowed grandeur.

The next great town hall to have the placing that a grand classical design deserves was Glasgow (Fig. 57). Its site at the head of George Square gives it enormous prominence. Its classicism is in many ways backward looking and might seem dull and weak were it not for the fact that the classical dress is skilfully disposed. The rustication and linking of the two lower floors lessens the weight of the whole, and the corner turrets with their domes and the enormous tower must be recognised as the beginnings of the move towards Edwardian baroque. William Young's building stands at the turning point of the style, and it is interesting to compare it with another of the designs for the building submitted in the competition. It is no surprise in Glasgow to find a severely classical design, but the design submitted by a little known architect called Bromhead preserves the old fashioned Roman classicism intact. He proposed a building completely surrounded by huge Corinthian columns and pilasters on a rusticated podium. There was to be no tower, only a massive pediment in the centre of the front. Beneath it the main entry was by way of a huge freestanding portico with Atlas figures flanking the doorway. The design is a complete throwback

57 Glasgow city chambers, William Young 1881–9

to the days of 'Greek' Thomson but was sufficiently convincing and interesting to merit publication in the *Architect*[12] which was generally quite discriminating in its choice of illustrations. It also reminds us that it was only the giant columns that could give real dignity in the larger classical buildings. They recur throughout the period up to 1870 in examples such as Liverpool (Fig. 11), Leeds and Stoke-on-Trent. Even the Birmingham council house (Fig. 2) achieves its effect almost entirely by the repetition of huge Corinthian pilasters. There the tower, porticoes and dome are less effective and little more than ingredients in the whole. Though they are needed to break the incessant rhythm, they do not provide a sufficiently effective counterpoint, and the main entry with its exaggerated porte cochère and mosaic-filled arch is especially clumsy.

Later large columns or pilasters on a podium were adopted in almost all the

58 Leicester municipal buildings, F. J. Hames, 1874–6 (*Builder*, vol. XXXVIII, 1879)

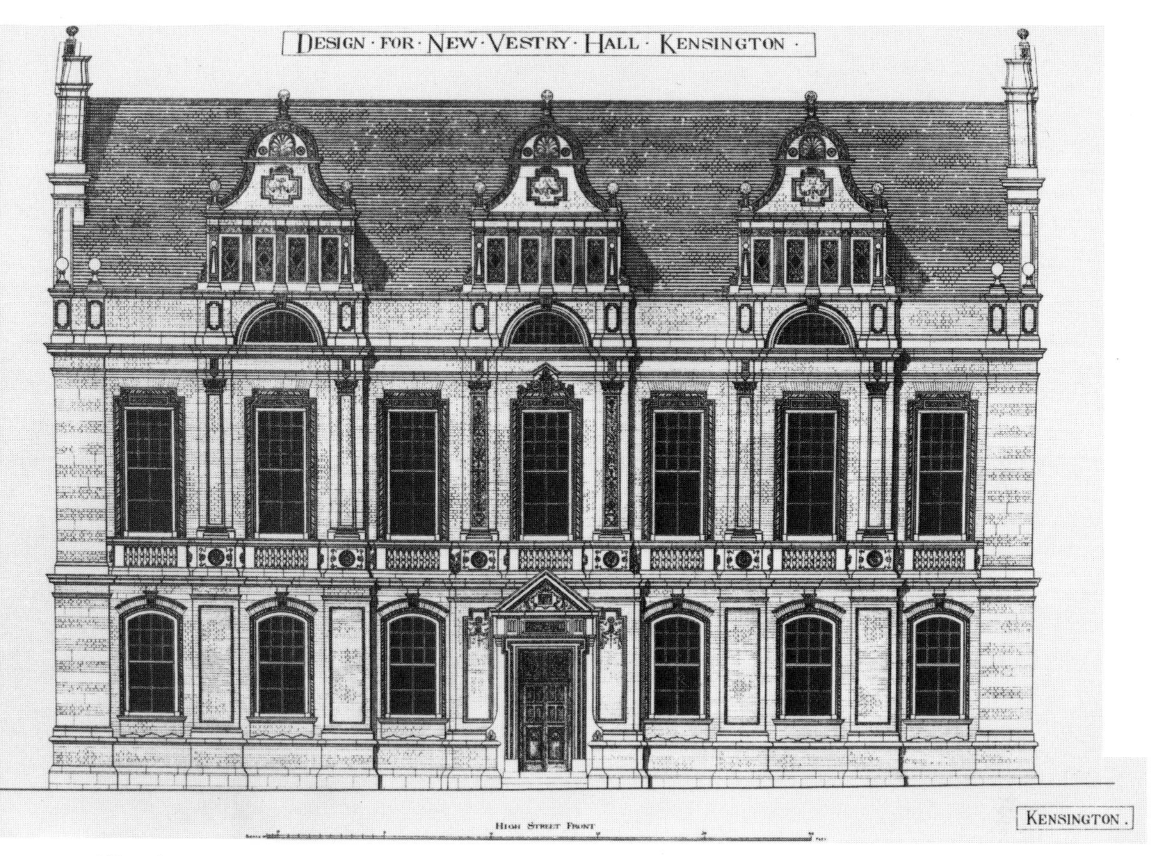

59 Kensington vestry hall, second premiated design, J. O. Scott, 1877 (*Building News*, vol. XXXIII, 1877)

baroque town halls, though there the use is rather different. In fact before Birmingham's return to traditional classicism new elements had given added choice in the field of town hall building. The 1870s and early 1880s were a period of rampant eclecticism which was taken to offer the best of both worlds in freedom of composition and grandeur of elements. In town hall building the change was ushered in by the adoption of the Queen Anne style for Leicester town hall in 1873 (Fig. 58). There F. J. Hames produced a very competent and varied façade that wrapped around two sides of a long block of different heights. He was able to give a rich entry, provide four floors of offices and allow for different ceiling heights just as Waterhouse had at Manchester. However he retained a much friendlier and more variegated façade with only a relatively small tower.[13] Pilasters were out, but the heavy cornice united the main façade while above there was room for a variety of gables and dormers with scope for applied and carved decoration as required. Leicester was a surprisingly successful composition and marks a turning point in town hall design. As might be expected from a former assistant of Nesfield, it displays almost all the characteristics of the Queen Anne style, and even in spite of its bulk appears quite intimate. However, perhaps because of this very intimacy, this was not a recipe that could be easily repeated and the Queen Anne town hall is hardly distinguishable as a separate type. Hames went on to produce designs for Leeds municipal buildings and Darwen town hall, but these have not survived. Queen Anne designs were a feature of the Kensington vestry hall competition in 1877, but in spite of their quality they did not appeal to the board and were not built. In fact, of the Queen Anne designs only those by J. O. Scott (Fig. 59) and J. J. Stevenson won prizes, taking second and third place respectively. The selected design, by R. Walker, was a safe mildly Italianate classical piece, and the most convincingly Queen Anne designs, by J. M. Brydon and E. W. Godwin, were not even placed. Of the two premiated designs even that by J. J. Stevenson, though recognisably Queen Anne, is hardly a textbook example of the style.

There are few other Queen Anne town halls. T. G. Jackson produced a charming little town hall for Tipperary (Fig. 60) that exchanges the traditional uniform of brick for roughcast. But in general brick town halls tended to lack the necessary dignity, and the style needed translating into stone for any real success. This was excellently done by T. E. Collcutt at Wakefield (Fig. 79) and in his design for Barrow-in-Furness town hall; but in the transformation it becomes harder to see these buildings as truly Queen Anne, and the tower of Wakefield town hall certainly owes nothing to the movement. Even a doyen of the style such as E. R. Robson stuck to a stone version in his design for Leeds municipal buildings (Fig. 61), and there is altogether too much regularity for that design to count as Queen Anne. In fact he later reverted to Gothic for the little town hall at Loftus-in-Cleveland (1879) (Fig. 62). The extensions to Pontefract town hall are one of very few other Queen Anne town halls, though the characteristic Dutch gables and moulded terracotta later gave their main character to several simple blocks like West Hartlepool municipal buildings. Similar motifs in a variety of materials were used by George Skipper in a group of town halls of the 1890s in Norfolk, but by then the Queen Anne style itself had become so diluted that such buildings are best described as examples of eclecticism. There are a few late survivals such as the design for Hitchin town hall (Fig. 63) that mixes a roughcast upper storey and deep coved cornice with a baroque entry, but that was not executed as designed and the consultant architect, E. W. Mountford, is best known for other styles. What the Leicester building had demonstrated, however, was that freely composed town halls could be dressed in other than Gothic clothes. Though Gothic

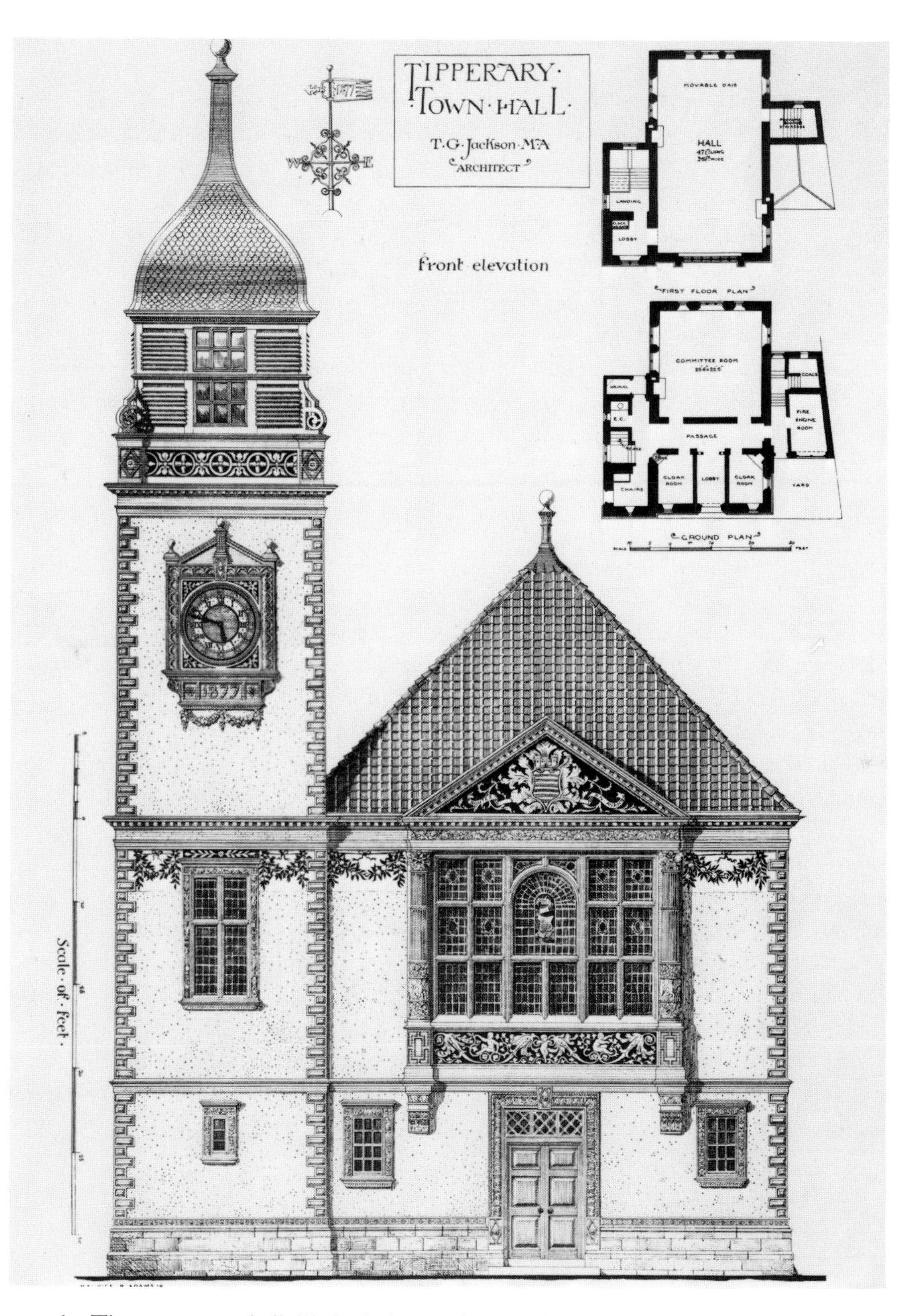

60 Tipperary town hall, T. G. Jackson, 1877 (*Building News*, vol. XXXV, 1878)

61 Leeds municipal buildings, unsuccessful competition design by E. R. Robson, 1876 (*Building News*, vol. XXXII, 1877)

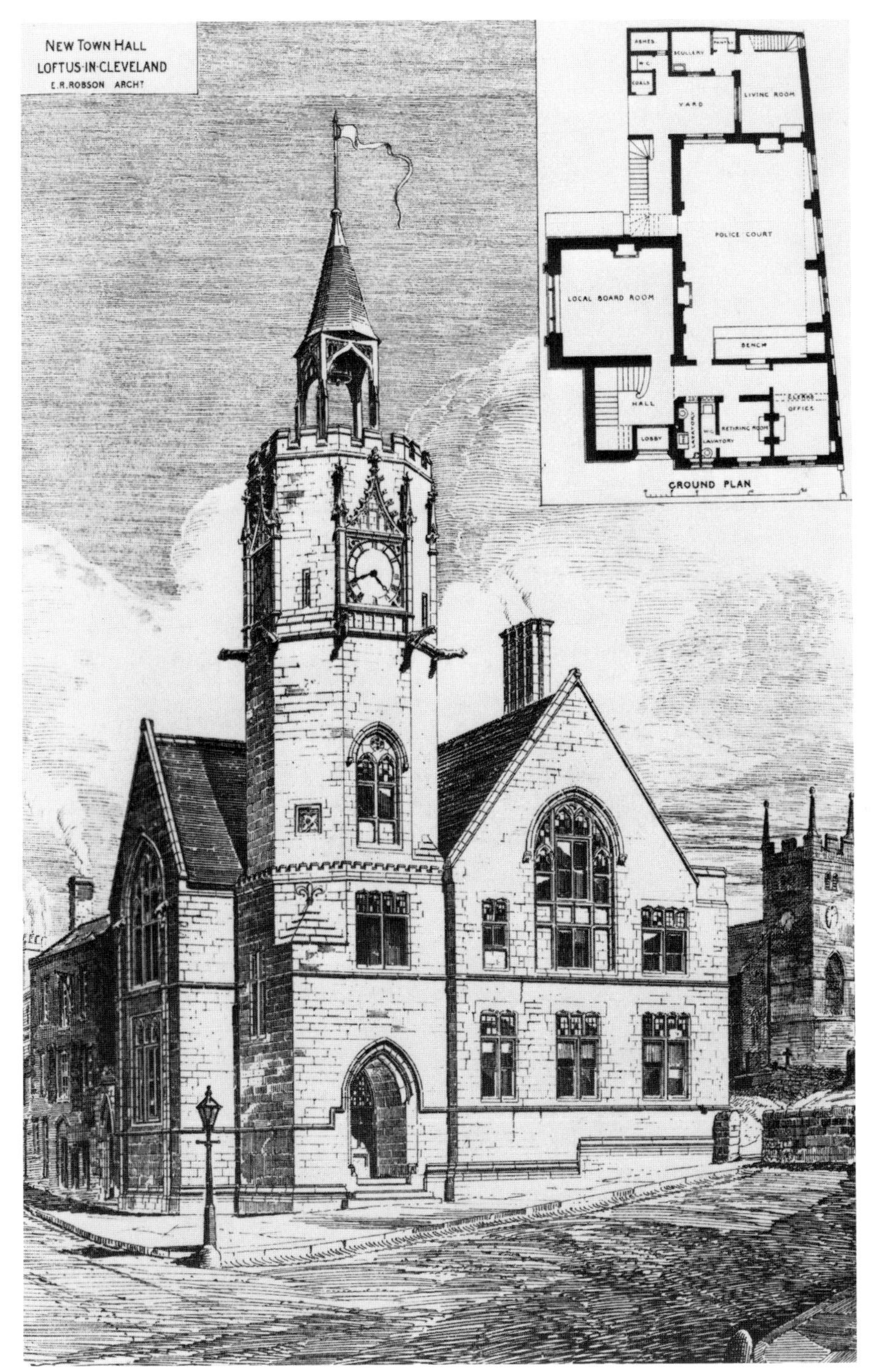

62 Loftus-in-Cleveland town hall, E. R. Robson, 1879 (*Building News*, vol. XXXVI, 1879)

63 Hitchin town hall, winning design, G. Lucas, 1898; built to a quite different design with E. W. Mountford as consultant, 1898–1900 (*Builder*, vol. LXXV, 1898)

was to survive for at least another decade (Fig. 31), architects had been offered a new freedom, and the way was open for a series of freely eclectic buildings among which the Queen Anne legacy was mostly found in its various Jacobean descendants which allowed both richer ornament and more formality. Collcutt's design for Barrow town hall with its arcaded first floor loggia between end pavilions should probably be classed with these rather than with Leicester.

Jacobean was really a mongrel version which translated more easily into stone but retained the large oriel windows and fanciful gables. It appears eventually at Oxford in H. T. Hare's town hall (1893). That building is seriously underestimated and incorporates a rich palette of styles. The façade is Jacobean with fine mullioned windows and elaborately carved gables which none the less agree satisfactorily with the medieval house that was to be incorporated into the design. The entry up steps brings one into a marble hall with a grand stair rising in a single straight flight to the main hall. This sequence is frankly Empire with its rich materials and heavy plaster decoration; but the second hall over the entrance is Tudorbethan with a dark hammerbeam roof and dark panelled walls. Perhaps the acorn finials in the roof are meant to make the ensemble Jacobean again. There is a crazy sort of logic in this belief that different functions required different settings. It was something that Norman Shaw understood very well, and he used it in his one town hall commission, as a consultant for the Bradford town hall extensions. The site architect was F. E. P. Edwards, the city architect, but the character of the work is clearly Shaw's. The outside might just be described as Gothic. It is certainly in keeping with the original block, but there was no attempt to repeat the insistent rhythms of the earlier section. The variety of window shapes in the extension, round, mullioned and segmental headed, acts more as a foil to the original, and the only strongly medieval features, and they are more Tudor than Gothic, are the two mullioned semi-circular bow windows of the hall. Inside the council chamber is classically planned as a Greek cross beneath a dome with marble columns and a circular top light. Yet above the polished panelling the whole effect is lightened by the Arts and Crafts character of the plasterwork with bands of vine leaves and pigeons and squirrels all to the designs of Ernest Gimson. The new mayor's parlour, by contrast, is gently Jacobean with a half-timbered overmantel and reproduction Stuart furniture. The hall is different again, and more nearly Gothic. Shaw was able to build into it his favourite dramatic fireplace element (Fig. 90). The main space is a short rectangle beneath a high arch braced roof, brightly lit only at its far end by the pair of huge mullioned bows which rise the full height of the room. Entry is by means of doors at the dark fireplace end which is separated from the main space by a large stone arch that frames the grand chimneypiece and turns this end of the room into an overgrown inglenook.[14] This is a fine conception, but it still does not complete the range. In 1914 Shaw advised on the new staircase which is an Edwardian baroque affair with twin stairs rising over a bridge to a square balustraded landing, rich with marble and stained glass, from which you can pass either straight into the original Gothic mayor's rooms or via a short passage to the airy council chamber and grand hall. The individual parts are all successful, but at this late date eclecticism was being strained to the limits and had generally been overtaken by municipal baroque.

Eclecticism was fresher in the years from 1880 to 1900 and produced some fascinating and characterful buildings (Fig. 64), especially in its more usual guise of Jacobean-Elizabethan-Renaissance. It provided a very necessary advance on the

64 Bury municipal buildings, unsuccessful competition design by F. H. Tulloch, 1891 (*Builder*, LXII, 1892)

repetitive Gothic of the late 1870s. Harry Cheers was a free user of this mode, and produced among others Hereford town hall where a suite of grand rooms and offices are all tucked under one huge red brick gable frothed out with turrets and a mass of strapwork in cream terracotta. There is even a semi-circular stair with a swirling iron handrail and art-nouveauish stained glass. Generally such aestheticism was avoided

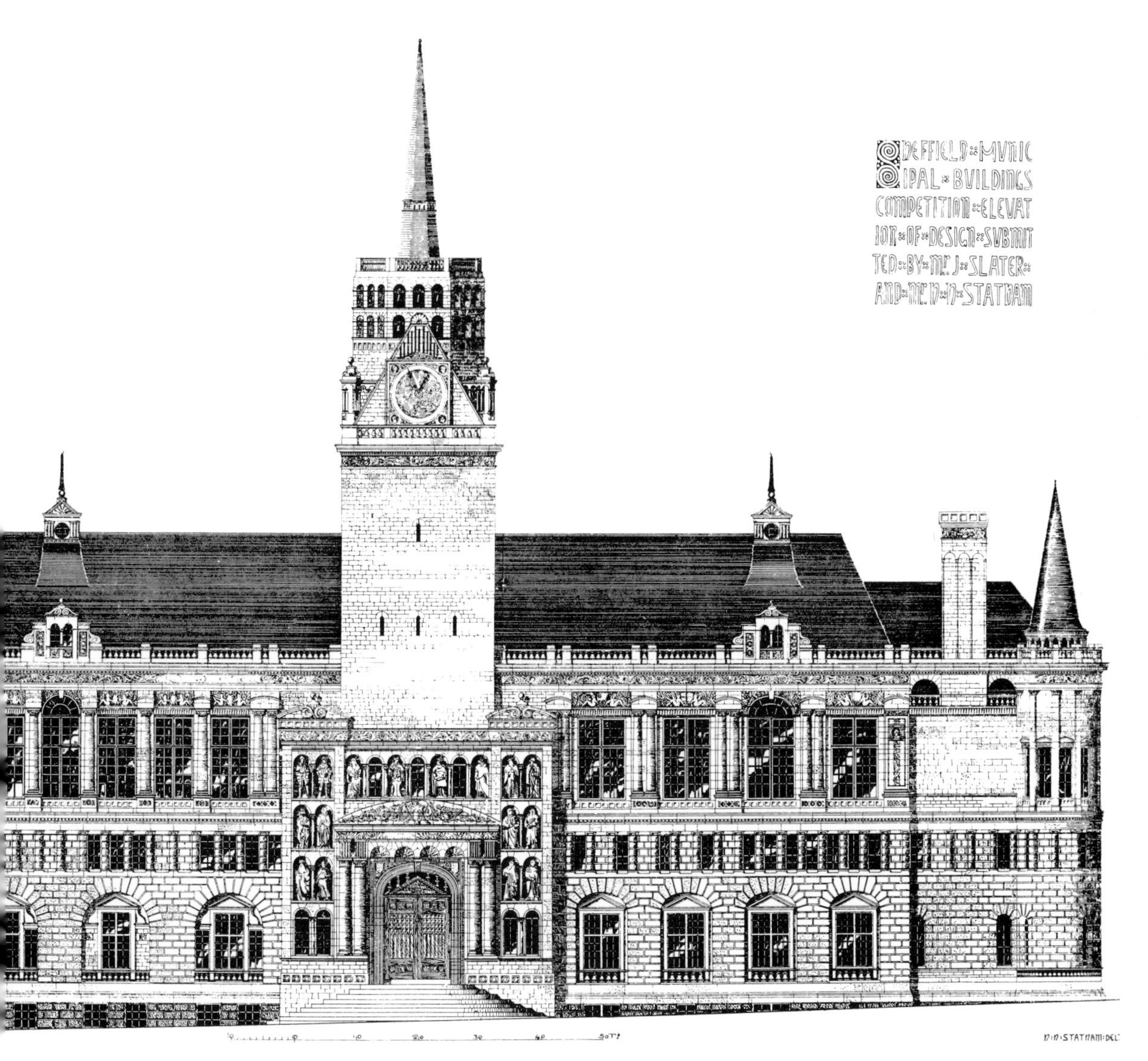

65 Sheffield town hall, unsuccessful competition design by H. Heathcote Statham and J. Slater, 1890 (*Builder*, LVIII, 1890)

in town halls, and Halsey Ricardo's design for Oxford town hall is as far as things went in that direction. His design is similar to some of Harrison Townsend's work but lacks any frankly art nouveau decoration. It is in fact as much a medieval castle front as an art nouveau design, and significantly it was not built. The wilder flights of eclecticism too were unacceptable, as we see with Heathcote Statham's extraordinary design for Sheffield town hall (Fig. 65).[15]

This brings us back to the problem of a symbolic language and its need to be both easily recognisable and yet varied enough to express the specific character of a town. Directly derivative buildings were equally unappealing, and another of the unsuccessful designs for Sheffield town hall offered an English version of the campanile at Venice. Mountford's winning design was successful because, for all its free composition and looseness, it was decked out with easily recognisable ornaments of grandeur—friezes, columns, pedimented windows and arched openings with carved spandrels. There was plenty to recognise here, yet the scheme offered enough variety to allow for free planning inside; and when Mountford was asked to extend the building in 1902 he had no difficulty in adding a further block that continued the same decorative pattern. The final section was built later still (1908–25) under another architect, though still to Mountford's plans, and manages to be a different piece that is still clearly part of the same whole. Sheffield town hall is probably the showpiece of eclecticism, but it had many successors and many smaller buildings are in the same mode. The importance of the Sheffield building is that it repeated the message of Leicester in an even broader vocabulary, that eclecticism really could be a proper vehicle for grandeur.

There was one further element in the pattern book that had materially helped town hall architects from the 1870s on, which deserves individual treatment simply because of its wide application in both classical and Gothic buildings. Most of the features of the eclectic town halls of the last quarter of the century derived ultimately from the Italian Renaissance or from Jacobean England; but from France the architects drew and used avidly the mansarded pavilion. This feature appeared as early as the 1860s where it was used in the winning design for Bishop Auckland town hall (Fig. 66) to give added dignity to an endearingly simple little domestic Gothic building. It was taken up especially in the 1880s, and was particularly useful in articulating the larger masses or those on awkward sites. It could be adapted to either Gothic or classical dress. At Dewsbury (Fig. 53) the pavilions make essential terminals to the tall façade forced on the architects by the steeply sloping site. At Middlesbrough (Fig. 31), one of the last of the large Gothic town halls, the corners of both the municipal buildings and of the town hall are stressed by pavilions which in the latter case serve no practical purpose but only give a sense of form to what would

66 Bishop Auckland town hall and market, winning design by J. P. Jones, 1860; built in a slightly modified version by J. Johnstone, 1860–2 (*Builder*, vol. XVIII, 1860)

otherwise appear an enormously extensive block. Their value as a corner feature had been appreciated by Waterhouse at Manchester and at Middlesbrough the practice is merely regularised. There a façade of nineteen bays is effectively broken into a mere five sections by the pavilions and the further subdivision by pairing the remaining windows helps to reduce the building to manageable proportions. The undoubtedly French mansard roofs sit quite easily on top of the workaday Gothic façade. The regularity of the pattern is a little uninspiring, but the architect did not avail himself fully of the pavilion principle, and his mansard roofs merely cap sections of the same flat façade. There is virtually no attempt to provide movement in the façade itself which thus has the character of a long linear block. Seen from the southern end the tower over the town hall at the far end does not tell sufficiently to offset the linearity, and the corner pavilions are a necessary alternative.

67 Taunton town hall, third premiated design, H. T. Hare, 1898 (*Building News*, vol. LXXV, 1898)

Of course the motif was most convincing when borrowed more nearly whole, and at Wolverhampton a decade earlier there is just such a façade. The trio of mansarded pavilions provide an effective substitute for a tower, and Bates' simple classical façade, with two layers of rustication, round headed windows to the piano nobile and a meagre allowance of pilasters for the pavilions, is turned into a convincing palace along the lines of so many *mairies* by the exaggerated mansard roofs. It is, of course, merely a front to a workaday brick building that runs away down the hill, but at only around £20,000 in 1870 it was remarkably economical. It was probably economy that resulted in the choice of this design without the all-important tower, yet the high crested roofs go a long way to ensure the dignity of the building.

However, there were limits to the scope of eclecticism, and the free treatment of French Renaissance themes can be seen as no more than a survival of other equally free translations of continental Renaissance forms in the mid-century. Still, with the growth of the corporate machine, there were more frequent opportunities to design really huge piles, and for these a new style opportunely arose. It is difficult to find any precise reason for the sudden emergence of the baroque revival which was so ideally suited to the, by now, more distant authoritarian bureaucracies of the great cities.

68 Wakefield town hall, unsuccessful competition design by Holtom & Connon, 1877 (*Architect*, vol. XVII, 1877)

Psychological association certainly isn't enough, and in any case the baroque recipe was successfully adapted to many public halls. It even appears in designs for smaller buildings such as Taunton (Fig. 67), where H. T. Hare successfully grafted restrained baroque forms on to a ground floor loggia that consciously echoes the old eighteenth-century market hall type. In fact it is probably fair to see in the baroque revival a slightly more scholarly form of eclecticism. The fact that one of its main sources was Wren and that there is also a considerable debt to Vanbrugh might be seen as a reaffirmation of the essential national roots of the style of these consequential buildings that housed a particularly English form of democracy. There is a hint of the new direction in the last version of the Leeds town hall that was built in Portsmouth from 1887 to 1890 where ogee cupolas suddenly appear on the corner pavilions. However, that was a definitely backward-looking building. There is a much earlier version of the theme in a design by Holtom & Connon for the Wakefield town hall (1877–80) (Fig. 68). This makes use of four small corner domes with supporting groups of sculpture. The design lacks the movement that would allow it to be called baroque, but indicates a strong link with the grand classical designs of the mid-century. Certainly the emerging baroque style was felt to be old fashioned and traditionalist, but that was just what was wanted in a municipal palace. Perhaps the first protagonist of the style was J. M. Brydon who first gained success with a design for Chelsea vestry hall (Fig. 45) that owes all its significant features to Christopher Wren. He followed this with another important commission for Bath guildhall where the problem was precisely to root the building in English classicism, for his twin blocks were to flank the eighteenth-century guildhall and merely extend its façade. Brydon was a thoroughly competent architect and he managed the Bath commission adequately. However his buildings lack any real élan, and, although they were early indications of the new direction, the first development of the English Renaissance revival has to be sought outside England.

Scotland provided two earlier major opportunities; and the birth of the style has, I think, to be related to the strength of the classical tradition, particularly in Glasgow. There the municipal buildings competitions of 1880 and 1881 resulted in a classical revival building by William Young in a heavy Renaissance idiom (Fig. 69). Its façade has already been described, and I have cited the corner turrets and cupolas as baroque touches. This building must rank as the first major municipal work of the Renaissance revival. Several influences can be traced within it, but the overall design is remarkably consistent. The tower is the most eclectic feature, but then there were no clear Renaissance precedents for a massive tower as a rising feature. The interiors with their succession of domed and vaulted halls, mosaic floors and ceilings leading to the final grand stair rich with orange and red marble would satisfy any craving for grandeur. If not fully baroque, this sequence approaches very nearly to the standard later set by buildings such as Stockport town hall. The winner of the first competition at Glasgow, George Corson, had in contrast merely enlarged on the well-tried mildly continental classical mode that he had used in the Leeds municipal buildings, exchanging the domes he proposed there for mansarded roofs. Most of the other designs were pretty wide-ranging in their choice of motifs especially when it came to the tower. A particularly massive and frothy version was submitted by Leeming & Leeming, another partnership with considerable experience of municipal competitions. However two more designs deserve a mention here. E. T. Salmon submitted a design with a low dome instead of a tower that is clearly inspired by the French Renaissance and is a foretaste of the Beaux Arts influence that was later to swamp the particularly English character of Edwardian baroque. Coe & Robinson, however, who took second premium produced a monumental classical pile topped with a domed tower of the same general plan as that at Leeds, but treated this time in a fully baroque manner. The design was not built, but was well publicised in the professional press and will have had its influence.

In the same way the abortive Edinburgh competition of 1887 marked a

69 Glasgow city chambers, entrance vestibule, William Young, 1881–9

significant development of the style. In the competition designs there the influence of the French châteaux and the survival of Scottish baronial was still evident. There were even some obstinately Gothic versions (with the usual Scottish offering of open crown spires). However several designs show the Renaissance revival firmly established. The design by Leeming & Leeming with five floors of rustication towards Princes Street was capped by a thoroughly convincing Wren style dome atop a two stage drum, and there were flanking corner cupolas on the High Street façade. This was a recipe that was soon to reappear in Belfast. J. M. Brydon also competed (Fig. 43) and also designed a great central dome, but he provides more extravagant flanking cupolas and a corner tower that is even more clearly baroque. A. Broad, a lesser-known competitor, designed a yet more extreme baroque domed tower, though his façade was more nearly in the Beaux Arts tradition. In fact a number of designs were produced in the early 1890s in a recognisably Beaux Arts idiom, but they were rejected and English baroque was the only acceptable style for municipal clients until well after 1900 (Fig. 70). The largest and grandest of the English baroque town halls were also built outside England in Belfast and Cardiff. Belfast city hall by Alfred Brumwell Thomas (1898–1906) relates directly to St Paul's cathedral, a huge pile that must have been an extreme contrast with the humble municipal offices (1869–70) that it replaced. Its success, like the Glasgow city chambers, is due very largely to its enormous bulk. It may be a historical accident that no town halls on that scale were required in England in the fifteen years from 1890 on when English baroque really swept the board. However, it is undeniable that on the really grand scale these domes, towers and huge façades of Portland stone (it usually is Portland stone) are dramatic and imposing. In the right hands they do not entirely lose the jollity of their predecessors. Cardiff city centre is a case in point where Lanchester, Stewart & Rickards designed just such a palace complete with domes, sculpture and a tall tower (Fig. 99). In fact they designed two palaces, one for the law courts and one for the town hall in a municipal commission as extensive as that won by Elmes at Liverpool two generations before. Their design is a thoroughgoing piece of civic pride and a fitting beginning to the development of the sixty acre Cathays park, and it is only to be regretted that they were not allowed to complete the row with their equally splendid design for the National Museum of Wales. Still Cardiff is the town hall with everything. There is a variety of fine sculpture perched on the roof-line and even a splendid bronze dragon atop the council chamber dome. Inside there is the magnificent sculpture hall with its yellow scagliola columns and bronze capitals that was soon peopled with bronze versions of various Welsh heroes and heroines. The mayor's parlour has a magnificent bronze fireplace and overmantel. The central hall, though less lush than some of its predecessors, is huge and well lit both by dormer

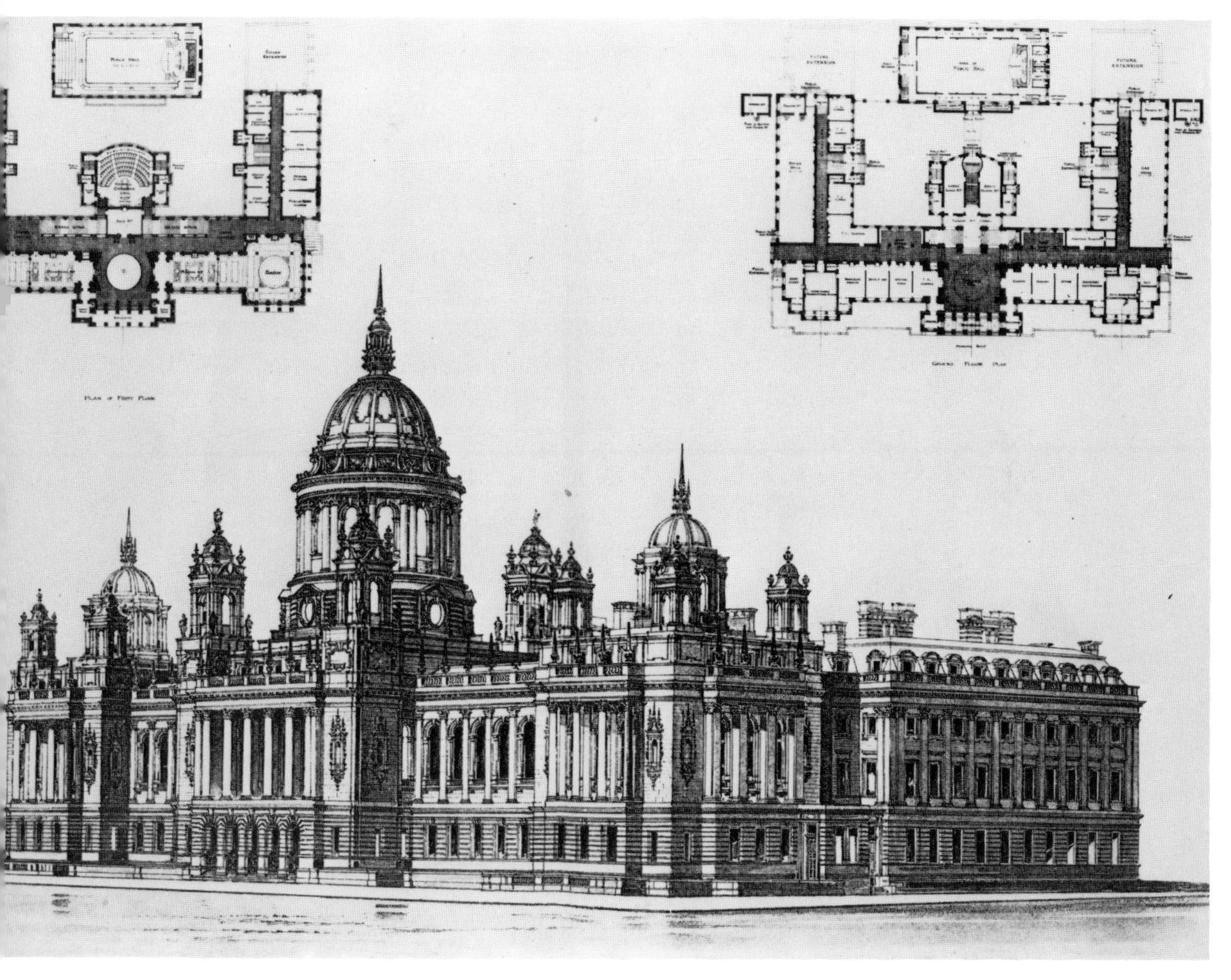

70 Belfast city hall, premiated design for second competition, Malcolm Stark and Rowntree, 1896 (*Building News*, vol. LXXII, 1897)

windows in the segmental ceiling and by a row of giant electroliers designed by the architects. For most tastes the scale of grandeur is altogether too much and the sheer bulk of the building makes it aloof, but it can never be dull.

A comparison between the Cardiff city hall and the town hall and municipal buildings at Middlesbrough shows how the baroque revival brought drama back to municipal buildings with a vengeance. Though it was impossible for many corporations to build on the scale of Cardiff, the acceptance of freer planning behind a façade did allow for baroque scene painting and in many cases only a dramatic façade

71 Colchester town hall, part elevation, J. Belcher, 1898–1902 (*Builder*, vol. LXXVII, 1899)

was needed. In fact the style could be adapted to quite small buildings, as the design by Wimperis for Surbiton municipal buildings amply shows. An exaggerated cornice and a couple of columns cleverly transform a very modest block into a quite imposing pile. Only slightly larger and more lavish in scale (it cost around £35,000 without its tower), Colchester town hall by John Belcher (Fig. 71) shows just how successful the style could be as a contribution to the townscape that adds drama and dignity without overpowering. The dress is red brick with stone dressings that run to heavy aedicules around the windows and afford an exciting play of light. The moot hall inside it suitably pillared and grand, and the tower that was eventually added completes one of the best pieces of civic display from the closing years of the nineteenth century.

72 Cambridge guildhall, proposed design, J. Belcher, 1898; scheme abandoned

Belcher was in fact a master of the style and also designed a similar scheme for Cambridge (Fig. 72) with projecting turrets capped with globes, a pillared balcony over the entry and a handsome ground floor loggia. The interior was to include a particularly sumptuous stair, but alas the building never materialised. Brumwell Thomas, however, after this piece at Belfast, did achieve a second extravagant building,[16] this time at Stockport (Fig. 73). There he produced a Portland stone façade in the wildest Baroque that is both more exciting and less daunting than the Belfast building. Though the grand rooms are all lavishly decorated, the actual façade is a façade and no more for behind it the rest of the building is freely laid out with the great hall to the side, and at the sides and rear the Portland stone gives way to cherry red brick. Stockport is to my mind the most tremendous of these town halls. Its Portland stone façade is certainly more strident than the design by H. T. Hare which took third place. He specified Darley Dale stone which would have given an altogether softer accent, though his design is in a similar baroque manner. In fact, there is considerable variety in municipal baroque, not only in materials but also in design. At Leigh in Lancashire, for instance, a local architect produced a cheerful and egregious composition, never quite completed, with a row of shops beneath exaggerated gables to one side while the Market Square front was tricked out with heavily blocked columns. The hipped roof and cupola are all that this design could support, but the interiors are thoroughly sumptuous with scagliola and dark polished panelling.

One should probably distinguish two strands of baroque revival. One was a more earnest Renaissance classicism that drew principally on Wren and Hawksmoor rather than Vanbrugh. The other was altogether more exaggerated in its motifs, and made freer use of different materials. The two streams are not totally distinct and a single architect might design happily in both ways, like Brumwell Thomas at Belfast and Woolwich. Others like E. W. Mountford would continue to draw happily on any number of sources while working in a broadly baroque manner. However the exaggeration of individual motifs seems to have been more fruitful as it was more adaptable to the different needs of different towns. It certainly allowed the freedom that makes Deptford town hall so successful. None the less the more serious classicism was often successful on a smaller, more intimate scale. One such building is a sensitive reworking of seventeenth-century classicism by T. L. Moore for the small town of Helmsley in north Yorkshire. It fills half of one side of the market square, yet it is not at all a grand building. Its gentle elegance and intimate scale are entirely appropriate. C. E. Ponting's design for the little town hall at Marlborough is another example that consciously resurrects the traditional eighteenth-century type. These simpler buildings, were, however, rarer, and until well into the first decade of the

73 Stockport town hall, detail of entrance front, Sir Alfred Brumwell Thomas, 1904–8; carving by Gilbert Seale

twentieth century the wildest baroque flourished. Thereafter there was a gradual growth in solemnity and restraint which arrived on the municipal scene in the shape of Ashley & Newman's ponderous extension to the Birmingham council house designed in 1907. This was the provincial counterpart of the London county hall, and like that building is a good deal less exciting than one might have hoped. The LCC competition produced a number of fine designs and Ralph Knott's winning version was far from unsuccessful. Its most exciting feature was the freestanding circular hall set in the recessed centre of the landward façade. This extravagance was early ruled out and the building reversed leaving the empty recess to face the river. Later the site was curtailed and the final building has often been criticised for weaknesses that result more from the diminution of the commission than from any failure by the architect. The economic situation in the country as a whole could no longer support baroque dreams such as Lanchester, Stewart & Rickards had submitted for the competition, and it was fortunate that Ralph Knott's design could be so extensively hacked about and still retain its unity. At Birmingham there was no cutting down on the scale of

London for the choice had been for a simpler rectangular design that filled the whole block with offices, art gallery and museum. The result is large and grandiose, but altogether too heavy and lacking in any dynamic formal arrangement. It was one of the first municipal buildings in which the ethics of combining steel frame construction with classical motifs, particularly in the arched bridge, really appeared to trouble the profession. But even without such crises of conscience this sort of megalomaniac building could not really be repeated, and after about 1906 the excitement was gone from Edwardian baroque. There was a swing back to simplicity in designs such as that for Dartmouth town hall by the young Vincent Harris that was so highly praised at the Royal Academy of 1906. This trend led ultimately to the simplified classicism that we see in such late buildings as Marylebone town hall (1912–18). These are the forerunners of the stripped classicism of the 1920s and 1930s, and the truly Edwardian development does not go beyond such buildings as Lancaster town hall.

Lancaster's town hall (Figs 39, 94) is a good example of the last of a kind. If not positively the last in date it was, oddly enough, the last work of its architect, E. W. Mountford who can almost be considered as typically late Victorian. His building for Lancaster is a heavy but restrained piece of baroque with a strong debt to Hawksmoor. The main feature of the front is a hexastyle portico with a sculptured pediment, and there is a central tower set somewhat back. There is a free use of linear rustication and blocking on the window frames, while each side façade has a pedimented feature supported on attached columns. The whole building is held together by a heavy cornice and entablature. The actual shape of the building lacks movement and is heavier than the best of Edwardian baroque. Indeed the effect is more of solemn majesty, an effect that is heightened by the size of the building in relation to the surrounding buildings. The grand manner of the interior is equally imposing and formal as we shall see later. The building epitomises the final stage in the development of town hall styles before the Beaux Arts and the *entente cordiale* diverted the stylistic stream and municipal extravagance became less fashionable. In fact Lancaster town hall is hardly an example of municipal extravagance for it was a gift to the town. After about 1905 corporate architecture was centred on more serious matters. Most towns were already provided with an entertainment hall that could be modified if necessary, while the provision of separate accommodation for the many other municipal enterprises such as fire brigades, police stations, school boards, technical schools, baths, libraries, etc., not to mention housing, occupied most of the municipal building energy. There was altogether less need for town halls of the old type and civic display became distinctly less fashionable.

9

Display: townscape and towers

One important element in the erection of a town hall as a display building was the choice of materials for the exterior. It went without saying that the best was required, but this generally meant expense and often caused problems. We have seen how in the Birmingham town hall Anglesey marble was used throughout, and was chosen as a material before the stone was presented to the town. At Leeds the building is mostly of local Yorkshire stone, but the problems of finding enough large blocks of sufficient quality[1] led to considerable worries as to whether the colour would match. In the end at least twenty-one different quarries were used and the stone for the columns came from as far away as Darley Dale. Stone was by far the most popular material for these buildings since it was obviously grander than brick though considerably more expensive. Thus though the assize courts in Manchester were only of brick and stone, there was never any question but that the town hall would be all of stone. That was specified in the competition instructions. At Middlesbrough the winning design offered an alternative of brick and stone or all stone, but in spite of some pressure for economy there is no record of any battle over the decision to build in stone. At Chester the cost led the corporation to ask for tenders of three kinds: for construction in stone, in stone but without the tower and in brick and stone. Though there was little difference between the cost of stone without the tower and brick and stone with, the choice was for stone even if the tower had to be abandoned. The quality of the stone was important too. It was fortunate that the many towns of the northern industrial belt had ready access to the excellent freestones of the Pennines which could build solid and take elaborate carving. Bradford, for example, was entirely faced with local Cliffe Wood stone. And such use of local stone could be a matter of pride as well as economy, and it is no surprise to find town halls of local Gwespyr and Penmaenmawr stone at Llandudno or Llanelli, though Yorkshire stone and Bath stone were imported to both these places for ornamental work. Rhyl has a town hall of Denbigh stone and Penmaenmawr setts with Wrexham stone dressings and Merthyr Tydfil town hall was built in local Pennant stone. In Cornwall, another area of plentiful stone, Launceston, St Austell and Truro all built town halls of local granite. Plymouth guildhall was of Cornish granite with walls of banded dark, light and reddish limestone with the addition of Portland and Mansfield stone for carved ornaments. At Glasgow, where there was a choice of good stone to hand, the pressure for quality even led to complaints that it was to be built of freestone rather than granite.

Of course there were areas where stone was not readily available. However, at Banbury, where the town is largely brick built though within reach of Costwold stone, the town hall is of dressed ashlar masonry. Even Ipswich, in the heart of the Suffolk brick country had a handsome plinth of red Mansfield stone and was stone faced. Brick town halls of the mid-century are not unknown. Kidderminster, Saxmundham, Louth, Grantham and Hartlepool (Fig. 74) are all examples, but they were generally in lesser towns and mostly have stone dressings. Patterns of coloured brick were relatively rare though yellow stock brick with red and blue bricks were used in some of the smallest buildings such as Hadleigh. E. B. Lamb's stripey creation at Eye is a notable exception, but there the diapers are filled with flint cobbles, a new use for an essentially local material. The better freestone was often moved long distances. Bath and Mansfield stones were the most popular, but Ancaster, Pennant and even Caen stone were used for details in many parts of the country.[2] There was also a strong demand for the harder stones for polished columns and stairs. Pink Aberdeen and grey Peterhead granite were the commonest in town halls, as in other buildings, but red Devonshire marble was also popular. At Saltburn on the north Yorkshire coast it was proudly boasted that the Devonshire marble pillars for the tower, supplied by Bluckler of Dawlish, were the largest ever quarried in Devon. For the most part, however, the very grime of the towns meant that it was unwise to indulge in polychrome structural stonework such as Ruskin preached, and buildings like Godwin's Northampton town hall are relatively rare. Banded stonework was used on a few buildings, and special occasions might require special treatment, as in the choice of knapped flint and stone dressings for King's Lynn town hall, an 1894 addition to a fifteenth-century guild building. Kentish ragstone with flint for the upper storey was used by Burges in a similar though more elaborate building incorporating the thirteenth-century Maison Dieu at Dover. Winsford in 1871 even built a half-timbered town hall to cope with the subsidence from salt mining.

Leicester was the first major town hall to break this predominance of stone. However, although the Queen Anne style was essentially a style of red brick and tiles,

74 Hartlepool town hall and market, C. J. Adams, 1865–6

the next Queen Anne town hall, at Wakefield, was faced in stone; and other such essential features of the style as tile hanging and exterior plasterwork were seldom taken up. After Leicester, though, brick was established as an acceptably grand material even in other styles. It was shortly followed by others such as Waterhouse's Gothic town hall of red brick with Ruabon terracotta at Hove in 1880–1. The 1880s and 1890s saw the same vast expansion in terracotta for town halls as in any other buildings. The range of inexpensive ornament it allowed made this material particularly attractive to the smaller towns such as Widnes or West Hartlepool. However its very cheapness also meant that it was less appealing to those towns who wanted to make a splash. Their needs were better met by the uniform of red brick and Portland stone that was gaining ground at precisely this time, especially in London and the south-east. This was frequently combined with a roof of green Westmorland slates and was used for such buildings as Rotherhithe (1895–7) or Eastbourne (1884–6) town halls. Finally the resurgence of the grand manner in the 1890s saw the increasing popularity of whole façades of Portland stone as at Stockport or Bethnal Green.

75 Darlington market and public offices, tower, Alfred Waterhouse, 1863–4

There was equal scope as we shall see, for the employment of a variety of rich materials in the interior, but the choice of materials for the façade was clearly crucial. The very fact that the buildings were designed to display themselves means that we must consider them as being at least partly window dressing. The façade was the key element in this and was often designed with the clear aim of making a telling contribution to the street scene. In this sense we should consider town halls not only as separate buildings but as features of the townscape. For this reason I have so far ignored the development of town hall towers since that was chiefly directed to this end. Indeed the advertising element was not only common to most town halls, it was also quite expressly a part of their function; and this explains the determination to build great and costly towers which were by and large without functional justification. The provision of a public clock was certainly more important in days when the mass of the populace did not normally possess watches, and when there was no radio to provide a time signal for those who did. But this can hardly explain the enormous and elaborate structures to support the clock, nor would it excuse the provision of expensive carillon machines such as those at Manchester or Bradford. At Leeds, indeed, the clock proved something of an embarrassment for Brodrick was unwilling to make so large an opening in his splendid tower. At Middlesbrough, where the tides to some extent governed the life of the town, there was already a clock tower in the docks by the time one was provided for the old town hall, and a further one was required for the new town hall, while the merchants, who might possibly have a real need for a

76 Manchester town hall, tower, Alfred Waterhouse, 1867–77

clock to fix their meetings by, failed to build the clock tower that was designed for their exchange.

A more excusable function might be the provision of ventilation shafts, but in practice these were rarely housed in the tower. Leeds has its four separate little towers, and Manchester also has two tall flues rising at the far end of the hall. The little town hall at Banbury is a relative rarity in using its tower to the full for stairs and the ventilating shaft. For the most part towers were frankly for show and no effort was made to justify them on any grounds of practicality. They might provide a handsome ante-room, as at Bolton, Bradford and Manchester[3] but they were virtually useless when it came to office space. A few were given over to storage of records and strongrooms (Leeds and Stourbridge are examples), but that was all. Yet there is no denying that town hall towers are important. At an early stage it was apparent that few town halls would tell by their bulk alone. The bureaucratic explosion of the 1860s and 1870s to some extent rectified this, but the great shops and banking houses were soon competing again, and the later towers, such as Sheffield and Cardiff, are often even taller in proportion to their buildings.

The need for a tower had some effect on the development of the styles too. A traditional classical design really required a central tower. The prototype, and still one of the very best, was Leeds (Fig. 21); and the effectiveness of this symbol is echoed in many subsequent copies. Central towers were also used on a number of major Gothic town halls such as Manchester (Fig. 76) and Bradford (Fig. 78). The precedents for central Gothic towers were, of course, the medieval town halls of the Low Countries; but the asymmetrically placed towers on buildings such as Plymouth guildhall (Fig. 34) probably came nearer to the romantic spirit that underlay the best Gothic designs. However the importance, elaboration and cost of these major towers made abundantly clear the aesthetic necessity of a strong vertical to offset the weight of buildings which stretched over increasingly long frontages. Bradford in particular, with a single frontage of 275 ft, relies very heavily on its tower for effect. Generally speaking, the central tower that was best suited to a classical design was less effective when seen along a street and really required an open square as at Leeds or Glasgow (Fig. 57) to show it off properly. In the case of Bradford the architects showed some skill in the placing of their tower. The best view of the town hall was not the main façade, now open to a carefully cleared space from which it was never meant to be seen. The composition is ideally effective from the Leeds Road where the line of offices curls round and the exciting top of the tower is seen in perspective with rather less of its plain stalk showing. Occasionally a grand classical façade with a tower could be achieved within the existing street plan if, as at Newcastle, the façade and tower formed the tip of a wedge and were seen down the whole approach road. Such buildings, though, lacked the dignity of a broad frontage, and the best of the classical town halls do front on to an open square. Leeds and Glasgow have already been sited, but the list would include Bolton, Portsmouth, Lancaster and Birkenhead, and in that their design required the open space that too can be considered as part of their contribution to townscape. The square was seldom there ready for the town hall, and, even when it was, the new building was usually designed to form an integral composition with the square. At Leeds the square was an entirely new creation, and the approach to the town hall, before the widening of the Headrow, must have been particularly exciting for the cliff of honey gold masonry formed the entire northern wall of the square.[4] And the value of such open spaces in city centres, great enough now, will have been particularly great at a time when few of the major urban concentrations had any public parks. Leeds, for example, with a population of 170,000 had only one park, the Woodhouse Moor, in the early 1850s. At Middlesbrough the Victoria Square gardens, laid out in front of the town hall in about 1890 to complete the scheme, are still the only open space in the centre of the town.

In a few cases such open space was ready to hand, and the corporations were able to benefit from the way in which their town's expansion was engulfing great mansions and to convert already existing palaces into fine town halls that give a different but very real dignity to their town centre. Warrington is undoubtedly the most splendid example with a grand mansion of 1750 by James Gibbs almost in the centre of the town. It was further embellished by the addition of a set of exceptionally fine cast iron gates by the Coalbrookdale Company; but, as these were a gift to the town, here was indeed a town hall on the cheap. Scarborough was another town to benefit in this way, purchasing and converting St Nicholas House and its park in 1894 as a replacement for its earlier smaller town hall. Runcorn, Cheadle, and Bingley are three further examples, while at Castleford, as late as 1914, the new corporation established itself in the only substantial villa in the town centre—a large but undistinguished brick mansion of 1873 (now demolished). Cockermouth was a small town with either less choice or more ingenuity, for their town hall is a converted Methodist chapel of 1841. However this desire to occupy buildings that were significant in the townscape, when simple purpose-built offices could certainly have been had, is worth noting in itself, and in cases such as Warrington it is clear that economy was not the sole motive.

None the less most towns were less lucky or less able to spare the space that would provide a setting such as Leeds created or Warrington acquired, and the majority of town halls needed to be features of streetscape rather than great static compositions. Godwin's Gothic town halls again showed the need for a tower, and all his early designs with their narrow fronts topped by a tower add up to an arresting vertical element in the long perspective of a street. At Congleton (Fig. 77) there is the

77 Congleton town hall, E. W. Godwin, 1864–6

added bonus of a side street which debouches almost opposite the town hall so that a full view of the tower dominates the second vista. This, however, was a chance benefit and the need was really for flexibility in the placing of the tower. Barry showed the way with his corner tower at Halifax that closes the vista down Crossley Street; and many others, such as Preston, followed. Rochdale (Fig. 36) was a good example of the tall tower as the final vertical in a straggling horizontal composition. Crossland's tower was 240 ft high (higher even than Manchester) and was a splendid Gothic caprice. A tower of seven stages with stubby pinnacles supported a slender octagon with gilded trumpeting angels atop its ogee arches. Above them a crocketed lead covered spire rose to a pedestal on which balanced a figure of St George slaying the dragon that was also fully gilded. This could be clearly seen from out of the valley, and must have been a landmark for miles. Waterhouse's replacement is a good deal less frivolous besides being a good 50 ft shorter.

The logical succession of orders controlled the extent of most classical towers, and the size of their stages was controlled by the relation of the size of their order to the columns of the main building (Figs 20, 21). Only the cap could develop into an extravaganza, and there are few outlines as satisfying as the concave dome and cupola of Leeds town hall. However, without such a massive base with its tiers of panelling supporting six huge columns there was a real difficulty in achieving the desired opulence and the required height. Lancaster town hall tower (Fig. 94), though a satisfying design, drops far too quickly below the roof-line as the ground falls away. A traditional alternative was the dome, and Liverpool town hall, its dome capped by a gilded Britannia, was an excellent prototype. Yet, oddly, there are very few domed town halls, and even the domed lights that frequently cover the council chambers are often concealed. Burnley is one of few town halls to sport a dome, but the effect is not very happy and the little dome needs to be propped up on a short tower to tell at all. Birmingham council house (Fig. 2) is the only nineteenth-century town hall with a dome as its main feature, and even there it is supported by the later tower of the art gallery. Without that tower the effect would be weak for the dome is small but set up on a high drum and capped by too tall a cupola. As a ceiling for the grand stair the inner dome is exciting but from outside it lacks the spreading grandeur of the great baroque domes. Belfast city hall in elaborating the dome of St Paul's cathedral could not go far wrong, though again the dome lacks width when seen above the fifteen bay façade. It badly needs the support of the little cupolas, also from St Paul's, that stand like outposts on the corners of the building. A much more successful and individual dome is that over the council chamber at Cardiff city hall (Fig. 99), which spreads its full width without a drum and yet gains height from its dragon finial. However that dome is only a secondary feature in a composition that reaches its climax in the

78 Bradford town hall, Lockwood & Mawson, 1869–73

elaborately crowned tower. Secondary domes or round-capped turrets occur in several places sometimes even two or three at a time and without towers. Such domes occur as supporting features in Wyatt's design for Manchester town hall, while the ten little ogee domes on the corners of Portsmouth town hall were a delightful addition to the Leeds–Bolton theme.

Towers much more than domes were the effective urban symbol, and for these the Gothic undeniably allowed greater freedom. There was virtually no limit to the number of stages in a tower, and almost any skyline of battlements, pinnacles and gargoyles would be effective. For added effect the composition could always end in a spire as do all of Waterhouse's tower designs. Some form of spire or tall cap was almost universal in fact, and Barrow is a rarity in ending with a flat roofed octagon.

79 Wakefield town hall, tower, T. E. Collcutt, 1877–80

North of the border there was even the occasional crown spire, but there was always scope for variety. Bradford town hall tower is a fine example (Fig. 78). It was scornfully likened to an exploding rocket but the effect of the open bell stage and swallow tail battlements is entirely delightful. Equally effective and individual is the tower of Wakefield town hall (Fig. 79) with its simple outline and medieval timber cap.[5] In fact towards the end of the century attention was increasingly concentrated on the upper stages. The Rochdale replacement of 1883, for a start, is free of decoration for the first 72 ft. However it was the classical designs that benefited most from this trend for they could now perch an elaborate cap on a stalk as tall as funds

80 Woolwich town hall, tower, Sir Alfred Brumwell Thomas, 1903–6

allowed. Salomons' design for Manchester town hall (Fig. 26) was a particularly successful early example,[6] but this treatment became more common with the advent of the baroque revival. A few architects avoided this general trend either doing without towers or producing versions such as Brumwell Thomas' cupola crown for Stockport town hall. Even that, though, was altered and propped up on columns so that the original design now forms the upper two stages of an open tower. The typical late towers are those like Sheffield, Colchester or Cardiff or those in the designs for Plumstead municipal buildings (Fig. 80) or Hull city hall. At Sheffield (Fig. 52) a very elaborate effect was achieved by an arcaded stage beneath four gables with similar arched openings, while an octagonal cupola, again with arched openings, is perched astride the roof. The addition of a series of Jacobean pinnacles completes the effect of richness, and there is no room for the clock which is set a good deal further down. For Plumstead (later built at Woolwich) more than one competitor designed the typical Edwardian baroque version with a simple tower topped by an elaborate clock stage with openings capped by heavy segmental pediments. Belcher's recipe for Colchester is similar, but the show stage, in stone on top of a plain brick tower, is of two layers and there is added sculpture. H. T. Hare's design for Colchester is more idionsyncratic, but the published drawing clearly stresses the importance of the tower by the exaggerated perspective. Cardiff too (Fig. 99) has a two-stage cap with sculpture both around its base and on the summit.

Visually the towers are often the most exciting part of these buildings, and it is significant that when the tower at Birkenhead was reconstructed in 1903 it was heightened by 15 ft. Some such striking feature became increasingly essential as the buildings grew in bulk and as the office blocks around them swelled also. There are few really dull towers, probably because the vertical accent is so vital. Even the Middlesbrough tower, plainly a derivatve of Manchester but set too far back behind the façade, adds an important emphasis to the street. Some towers were never built; but in general these buildings with their towers provide landmarks that are visible even from the depths of the narrow streets, and which originally stood out as distinctive among the chimneys. Town hall towers provided a necessary point of reference for any one looking at a town, and their individuality helped to stamp everyone's town hall as being particularly his own. The buildings were, or should have been, open to the grandest and the least, especially if they contained a large hall. Social barriers did in effect mean that only certain classes actually penetrated the holy of holies, but there was absolutely no bar to seeing the outside or looking at the tower. Thus these outside symbols, aggressive but always individual, must have entered into the consciousness of every citizen as part of the character of their town. Smaller towns had to make do with humbler symbols, and there is a large second rank of cupolas and turrets performing the same function in places such as East Retford or Thornaby-on-Tees. Sometimes, as at Darlington, Congleton (Fig. 77) or Barrow-in-Furness, we can see the symbols as they were meant to be seen, not crowded in by a forest of glass and concrete towers. It is easy to see what an important contribution they made to the streetscape.

This is not only a matter of their direct physical impact. The development of a whole area was often involved in or followed immediately on the building of the town hall. Even though the area might not itself be large it could nevertheless be significant. At Leeds the town hall and square, built on the site of a single house and garden, effectively altered the balance of the whole town and led to a great development northwards and westwards from City Square, the former centre. Rochdale town hall transformed a derelict and marshy river bank into a huge romantic Gothic plaza, and a whole block of slum property was cleared in the process. What became of the dispossessed is not clear, and they will certainly have suffered in such cases. Their numbers were relatively small, and there was no compulsion to rehouse them. If the problem had been raised it would probably have been argued that the prosperity eventually resulting to the whole town would improve the lot even of the dispossessed. Nevertheless this is a flaw in the grandiose plans of civic builders which today's conscience cannot excuse. Only by the end of the nineteenth century were the city centres sufficiently clear of population for the problem to disappear. Earlier we find concealed little unpleasantnesses such as the removal of eighteen houses in two courts (not to mention six street front shops and houses, a tube manufactory, stables, piggery and slaughter yard) simply to build the relatively small bulk of Birmingham town hall.

One cannot ignore this uncomfortable feature of the general improvement. The problem appears scarcely to have been recognised by the builders for there are very few references indeed to the needs of the dispossessed. What was important to the town hall builders was the provision of a fine new building as a symbol of an advancing town. It is more significant that almost all town halls were either part of or involved a larger new development. That these buildings did nothing to solve the problem of the slums and may even have contributed indirectly to their formation is really beside the point. Even when the slum problem was recognised no ready solution was seen, and scarcely any of the corporations were to any great extent involved in housing before the Great War. The town hall builders were concentrating on the business of showing a stability that was not a sham, and their buildings were not intended to conceal the multifarious problems of urbanisation. Thus when once the architects were presented with a site they seldom felt any compulsion to respect what was there before, but set about producing buildings which for all their humdrum and derivative character often pointed development in a particular direction, and not infrequently stamped at least the local development with their own character, as at Halifax or Manchester.

This is a less tangible element than the direct impact of individual buildings, but it is none the less important and very much a feature in the development of the collective urban consciousness. The relative success or failure of these buildings was due to the length of the corporation's purse and to the accidents of creativity in their architect. It is certain, though, that the resulting buildings are, for good or bad, often the strongest single element in the development of a visual impression of a city. We cannot be sure how far this affects the citizens though it undoubtedly does. And as it is the outside of these buildings that is most seen so it is their façades and especially their towers that do most to advertise their town. They are in short a factor in the development of the community consciousness, and help to form the character of the town. The fierce local pride that one still encounters is often focused on and by these buildings, and it is fair to assume that their influence was more powerful when they were new. Without their town halls towns would seem as nebulous and soulless as villages without a pub or parish church, and the buildings should be valued accordingly.

10

Decoration: painting and sculpture

The absorption of a distant symbol passed in the street is not the full tale of the effect of town halls. It was an important part of their function, which does not always survive today, that they were open to all ranks of society, or rather polite society. It was also an avowed aim of their builders that they should be widely used and would thereby help to bring the different ranks of society together. Their builders also expressed the pious hope that the buildings would serve to raise the taste of the populace. Two features of the full town hall were especially geared to these ends, the great hall and the adornment of the building with works of art. These two can conveniently be studied together for their provision was really in addition to the strictly functional requirements of office space and courtrooms. Yet such luxury was never regarded as foreign to town hall building. The availability of a public hall within a town hall, and the resulting public access, does a great deal to modify the character of these buildings as well as affecting their form. Sculptural and other decoration need not be connected to public access, but the presence of a grand hall was usually the excuse for such display, and even where there was no public hall, as at Bradford, the decorative display was still aimed at public view. In fact these luxuries were the chief vehicle for displaying civic pride without which these buildings would be meaningless. Consequently a great deal of store was set by the extent and quality of the decorative detail. At worst the measurement of ornament by the yard could show the wealth of a town; at best the use of sculpture, painting, mosaic and stained glass could proclaim the specific history of the town and show its aspirations. However the mere multiplication of ornament did not ensure success. In the first place mere repetition would inevitably look mechanical, and with the limited language of classical motifs could lead to imitation and invidious comparisons. One has only to compare the grand organ case in Huddersfield town hall with the still more splendid and vigorous original designed by Brodrick for Leeds to appreciate the limitations of this sort of copying.

It might be thought that the classical styles were somewhat limiting even in the use of sculpture. At any rate the pediment remained an extraordinarily difficult space to fill throughout the period, as F. W. Pomeroy's rather stilted composition[1] at Lancaster (Fig. 94) shows. On the other hand a Gothic style would allow the placing of niches and carved gargoyles and figured finials in a much freer way, and should therefore have been more easily adapted to the needs of individual corporations. Once the spare Neoclassicism of the early part of the century was past, the possible extent, cost and placing of ornament and sculpture might have become a factor in swaying corporations towards a Gothic style. However this does not appear to have been the case and we need to re-examine the basic differences between the two approaches to sculptural ornament.

The influence of Ruskin was undoubtedly considerable in fostering the belief, apparent from the mid-century on, that the only good ornament was that copied from natural form. Such buildings as Northampton town hall display his doctrines almost programmatically. His opposition to classical motifs—he selected the Greek fret as particularly ugly—was the natural concomitant of his fervour for the Gothic, but led him to a decidedly uneasy position when it came to the use of figure sculpture on buildings. This was admittedly the supreme achievement of Greek art, and in the first edition of *The Seven Lamps of Architecture* he was clearly more interested in gargoyle figures. He felt that perfect sculpture in architecture could be dangerous and was 'not to be regarded at first, nor to be obtained at the cost of purpose'; in short it was an 'architectural coxcombry'. His position was that the use of sculptural decoration was primarily to accent form and to provide contrast of tone and texture. By 1880, however, even Ruskin had quite changed his mind, and in a note to the new edition claimed 'sculpture should precede and govern all else. The pediment of Aegina determines the right—and ends controversy'.[2] By then, however, his original preaching had been fully absorbed and sculpture and ornament were being used as mere accents on the buildings. At Manchester the majority of the carved ornament is totally mechanical, and most of the few figures, by Farmer & Brindley, are too small and too distant to tell in their own right. There is nothing about the carved ornament of Manchester town hall that really lives up to the underlying aspirations of Ruskin and the convinced Gothicists. At Bradford the same firm were responsible for the unusually complete gallery of figures of monarchs on another Gothic building, but again the mechanical placing deprives the collection of much of its liveliness and reduces it to the status of patches of texture. Used in this way there was no real distinction between classical and Gothic sculpture in the last quarter of the century at any rate. And it could be argued that the strict rules governing its placing on classical buildings generally made them more successful since less imagination was necessary.

The confusion did not entirely obliterate the distinction in approach between classical and Gothic sculpture, but after the 1860s it was increasingly blurred. Originally classical sculpture had been exclusively allegorical and full of general moral allusions. The carved tympanum of Leeds town hall (Fig. 83) is one of the best examples. Gothic sculpture on the other hand was more specific, and could be used to illustrate local legends rather than personify the town. The elaborate iconography of Rochdale (Fig. 92) sticks more or less to this recipe. However there are too many cases where buildings in Gothic or classical dress use sculpture as the opposing style should for the distinction to be clearly drawn. Even at Rochdale much of the iconography is allusive rather than descriptive; and in Manchester town hall there are figures of Truth and Justice, two prime allegorical figures, in the fireplace of the reception room. Of course the frequent inclusion (though not at Manchester) of law courts in town hall buildings could have meant that those particular figures had developed into essential attributes with no more allegorical value than the inevitable portrait of the Queen or St George and the dragon. However the allegorical use of sculpture on Gothic buildings was not confined to this, and at Middlesbrough there are four fine figures by H. T. Margetson representing Music, Literature, Painting and Commerce (Fig. 93). The whole conception of Norman Shaw's fireplace in the Gothic hall at Bradford (Fig. 90) is allegorical, and one figure is even described as Icarus.

There is a certain honesty about this confused approach to allegorical sculpture. The message, if it can be called such, of a town hall was in one sense very general and was connected with high aspirations of moral and aesthetic improvement. The Gothic contribution of particularised sculpture was important in distinguishing one town from another, and it is no surprise to find Drake atop the tower of Plymouth or cherry trees in the capitals of Northampton. The whole great scheme of paintings for Manchester was designed to display the history of the town; though it must be admitted that several of the paintings are at best of only general relevance to the city. Mostly the great classical buildings stuck to purely allegorical sculpture and abstract ornament, but the spread of eclecticism did allow the rules to be bent and Sheffield, for instance, has two fine friezes, one illustrating the various local trades, and the other the local legend of the Dragon of Wantley. The Edwardian baroque staircase in Bradford town hall has a similar illustrative panel, and there are other instances that show how the baroque revival of classicism retained elements of this essentially Gothic approach. Deptford, for instance, has a row of individual naval heroes to give point to the identity of this Thames-side town. At Colchester, the supreme example

81 Colchester town hall, council chamber, John Belcher, 1898–1902 (*Builder*, vol. LXXVII, 1899)

82 Leeds town hall, carved keystone to basement floor, Cuthbert Brodrick, 1853–8

of an Edwardian baroque town hall, the tower is capped by a figure of St Helena, the patron saint of the town, and the Corinthian capitals of the façade are enriched with ears of wheat, roses and oyster shells in marked contrast to the allegorical calendar on the ceiling of the council chamber (Fig. 81). There are many further examples that illustrate this inconsistent approach to sculptural and other decoration. Artists and architects were required to make both specific and general references in the same decorative scheme, and so the blurring of the two approaches was probably as inevitable as it was welcome. There was some historical development in the approach to ornament, but this seems most closely linked to the growth of towns and the amount of wealth available for these buildings. The difference in wealth between the towns was also the principal factor governing the amount of ornamental display throughout the period.

To begin with there was relatively little in the way of grand display, and town halls such as Salford (Fig. 3) and Oldham are virtually free of carved decoration and their assembly rooms have no lavish plaster ornamentation. The more lavish interior decor of Birmingham town hall belongs to the late 1840s.[3] Thereafter Liverpool and Leeds (Figs 82, 83) showed the way with the full gamut of sculpture, tiling, plaster and paint. It remained for the Gothicists to add stained glass and even freer use of carving. The great decades of sumptuous decoration were the 1860s and 1870s, in buildings such as Manchester, Rochdale, Preston and Bolton. In the 1880s the tide

83 Leeds town hall, carved tympanum over main entrance, Cuthbert Brodrick, 1853–8, sculpture by John Thomas, 1858

began to ebb somewhat. There were still grand schemes—the Liverpool sculpture competition (Fig. 88) dates from 1882 for instance, though it relates to a mid-century building—but the continuing pressures of urban living were beginning to work against the idea of communal display. External sculpture continued to be common: it is often extensive and some of it is fine. Generally though, there was a decrease in the elaboration of the public halls, and decoration was more and more confined to elaborate plasterwork and coats of arms. One tradition, however, did not die, and that was the representation of some local history or legend in the ornamental programme. This tendency in fact increased and superseded the many impersonal figures of Justice and Prosperity. Heraldry was a continuing obsession, and of course the lion symbol of authority was ubiquitous (Figs 22, 84).

It will not be possible to catalogue all of even the major examples, and the variety of extent and development really precludes any attempt at a chronological survey. I

84 Manchester town hall, hall ceiling, Alfred Waterhouse, 1867–77

shall therefore deal with these features building by building taking the whole decorative scheme of hall and sculpture together as far as possible. I shall confine myself in general to artworks that are an integral part of the original scheme, ignoring the many fine examples of sculpture and painting commissioned to fit into completed buildings. One has really to begin with Manchester where Ford Madox Brown's great series of paintings are often regarded as the high peak of municipal art patronage. Indeed the interior of Manchester town hall is particularly rich in this way, though even so the intended scheme was by no means completed. From the moment of entering the building the effect is total and leads to a splendid climax in the great hall. The entrance steps are of Irish granite which gives way to a floor of marble and porphyry patterned in opus Alexandrinum. The panels of the ribbed vault of the entry are filled with a mosaic of foliate patterns mostly in red and gold, while the ribs themselves are alternately plain or carved with a simple double ball motif which echoes the berries in the panels. All this is typical of Waterhouse and the quality is either heavy or sturdy as you prefer. After the entry comes the waiting hall, and exciting colonnaded space sometimes known as the sculpture hall which marks its intention.[4] One of its earliest inhabitants was a statue of John Bright by Theed, and it was quickly peopled with a fine collection of portrait busts. The main passage has a vaulted roof and tiled walls with a shallow patera motif at intervals. Symbolism begins with the pattern of cotton flowers in the floor mosaic, but all this is hardly seen for attention is drawn straight to the grand stairs which are the only light source for the corridor. Each half of the double stair is lit by three tall windows filling two sides of their octagonal apsidal space. Above, the panels of the vault are rich with gold stars on a blue ground, while a traceried arcade marks off the landing area (Fig. 49). The three secondary spiral stairs are enriched with treads and paired columns of English, Irish and Scottish polished granite.

So far the decoration has mostly been no more than vaguely Gothic, but the landing begins in earnest the symbolism of Manchester. The floor is of mosaic with a pattern of alternating rows of bees to symbolise industry, while the cotton flowers appear again in the passage floors. Overhead the roof light is filled with drawings of plants connected with the cotton industry and panels to be filled with the names of mayors of Manchester. From the landing the public might pass into the great hall while a more select crowd would also be invited into the banqueting suite. The decoration of the latter is something of a disappointment. There is solid panelling, diapered walls and richly moulded ceilings some with coats of arms but the sculpture and painting are not as extensive as was hoped and the windows throughout the building have only the simplest patterned glass. The original furniture was substantial and the hangings were fine;[5] however, the overall effect is rather less successful than the grand stair. The main anteroom is a particularly cramped space beneath the tower whose arches even deprive the little area of light from the windows of the projecting bay. Perhaps the original decoration in gold and black counteracted this effect. Still it must be admitted that decoration of this sort was not a particularly strong point in Waterhouse, and he had wisely intended to rely on experts. He managed to get extra money for stone fireplaces which are handsome features. The finest is that in the reception room which is of alabaster with figures of Truth and Justice by Farmer & Brindley. Behind the arcade of the overmantel hangs a brocade with more bees. In the council chamber (Fig. 48) the walls were topped with a painted frieze to Waterhouse's design with the arms of various other Lancashire towns set against a pattern of the cotton plant, but the drawing is mechanical and does not compare with the equivalent work at Rochdale. Waterhouse clearly wanted to decorate the four rooms of the banqueting suite much as he did the great hall, and he intended to have panels with paintings round the walls. He was still pressing for this in 1895 when he wrote urging the council to contact the painters they had approached seventeen years before. These were Calderon, Yeames, Richmond and Walter Crane who wanted to decorate the ante-room with subjects connected with India. Waterhouse suggested landscape for one room to include the building of the Thirlmere reservoirs (the greatest work of Manchester corporation), the ship canal and the old halls of Lancashire. Another committee member suggested four literary themes, Shakespeare, Milton, Spenser and Chaucer for the four rooms. Nothing

85 Manchester town hall, great hall, Alfred Waterhouse, 1867–77

86 Manchester town hall, great hall, premiated design from second stage competition, J. O. Scott, 1868 (*Building News*, vol. XVI, 1869)

came of these schemes, and indeed it was 1892 before Ford Madox Brown completed the last of his twelve panels for the great hall.

The hall is the grandest, though not the most exciting, space in the building (Figs 84, 85). It is an effective climax to the processional route up the stairs, but it is a less entrancing space than the arcaded landing. It is a vast space, 100 ft by 50 and over 60 ft high, and Waterhouse managed to avoid the intrusive galleries that were so often needed.[6] The elaborately painted ceiling is the first feature to take the eye, but its richness is amply balanced by the series of large painted panels above the dado. The rest of the hall is rather bare. The original gold and black wrought iron chandeliers survive, but are somewhat lost in the vast space. The large organ case is not as lavishly carved as many others,[7] though the vault of the organ compartment is powdered with stars. Waterhouse found the problem of large statuary in such a space difficult but intended to have three life-size figures, Villiers, Cromwell and Queen Victoria in niches beside the organ and between the doors. In the event only a bust of the Queen arrived and Noble, the sculptor of the Cromwell figure, did not like the position so that statue was never put up. The statue of Villiers by Theed still perches alone in its cramped niche by the organ. The ceiling, however, and wall panels are ample treasure in themselves. The ceiling is of hammerbeam shape but filled in with flat panels on which are painted the arms of the various cities and countries 'with which Manchester is most intimately connected in trade'. For the benefit of the generality the panels are also clearly named, and the whole effect is of a rich profusion of red and blue amply set off by a good deal of gilding. Ford Madox Brown's paintings are much less strident[8] and their generally warm tone blends in admirably. The pictures are a series of large-scale figure compositions which were supposed to illustrate the history of Manchester; but there was a good deal of argument over what constituted Manchester's, as opposed to Lancashire's, history. The Romans, Christianity, the Danes and medieval weavers together with a Civil War scene give a sense of history while stressing the importance of trade and civil liberty. Humphrey Chetham stands for education and the care of the poor, while Crabtree, Dalton and Kay all illustrate the forward march of science. Not surprisingly the suggestion of a panel showing the Peterloo incident was turned down, but the lack of reference to transport is a surprise. The opening of the Bridgewater canal fills the gap, but is hardly the most apposite reference for the 1870s. Actually even that subject was an afterthought and was chosen instead of the opening of the Liverpool and Manchester railway to replace the Peterloo panel. Ford Madox Brown disliked it too, and it was the last panel to be finished.

This grand series of paintings is the only such municipal commission to be completed, and is as important as it is rare. Originally the commission was to have been shared between Ford Madox Brown and Frederick Shields, a close friend of Waterhouse, but he withdrew so that the whole series now has a unity of style as well of approach. The paintings are not often enough seen and tend to be undervalued; but their existence is a reminder of what might have been had the scheme been carried through for the other rooms as well. Unfortunately there is no tradition in English town halls, as for instance in France, that would insist on a whole scheme of artworks as an essential part of the building. Generally town hall architects did better to stick to sculptural ornament which might be seen as merely so much carved decoration to be bought by the yard from firms such as Farmer & Brindley, Thomas Earp and his successors or Harry Hems. All three of these did regular work on town halls, and it was Farmer & Brindley who got the contract for the carving on Manchester town hall. Not that that allowed them a lot of scope, for Waterhouse was even more sparing on the outside of Manchester town hall than usual, and sculpture forms no part of the main decorative scheme. What they did shows the usual solidity of their style which suits Waterhouse's building but is in marked contrast to the liveliness of contemporary work by Earp at the police courts or earlier at Rochdale. Here there were two roundels illustrating the old styles of spinning and weaving, thirty small coats of arms and a bare dozen statues on the whole building. These included the small St George set so high on the tower as to be invisible and the insignificant Agricola over the entrance. The rest were mostly monarchs, including Edward III who first brought Flemish weavers into the country, and are set in niches in groups on the rear façade and on the Albert Square—Princess Street corner. Their contribution to the whole scheme is minimal and compared to the paintings they are a disappointment.

A better standard is found at Halifax (Fig. 87). The sculpture there is by John Thomas of London and consists of four allegorical groups on pedestals at the base of the spire. Each group is flanked by two small lions and there are further figures like pinnacles at the corners of the spire. There is a blindfold head of Justice over the entry, but the richest part of the whole scheme is the army of putti sliding out of the spandrels on the more visible parts of the hall. There are in fact twenty-four of them and those on the front of the building flank keystones carved as large bearded heads. This is a splendidly organised scheme supported by further carved floral ornament at all stages of the building, not to mention the rich balustrades, elaborate cast iron cresting and plump scrolly lamp standards. The carving here is far from mechanical and each of the putti is carefully distinguished by pose or by the symbol in his hands (harps for the arts, scrolls for learning and the sword and scales for justice) so that there is a constant play of variety. It is a pity that the planning of the interior did not call for an equally elaborate scheme inside. The planning of the hall as part of the

87 Halifax town hall, Sir Charles and E. M. Barry, 1859–62; detail of façade with carving by John Thomas

circulation space made this rather more difficult, and the chief effect is the general sumptuousness of the plasterwork and the ornamental balustrades. The putti reappear less convincingly in the spandrels of the first floor arches and the original intention was to supply a complete set of statues on pedestals between the doors of the ground floor. Subsequent redecoration too has done a great deal to remove the effect of glowing splendour, and it is almost a surprise to find three good paintings, one by Daniel Maclise, filling the blind arcade of the landing.

One tends to expect town halls to display only rows of mayoral portraits, but though this is often the case they are the accretion of years and were seldom the intention of the designers. The professional press was constantly reporting the decoration of the Parisian *mairies* and the *hôtels de ville* by sculptors and painters of note such as Barrias, Boulanger, Bonnat, Delaunay and Puvis de Chavannes. Vienna was another much flaunted example with its three huge frescoes by Hans Makart and works by half a dozen other artists. The leaders of the provincial artistic élites in this country were often keen to emulate this, but were never able to achieve their aim. Birmingham and Liverpool provide interesting examples of the failure of this sort of scheme. The failure is, I think, less due to actual parsimony and the difficulty of costing artwork than to the fact that real works of art only repaid the sort of leisured study that was not likely to be afforded the façade of a town hall. There was felt to be a distinction between ornamenting a building, which was legitimate advertising, and adding to a building works of art, which were no part of business or practicality.

In the early 1890s Birmingham launched an imaginative scheme which might have bridged this gap by uniting the aims of education with the opportunity to indulge in aestheticism at little or no expense. It was proposed to provide paintings for the large panels under the windows of the town hall that would illustrate the history of Birmingham. There was an obvious echo of Manchester here, but instead of wasting money on an artist these panels would be painted by students of the Birmingham school of art. There would be some control over the tone range to ensure uniformity, and quality was to be guaranteed by the approval of both detailed sketches and the cartoon before work began. At least six panels were completed by students such as H. S. Meteyard, J. M. Baylis and Kate Bunce (whose uncle had proposed the scheme), but the idea was unaccountably abandoned and the panels have long since been painted out.

The saga of the sculpture for Liverpool's St George's hall is better known and amply illustrates the problems of foisting an extensive artistic commission on a corporation where there was no ready tradition of art appreciation. Elmes intended the great building to be fully decorated with external sculpture to match the rich interior. The splendour of the inside with its elaborate Minton tile floor, quite the largest and most lavish of any town hall, fully matched the expectations of the massive architecture. The actual decoration was largely the work of Cockerell and was on a truly Roman scale. The plaster caryatids of the little concert room are well known. There were also angel trumpeters on the organ and yet larger angels in the spandrels of the vault. The ceiling was richly coffered, coloured and gilded and the walls made splendid with red granite columns and green marble panels.[9] The outside was intended to match this in richness as well as in bulk, and Elmes planned a series of twenty-eight relief panels and twelve figures on pedestals between the columns of the north portico as well as bronze groups and of course the great pediment and four lions for the eastern end. Only the four lions and the pediment arrived by the time of the opening and now even that has been taken down and broken up by the city engineers. The great pediment was a typical piece of mid-nineteenth-century symbolism and more overt than Manchester. It was described as conveying its meaning with an obvious clarity as all public buildings should. There was to be no mistaking the message of the Arts bearing tribute to Britannia while Mercury led up Asia, Europe and America. Britannia sat holding the sword of power in her right hand while with her left she raised up Africa (who was 'represented in a posture of gratitude and humility' with her sons in her arms) the breaking of whose chains was the work of Britannia to whom she pointed. Only the contemporary description can convey the belief in the total goodness and gentle might of Britannia and through her of Liverpool also. This was a good recipe repeated, as we shall see, at Leeds and Bolton among others. The other decoration was presumably intended to continue the theme, but had to wait for a competition of 1882, and the designs then proved too artistic for the corporation. Thirty-nine sculptors competed, and T. Stirling Lee was placed first with a scheme of six panels showing the attributes and results of Justice (for the court function), six more with the causes and results of National Prosperity (a nice reminder of the source of funds for the building), eleven panels for Music and the Arts showing Orpheus, Tubal Cain and the nine Muses while the remaining four were to be made up with emblems of the arts. For the figures on pedestals between the columns he intended representations of the Scientific Discoveries of Our Time and four large groups facing north, south, east and west were to show the spread of civilisation and colonisation. The first six panels were to show the childhood, girlhood, womanhood, administration, result and final end of Justice; but when the second panel actually portrayed Justice as a naked lady the corporation, fearing that the obvious symbolism was drowning in the extremes of bohemianism, ordered the whole scheme stopped. The dedication of the building might be 'artibus, legibus, conciliis', but the first of these was not to be allowed a free rein. Three years later the corporation only grudgingly accepted Rathbone's generous offer to pay for the remaining panels and their installation himself. He was allowed to put them up for a five year trial. Twelve panels were set up and are still there, one with the ironic caption, *Liverpool, A Municipality Employs Labour and Encourages Art* (Fig. 88). Orpheus and the Muses never arrived, and the intended bronze groups were supplanted by a family of marine lamp bearers and a scattering of municipal dignitaries.

At Liverpool the building itself is so tremendous that the lack of will is not damaging, and the uncarved panels are hardly noticeable. In smaller towns such a failure could be disastrous, and fine art stood a better chance if it formed an integral

88 Liverpool St George's hall, *Liverpool, A Municipality Employs Labour and Encourages Art* from the second series of panels by T. S. Lee, Conrad Dressler and C. J. Allen, 1894

part of the surface decoration. In this sense Gothic, which required gargoyles and carved capitals, was a better bet, and Godwin's Northampton façade (Fig. 54) is a splendid example. 'The whole front, indeed, may be said to be animated'; his work 'manifests in every coign and capital a perfect wealth of thought, imagination and research.'[10] The most obvious feature is the set of eight life-size statues of monarchs set high up between the first floor windows, but the narrative carving spreads over the whole front and is as inseparable from the bands of foliate ornament as they are from the polychrome stonework. This total integration allowed Godwin to complete an

89 Northampton town hall, great hall, E. W. Godwin, 1861–4 (*Building News*, vol. X, 1863)

elaborate iconographic programme that ranges from the straight historical authoritarianism of the monarchs to whimsical morality and local history. There is the usual figure of Justice beside the door, joined this time by Mercy, but the chief interest is in the relief panels over the lower windows showing the local trades. Local interest is continued inside with cherry tree capitals recalling the local orchards, while other capitals show fables such as the cock and the jewel, the suicidal donkey and a monkey running away with a kitten to the great dismay of the cat. This is romantic Gothic of the best with something to please everybody. The same level of decoration was continued in the interior where the thoroughly medieval hall has a richly carved wooden roof supported on elaborately decorated iron ribs (Fig. 89). There are round stained glass windows by Heaton, Butler & Bayne and a seasoning of higher art was intended in paintings by Colin Gill showing Moses and the law and Alfred the originator of English law; but even this didactic element was to be softened by further paintings of scenes from Tennyson's *Idylls of the King*. There is much more sense of enjoyment here and less of the earnest admonition of the Liverpool scheme, but alas the original paintings, even if they were completed, do not survive.

The freedom of Gothic, however, was not always used in this way, and schemes could be as firmly authoritarian as at Liverpool. Bradford town hall, like Northampton, carries a series of life-size monarchs in niches. This time there are thirty-five of them with Cromwell included for good measure and democracy. The statues are the work of Farmer & Brindley and the craftsmanship is sound, but on the second floor they are set too high for any character to tell. They are reduced to the role of supplying a decorative rhythm and indeed form almost the whole of the decoration. The only other elements are simple foliate capitals and bands of small square panels with shields. Victoria, by the main entrance, has a backcloth of squared leaf ornaments that is frankly dull. It is not that the scheme is a bad one, but that it was not conceived as rising beyond mere decoration, and the boast was in the quantity of the statues rather than in their quality. Specifically local history, too, was ignored, and the local fable of the Cliffe Wood boar, a splendid medieval tale, had to wait for inclusion until the arrival of Norman Shaw's Edwardian baroque staircase in 1914. Even then it was squeezed into a miserably small panel and lacks the power of Shaw's hall fireplace where he retained a more medieval flavour (Fig. 90). Oddly the figures are a throwback to the typical classical mythology of commerce. The theme is Progress and the central figure is Prosperity, winged and holding a laurel wreath and sphere. She is flanked on one side by Music, Literature, Architecture (with a plan of the old council chamber), Sculpture and Painting and for some obscure reason a boy strapping on a belt. He is sometimes called Icarus, or perhaps he is Cupid or merely symbolic of youth. The other side of Prosperity is filled, predictably, with figures of the local

90 Bradford town hall extensions, 1903–9, fireplace in banqueting hall, R. Norman Shaw consultant, sculpture by Earp Hobbs & Millar

industries and Commerce with Mercury's staff. There is also one putto holding a fleece while another pours out a cornucopia. The iconography is less insistent than at Liverpool and the figures make an impressive crowd on the mantelshelf. They are the work of Earp, Hobbs & Millar, a continuation of the firm of Thomas Earp whose best work is seen at Rochdale.

Rochdale provides an opposite example to Bradford, for there is endless variety in the carving and the whole building demands to be seen as an artwork. There is little that is didactic about the carved stonework and the usual statue of Victoria and the figures of local worthies never arrived. Yet, quite apart from the tracery of the windows, the whole exterior is alive with interest and Thomas Earp made full use of his opportunity to carve heads and beasts on every drip moulding and parapet available, though the sides and rear were of course left virtually bare. His repertoire is symbolic rather than illustrative, but there is a fine menagerie of heraldic creatures and a whole population of medieval heads, interspersed with the occasional typically Victorian tonsure. The whole building has an elaborate and detailed iconography. The phoenix and salamander of the fire station have already been described and there is also an owl, since fires were most to be feared at night, and a dog, because dogs had been used in the early days of the fire brigade. The human heads on the drip mouldings are less exciting, but the rangy vigour of the animals is outstanding. There are plenty of lions (over the porte cochère and as bench ends in the borough court or over the doors of the council chamber) and a number of excellent doglike or dragonish beasts ranging from elegant brass greyhounds for fire dogs, through the splendid pairs fighting on the porte cochère, to the outright dragons among the gargoyles. The whole scheme also has a strong tone of the whimsical that would have appealed to William Burges, and the decoration of the interior ranges from carving to stained glass to

91 Rochdale town hall, W. H. Crossland, 1866–71; detail of Minton tile floor in entrance hall designed by Heaton, Butler & Bayne

heraldic tiles and wall painting and even includes a major picture. Animals reoccur but there is a wider range inside. On the walls of the borough court the dogs turn into hounds of justice crouched in a frieze of springy foliage, crowns, fleurs de lys and Tudor roses. The heraldic turn reaches its heights in the Minton tile floor (Fig. 91) of the exchange which consists of elaborate panels with royal arms, lions, several varieties of rose, thistles, shamrocks and the rest. It is a splendid conception echoed in the arms of the countries with which Rochdale traded (and of the other Lancashire towns, Yorkshire cities and ports of Britain) that fill the windows of the exchange hall and the nine great three-light windows of the stairs. The scheme is the same as was used by Waterhouse at Manchester, but predates it and is here handled much more boldly and extravagantly. The heraldic colours of the stained glass are particularly effective. There is also the same reference to trade in the carving of appropriate plants in the tracery of the windows.[11] The great hall is if anything still more magnificent with a monstrous hammerbeam roof whose great lever beams, carved into distinctly solid angels with gilded wings, originally clutched gasoliers (frontispiece). The walls are covered with an ultra-rich diaper pattern of foliage in black and indian red that includes bursting cotton pods. The panels of the roof are painted with coats of arms, though in the interests of the overall pattern, the lions of Lancashire are all turned to face the platform. The east end of the hall is largely covered by Henry Holliday's large and dull painting of the Magna Carta, specially commissioned but virtually invisible because the hall is darkened by the series of stained glass windows which form the chief treasure of the building. These, designed by Bayne of Heaton, Butler & Bayne, are a complete series of full length pictures of kings and queens of England rounded off with Victoria and Albert facing each other down the length of the hall from two rose windows in the gables. The Queen is surrounded by the badges of the various noble orders (a nice piece of wishful thinking) while her consort has emblems of painting, sculpture, science, architecture, commerce, manufacture and, odd but not forgotten, agriculture. There is not the same scale here as at Manchester nor the same expense,[12] but the effect is of much greater richness and variety. Indeed decoration on the same scale does here spread to all the main rooms. The stained glass spreads to the borough court with nine full length portraits of great Englishmen connected with the development of the law. The scarlet robes of the three great jurists form a backdrop to the judge's throne. The council chamber (Fig. 56) is an unusual space with its ceiling supported on pierced Bath stone arches with carved foliate decoration. The door cases are richly carved and panelled, the windows contain the arms of Peel, Arkwright, Salt and the Duke of Bridgewater, but in this room the wall painting is the chief interest. Above a simple rectangular diaper with stencilled patterns of bursting cotton pods and teazles is a frieze of twenty-two panels illustrating the crafts of weaving, spinning and textile printing. These are separated by paintings of the different plants used in the manufacture of textiles.

This still leaves a whole series of minor rooms each with an individual scheme. The committee room had a further richer diaper and a boldly drawn frieze of the bear, beaver, lion, tiger, fox, stag and tailor bird to suggest primitive clothing, and a panelled ceiling illustrating the trades of the town and the new borough arms. Four white angel corbels seem quite out of place. The refreshment room was not a success with easel-type pictures of game alternating with conventionalised fruit and flowers. Only the carved game birds on the corbels survive. The mayor's rooms are the final delight. The mayor's parlour is decorated as the fabled garden of the Hesperides which may have caused some wry mirth. The trees of the garden spread across the ceiling guarded by dragons and with their boughs alive with humming birds. The beams are patterned with trailing vines and inhabited by storks while the humble British birds find their place in the frieze, and the windows represent the four seasons. Only the fireplace tells no story being merely a conventionally enriched Tudor arch. Perhaps more delightful yet is the mayor's reception room. The windows symbolise morning, noon, evening and night while Jack and his beanstalk fill the window jambs. The frieze symbolises night and day and shows the story of King Wren, while the beam ends are painted with other scenes from Aesop's fables on a gold ground. The final touch of whimsy is the carving of the four corbels to show two of the chief supporters of the scheme (Fig. 92), the architect wearily toying with a pair of dividers and the mayor clutching his new town hall.

It must be admitted that the scheme is uneven and the symbolism varies from the too obvious to extremes of abstruseness. The whole building was criticised at the time for eclecticism in drawing so freely on different periods of Gothic. Yet in spite of the carefree composition and the awkwardness of several features, this building with its splendid decoration, rich, rounded and nicely passing the border of vulgarity, is the epitome of civic pride. This particular brand of richness was never surpassed in Gothic and only seldom equalled in the classical temples such as Bolton. There are plenty of lesser examples. Middlesbrough, for instance, has a hammerbeam roof with particularly coarse dragon and eagle head terminals. There are also the four symbolic figures (Fig. 93) by H. T. Margetson who provided the classical equivalent in an elaborate pediment at Portsmouth. The nearest equals to Rochdale are both contemporary. Plymouth had a good ration of carving by Trevenan and by Richard Boulton fresh from Northampton and Congleton. This included the statue of Drake atop the small tower and a statue to cap each of the many gables. There was plenty of stained glass too by Heaton, Butler & Bayne and by the local firm of Fouracre & Watson. Another rich town hall, now unfortunately destroyed, was G. G. Scott's

92 Rochdale town hall, W. H. Crossland, 1866–71; detail of decoration in mayor's ante-room, carved corbel, portrait of G. L. Ashworth, by Thomas Earp

building at Preston. This had the typically Scott feature of elaborately decorated cast iron beams. The main stair wall was covered with an allegory of Manufacture and Commerce above full-length portraits of a miscellany that included Caxton, Linnaeus and Robert Peel. This building was also famous for its stained glass which was entirely heraldic with plenty of repetition of the arms of Preston and the red rose of Lancaster. The hall walls sported pictures of thirty-six celebrities, musical, literary, artistic, scientific and entrepreneurial. Clive, Wellington, Raphael, Davy, Chaucer and Dr Johnson were all part of this surprising crowd. And there was further marble inlay, carving and sculpture throughout the building.

The decade from about 1865 to 1875 saw the high tide of this sort of narrative adornment that was so suited to full blown Gothic. The trouble was that real success required the spread of paint, carving and stained glass to almost every part. This might be all very well if the necessary extensive funds were there, but there was a danger that too little ornament would make a building look damagingly bare. Equally, too much mechanical repetition would with difficulty avoid monotony. The disastrous results of this can be seen in some town halls of the 1890s when cheap terracotta ornament could be applied almost without thought. Fortunately by then

93 Middlesbrough town hall, G. G. Hoskins, 1883–8; figure of *Painting* by H. T. Margetson

94 Lancaster town hall, E. W. Mountford, 1906–9; pedimental sculpture by F. W. Pomeroy

the growth of eclecticism and the English Renaissance revival had reduced the place of carved and painted decoration to the mere provision of a variety of textures and isolated sculptural groups high up above close scrutiny. At the extreme end of our period the effect could be achieved by a veneer of rich materials. The interior of Lancaster town hall (though now disfigured by the insertion of fire doors) shows this especially clearly with the corridor walls entirely covered with a marble veneer while the main rooms are all panelled in oak. The effect is certainly rich, almost sickly, but is achieved entirely without sculpture or painting and there are only two stained glass windows. The entrance hall is floored with black and white marble while the stairs are pure white. The walls are panelled throughout with a simple arcaded pattern of dark and light marble—dark vert bella and light Swedish green for the vestibule, grand stair hall and first floor corridors, and emperor's red and the darker orange fleury for the ground floor. There is none of the implied camaraderie of the medieval guilds, but the formal splendour is undeniable. Almost the only decoration outside is a rather dull pediment by F. W. Pomeroy (Fig. 94)[13] showing King Edward VII flanked by dolphins to show sea power and two figures of loyalty and truth (or maybe justice) while two cherubs hold coats of arms and two lions' heads stare out of the corners. There is a solemn dignity here that is of a different order from the gay abandon of

Rochdale forty years earlier. Hampton's Victoria monument in front of the town hall, and designed as part of the same scheme, has more narrative richness in the panels of the pedestal, though the figure of Victoria herself, staring beadily across at her son, is every bit as wooden as he.

In fact Mountford and Pomeroy between them had created a more joyous and richer scheme at Sheffield using similar materials but in a more traditionally Victorian freedom. There the grand stair (Fig. 29) was lined at Mountford's insistence with red Devonshire marble, and below the landing balustrade runs a fine frieze in Darley Dale stone illustrating the local tale of the Dragon of Wantley. This is much more in the rich narrative tradition that displays a specifically local pride. Outside Pomeroy also created two 36 ft long friezes illustrating local trades and there were further pairs of figures in the spandrels of the arched entrance. The final touch for this steel town was the figure of Vulcan on the roof of the tower, modelled, say the guidebooks, from a grenadier guardsman. The figure has been credited to both Raggi and Pomeroy, but it was evidently a good piece of sculpture, part of a decorative scheme of high standard and a useful contrast with the rather thin carved ornament elsewhere on the building.

The tradition of narrative or locally symbolic sculpture never entirely died, though it ran rather thin at times. It began in the early 1860s with such items as the statue of Marvell on the Hull town hall which formed only one part of a rich overall scheme. An example from the 1890s is Lawson's dignified set of friezes on the Bath guildhall extensions. There was some resurgence around the turn of the century with items like the panels for Rotherhithe town hall by E. M. Roper that showed the docks and timber trade in the Thames around 1700. A similar but better known example is Deptford town hall with its specific and general nautical references. The local references were generally more imaginative than the grander, more generalised compositions that began with the St George's hall at Liverpool and ended with examples such as Lancaster. In between, all four main versions of the Leeds theme (Leeds, Bolton, Portsmouth and Morley) have similar grand compositions, the last three filling a pediment. Leeds is probably the best with a group by John Thomas of London in the tympanum of the entrance (a rather more manageable shape than a pediment in any case) (Fig. 83). Leeds sits enthroned fostering both the arts and sciences. There are five symmetrically grouped figures, all massive draped females who are in effect spiritual descendants of Britannia or Roma. The arts, not surprisingly, are surrounded by a collection of classical accoutrements including a head of Athene, but in this case their weightiness and distance nicely match the enormous pomp of the building. Such classical piles called for a quality of sumptuousness that was never quite the same as the ingenious richness of the Gothicists. In such a building actual sculpture was confined to a few regular spots,

95 Leeds town hall, Victoria hall, Cuthbert Brodrick, 1853–8 (*Building News*, vol. IV, 1858)

and the rest of the effect was produced by more mechanical decorative features, and the language was well understood. The fasces proclaimed law and order, lions the power of the corporation and of the law, while the useful putto was easily transformed into Mercury, 'symbolic of order, peace and prosperity'.[14] These could be easily embellished with acanthus scrolls, urns and sets of hoary heads, presumably giants of labour, on any convenient keystone (Fig. 82). In the great hall at Leeds the Corinthian capitals were further enriched alternately with ram's heads for the woollen trade and owls for the city.

To all this was added the rich polychromy of paint, and the interiors of such buildings were particularly gorgeous. Later generations insisted on at least a veneer of marble or its actual counterfeiting with scagliola, but the mid-century was a riot of painted effects. The great hall at Leeds is one of many examples, but the quality was ensured by the employment of J. G. Crace as the decorator (Fig. 95). His work has now been painted over and the proportions of the room quite spoiled by the intrusion of a huge gallery, but a portion of the original work survives in the lost space beneath it as a tantalising glimpse of the feast described by the contemporary press. The colour of the walls was 'a quiet green' (it is actually a strong olive),

> relieved by marginal borders of fret ornament in a deeper tone of the same colour, outlined with maroon. The bold projecting columns are in imitation of Rosso Antico marble, the enriched capitals being of bronze and gold. On the upper fascia of the wall, in a line with the capitals are a series of appropriate inscriptions,[15] in bold character on a deep violet ground margined with green, and relieved by coloured lines and ornament. Below the base line of the columns, the wall, forming a high dado, is in imitation of Verde antique and other rare marbles. The entablature above the columns is of a quiet (sic) stone colour relieved with gold and bronze, and the frieze is in imitation of the same red marble as the columns. The fine circular roof is divided into compartments; the main lines leading from the columns have leading ornaments and mouldings in bronze and gold. The general tone of the ceiling is a light neutral vellum colour with margins of citron and grey relieved in the grounds of the ornaments by maroon red or blue.[16]

And mere paint was not all, for the ceiling plaster was deeply moulded (Fig. 96) and the spandrels enriched with plaster putti and more ram's heads and owls. The same painted feast spread over the rest of the building eked out with Minton tiles in cream with pale blue and pink palmettes and a whole range of classical motifs to the floor of

96 Leeds town hall, detail of plasterwork in Victoria hall, Cuthbert Brodrick, 1853–8

the entry. Even the graining of the doors was done in a selection of patterns, walnut and pollard oak, etc., to show the different status of the different departments.

For classical town halls Leeds was undoubtedly the high Victorian moment, but the tradition did not stop there. At Bolton the whole tempo is slightly raised, though the quality of some of the work rather let the scheme down. In the first place the outside sculpture now ran to a whole pediment in which is the expected theme of the goddess Bolton flanked by Manufacture and Commerce. There is also a negro boy offering a basket of cotton and Earth pouring forth gifts from a cornucopia. The other

97 Bolton town hall, W. Hill and E. Potts, 1866–73, organ in great hall by Gray & Davidson, case probably by Simpson & Son, London

side of the pediment is matched with a boy holding the prow of a ship and a figure of Ocean who between them symbolise the extent of trade. The composition, by W. Calder Marshall, is no better and no worse than the Liverpool or Leeds versions, though its position high over the massive columns stresses the aloofness of it all. Inside, having passed through the cramped grand entry into a small dark passage one reached the hall, or you could climb (though there was no grand stair) to the banqueting suite on the first floor. Here the sumptuous tradition was continued, though a clear ten years later than Leeds the standard of craftsmanship in classical figure drawing had fallen off rather (Fig. 97). The painted figures with trumpets in the hall were so poor that they were soon painted out. The surviving plaster figures are thoroughly coarse, though the floral ornaments are excellent. Since it was the decoration of this building more than anything else which attracted attention it is worth looking in detail at a sample. Here the rich painting also involved some local pictorial reference like Rochdale and the other town halls of the same decade, but it was the colour and pattern that were the strength of this scheme. The general plan was to have warm and brilliant colours in the hall and banqueting room and more sober tones in the council chamber. The more sober tones gave this scheme:

> the wall opposite to the windows is diversified by shallow arched recesses corresponding with the windows, and the end next to the Mayor's Parlour is further emphasised by the introduction of pilasters on each side of the state doorway. In addition to the principal cornice at the angle of the ceiling, the wall is further broken, horizontally, by a string course carried round it about three fourths of the height from the floor; and the lower part of the wall is faced by a very rich and elaborate parquetry wainscot, with a plinth of dark and light wood contrasted, the mouldings marked out in strong lines of black and light tints and above this an intersecting pattern of various coloured woods carried round the room, the whole finished by mouldings in various tints, as below. . . . The rest of the decorations of the room are carried out in colour. The ceiling which is subdivided into numerous panels is richly decorated. The elephant's head—emblem of the corporation—being introduced with gold and honeysuckle scroll work round it. Some of the panels are grounded of a brilliant red while others are contrasted in black and the whole bounded by a laurel border, gilded and supported by a deep cove, which is filled by a trellis diaper in vellum and salmon colour, relieved with gold. The entablature runs beneath, and is coloured a warm drab enriched with gold and ornaments. The frieze in it is panelled with a series of tablets, bearing the names and dates of office of the mayors of Bolton from 'Darbishire', the first mayor in 1838, to 'Cannon' at present. At intervals round the walls beneath, arranged in canopies and painted on a gold ground are emblematic female figures representing fifteen of the Industries of the locality, and under them again the walls are divided into panels of deep red, relieved with scrolls in black and gold, and alternated with narrow flat pilasters in brown and pale blue.[17]

The critic went on to complain about the vain repetition of the elephant's heads staring down from the ceiling and the poor quality of the figure drawing. He also objected to too much 'vegetable gold' generally and to the pictures of food in the banqueting hall. 'It is difficult to say what is the satisfaction to be derived from seeing, as it were, the ghost of your dinner running round the room, while the corporeal substance is on the table.'[18] Nevertheless it was felt that Bolton town hall had succeeded in providing a properly sumptuous setting for the municipal aristocracy. It only remained for these princes to surround themselves with fine furniture and corporate silver and jewellery to complete the dream. The furniture at least was often specially designed by the architect, but like the decorations such extras seldom survive intact. At Bolton a few pieces remain to indicate the extent of such lavishness. A better impression is, or used to be, given by Morley town hall which retained virtually all the original furniture made by Christopher Pratt of Bradford.

The lush schemes described are, of course, only the high points. Sculpture, paintings and elaborate stained glass might be ruled out by finance, but there can have been very few town halls that were not adorned with a good deal of colour and gilding. Even now that it has lost most of its original painting, the little council chamber at Oldham (Fig. 47), one of the few civic failures, with its original furnishings retains a good deal of the comfortable dignity that was so important a feature of these buildings. Indeed this sort of display was probably cheaper and just as satisfying as the provision of fine art. After all one did not go to the town hall to see art. Town halls were business buildings and for most of these practical men business was entirely distinct from art. Decoration was a different matter, more like a quality finish, and anyway essential to the advertising character of the buildings (Fig. 98). As the high-flown aspirations for general moral and aesthetic improvement as a result of town hall building came increasingly to be seen as futile, so the pressure for purely artistic adornment lessened. Educational elements or local interest might still be allowed, but by the end of the 1870s it was obvious that 'art' decoration, though a desirable luxury, would be reserved for the richer and larger towns. The artistic world continued to write urging more employment for themselves, and the architectural press frequently noted the importance of such work in Paris and elsewhere on the continent.[19] There was, however, no way of proving that such extras had any practical function beyond advertising the wealth of a town. In spite of the efforts of local benefactors, that were at best piecemeal, there was no continuance of the elaboration of the 1860s and 1870s. Art as an integral component of town hall building was frequently stillborn and its manifestations at the turn of the century are too often sterile.

There are a number of exceptions among the larger baroque town halls, but there are few cases comparable to Cardiff where P. R. Montford produced a fine and extensive series of sculptural groups. In general the baroque grand manner relied on an overall impression that gave the effect of richness but without the fussiness of the

98 Birmingham council house, banqueting hall, R. Yeoville Thomason, 1874–9

99 Cardiff city hall and law courts, Lanc

rt & Rickards, 1900–4 (*Builder*, vol. LXXIV, 1898)

100 Leigh town hall, J. C. Prestwich, 1904–7; balcony with carved support by Farmer & Brindley

earlier generation. Stained glass, mosaic, plaster and marble remained common and more of these interiors survive at places such as Stockport or Colchester. However, the symbolic language of the sculpture was in general more restricted and, apart from the survival of Justice and occasionally Plenty, the most common figures are nameless giants or hooded matrons like those that sit brooding on Colchester and Cardiff town hall towers. There were a few among the less grand conceptions that aimed for some elaboration of iconography. The series of huge figures in low relief that represent the industries of Cheshire on Crewe municipal buildings are not unsuccessful followers of their nineteenth-century prototypes. They were the work of F. E. Schenk who had already executed some notable municipal commissions, among them sculpture for Oxford town hall. Other artist-craftsmen became well known in this sphere in the Edwardian period. One such was Gilbert Seale who provided all the carved swags for Lancaster town hall, and the fibrous plaster ceilings for Walsall municipal buildings.[20] These included a pair of fleshy mermaid figures over the council chamber door, but in general this sort of work was restricted to more or less elaborate swags and scrolly foliate borders. Indeed in the Deptford town hall, whose external nautical frieze, statues of naval heroes and Neptune figures effectively continue the old tradition, there is no figure carving in the interior decoration at all, though again there are a couple of rather squashed plaster mermaids over the council chamber door. The emphasis is on quality of workmanship and the superb ironwork of the stair rail is equal to the best that earlier generations produced. The tradition of large-scale figure painting did not altogether disappear, but good examples are rare and there were better patrons among the major shipping and insurance companies. Even in so auspicious a place as Chelsea the figure panels are a disappointment and do not constitute a scheme of decoration. There was a competition in 1911[21] which promised well, with Sargent, Wilson Steer and E. A. Rickards as a jury. However, the winners, C. Sims, F. O. Salisbury, Mrs S. Florence and Miss G. Woolway, were none of them outstanding artists, and the resulting scenes of local history are merely pedestrian. It was not until such extravaganzas as Stockholm town hall had demonstrated the importance of artwork on the grand scale in the mid-1920s that there was much revival in English municipal patronage of the arts.

11

Town halls in use

The stress on function in design and decoration demands a brief look at the use of these buildings by way of an epilogue. We know immediately the use of the operative offices and of the courtrooms, and we can to some extent recover the story of the functions of the halls. However, the junketings at the opening ceremonies also provide an interesting insight into the forms of worship these temples were most fitted for and how they related to their community.

The direct bureaucratic function has been discussed earlier, but it is worth remembering how important the concentration of functions must have seemed in the period before about 1890. Indeed until the advent of the telephone there must have been some real saving of time and corresponding increase in the efficiency if the various departments were gathered in one building. The real need, too, for adequate public space is evidenced by the number of buildings put up by public subscription, and no town hall is really complete without its great hall. The use of these halls provides an important direct link between the citizens and the seat of their local government for they allowed the use of the town halls by the citizens on their own terms. It was argued that they were in the nature of a public service and so did not need to be run commercially and hire charges could be kept to a minimum.[1] Even the long term financing made possible by the local government loans helped the corporations to keep the hiring charges down. The result of this was that the halls were used for a wide variety of functions, all strictly reputable, which brought the buildings into the daily ambience of many, indeed of most, of the townspeople. The assumption has to be, and there is some evidence for this, that it was the conscious policy of the corporations to foster such widespread use. The halls were genuine multi-purpose spaces throughout the period, and even those that were originally built as concert halls, like Birmingham, were also used for other meetings such as political gatherings or the civil service examinations or even for drilling volunteers.[2] Even today town halls are regularly used in this way for a host of activities ranging from baby shows and wedding receptions to wrestling and religious revival meetings. The survival of this variety is a measure of the success of these buildings; and the use was, and in most cases still is, extensive. Within a year of opening, the wear and tear on the Leeds town hall was such that 'parties using the Victoria Hall for tea purposes (were) not allowed to remove the tables afterwards',[3] and there was already pressure on the space that led to requests for the use of the civil court as a secondary ballroom. Here, however, propriety stepped in and the request was 'not entertained'.

The corporations had to serve their townspeople, but they also felt compelled to 'improve' them. This earnestness was probably part of the reason for turning down a request by the celebrated Blondin to walk the tightrope in Leeds town hall. Bradford was more latitudinarian and the St George's hall catered for General Tom Thumb and the Two Headed Nightingale as well as for Paderewski and Patti. Nevertheless it was in music more than anything else that these town halls were used to improve taste. Huddersfield town hall is an extreme example of a type where a huge public hall for choral concerts on the grandest scale quite overpowers the little huddle of offices built up against it.[4] Organs were almost *de rigueur* and huge four manual instruments were not uncommon (Fig. 97). The larger towns even appointed salaried organists as part of their musical educative programme. At Leeds the city organist received a salary of £200[5] per annum in 1860 for which he was to give not less than a hundred public performances. The high hopes of these schemes were not often fulfilled, and by 1865 it was clear that the regular concerts in Leeds (with tickets at 6*d*. and 3*d*.) were very far from covering costs. It is a measure of the council's belief in the importance of such improving activities that they continued to subsidise them.

How far these buildings actually elevated taste is very much in doubt, but there was certainly a sense in which the wide appeal of the whole range of activities catered for in the one public room fostered a sense of community. In this the buildings have made a significant contribution to the development of the towns. A much better documented and more obvious contribution, however, is their contribution in the ceremonial field. Public celebration and rejoicing was a feature of the age, and town halls provided both a backdrop and an occasion for some of the most lavish festivities. The laying of the foundation stone was the first opportunity, and one that was not often missed. Bolton is unique in having no celebration at all as a result of the strong feelings engendered after six years of argument over the cost. Generally speaking this was an occasion for displaying confidence in a new and expensive scheme. It did not do to advertise too widely before the building was up, and these ceremonies were usually led by the mayor[6] or the chairman of the town hall committee who could be relied on for a speech explaining the need for the building and the benefits to be gained by its grandeur. The popularity of these events is evidenced by Rochdale where there was a grand procession. At Gateshead the crowds were such that the stand erected for them collapsed spilling 500 citizens in a heap. Fortunately there was only one fatality.[7]

Yet if the beginning of a building was significant its successful completion was even more important and was the occasion for a town to measure itself against its neighbours and claim its new status. Rochdale is a relative rarity in being unable to entice any nobility to open its extensive municipal palace. Both Gladstone and the Princess Louise and her husband, the Marquess of Lorne, were applied to but declined. Wherever possible a town would invite the biggest name available, and for the few towns that succeeded in collecting royalty success was ensured. Leeds town hall was opened by the Queen herself in a blaze of triumph which included a huge procession designed not so much to show her Leeds as to let Leeds see her. This first royal visit to Leeds marked an important advance for the borough and was the excuse for extended rejoicing. The royal party spent the previous night in the mayor's house vacated for the purpose, and Prince Albert with typical thoroughness climbed to the top of the unfinished tower with Brodrick and 'entered freely into conversation on the subject of the building'.[8] The procession the next day began by passing the massed crowds of 26,809 Sunday School children with their 5,301 teachers who hoped optimistically to control their charges by providing great placards with slogans 'Prepare to Cheer', 'Sing!', 'Silence!' and 'Dismiss'. The rest of the route was lined with constables assisted by 21,150 members of Friendly Societies wearing a special uniform of white gloves and a laurel leaf in their buttonholes. The route was extravagantly decorated and one enterprising shopkeeper even perfumed the air outside his shop. The corporation had provided a triumphal arch 35 ft high topped by a trophy of banners which concealed the new building until the whole pile burst into view across the newly named Victoria Square. Inside, the Victoria Hall was adorned with a deep crimson velvet carpet specially made by Crossley's of Halifax and there were specially made chairs for the royal party upholstered with cerise satin, which one hopes did not clash too badly with the Queen's 'rich mauve silk dress with elegantly brocaded flounces and . . . bonnet of the same material trimmed with green flowers'. Every effort had been put into an enormous display. The mayoral suite was decked with potted plants and ornaments borrowed for the occasion. The local gentry obligingly loaned a further forest of plants for the great entrance steps, and the corporation provided at their own expense newly designed full dress robes. Victoria and Albert both made eulogistic speeches, and collected half a dozen loyal addresses. The Queen then knighted the mayor and withdrew for luncheon in the Mayor's apartment; after which they drove hurriedly to the station to catch the train for Balmoral.

The episode had all the accoutrements of pageantry and the celebrations continued with a dinner and ball for the select few and illuminations and a gala for the populace. There is a curious modernity in the comment of the radical *Leeds Times* that 'we cannot explain or control the feelings, half curiosity and half homage, aroused by royalty which interrupt the normal tenor of an industrious money making people'.[9] And the celebrations did not stop with the royal visit. There was, of course, a music festival, but more significantly, the town was selected as the venue for that year's meeting of the British Association. The publicity was enormous and effective and there were so many visitors that special trains were run from Bradford with the day return ticket acting as an entrance pass to the building.

The Leeds celebrations were some of the grandest, and Rochdale a decade later could not match them. There was much less coverage of the building in the national press and no noble visitors. Two local MPs were present along with the Bishop of Manchester, but the building was actually opened by the mayor. There were less visitors too, only some 4,000 in the first three days of opening, which contrasts with Bolton's crowd of 150,000 in the streets when their town hall was opened two years later. One is tempted to assume a certain weariness at the rising costs at Rochdale, though the actual money came out of the profits of the gas works and not out of the rates. Still the celebrations were considerable. The corporation spent £1,000 (the Leeds festivities cost the corporation £9,000) and besides the inevitable banquet and ball there were commemorative mugs and medals and banners in the street.

None the less, as part of the purpose of these buildings was self-advertisement, it was always a good thing to have outsiders to see the splendour, and an important celebrity was very much to be desired. Bolton could not entice the Queen in 1873 but did attract the Prince and Princess of Wales, and again we have a picture of a hugely enjoyed expensive spectacle. The procession ran to forty-three carriages full of notables, and the mayor's coach was provided with heralds in front and footmen in gorgeous liveries specially imported from London for the occasion. Their Royal Highnesses were welcomed at the town hall and there were the usual speeches followed by a hasty banquet after which they had to hurry along for the London train. But again the celebrations ran on well into the night with elaborate illuminations, lamps with crystal Prince of Wales plumes and Brunswick stars, and even an electric light to illuminate the town hall which must rank among the earliest attempts at floodlighting. There was a balloon ascent too and fireworks as well as a grand concert and full dress ball. The effort put into this display is shown by the formation of a special Banquet Committee, Music Committee, Ball Committee, Decorations

Committee and even a Special Finances Committee. Street decorations alone cost the corporation over £1,000 and ran to Venetian masts and banners along the whole processional route. And the local clubs and trades joined in producing such delights as a 'specimen of Bolton industry in the shape of a quilt bearing a representation of the town hall'.[10]

Wherever there was scope and the town was large enough we find the same elaborate celebrations. Middlesbrough, perhaps being lucky enough to coincide with the Royal Jubilee, was also opened by the Prince and Princess of Wales. The celebrations were as grand as could be with a profusion of flags and bunting and the march of progress signalised this time by the novelty of having the Princess start the town hall clock by means of an electric button concealed in her bouquet. Middlesbrough was one of many towns to celebrate the event by producing a handsome commemorative booklet which in this case contained a description of the special decorations in the rooms temporarily fitted up as retiring rooms for the Prince and Princess. The details indicate the extent of the extravagance of these occasions. The Prince's room, for instance, had gold brocaded satin wall coverings formed into panels by bands of crimson antique silk plush. Both rooms were lavishly fitted up with decorative 'objects', and among those in the Princess's room was a pair of great turquoise vases of Linthorpe ware that were subsequently sent to her as a present.

Yet there was always more to these displays than merely the showing off of visible splendour to distinguished outsiders. These occasions were really celebrations of successful trade, festivals of capitalism for which the town halls provided the only possible backdrop. It was good to be reminded of the success and variety of the enterprise of one's town, and useful to show this to colleagues and rivals. Thus a trades procession was also an important and integral part of the festivities. At Manchester, while it was publicly regretted that the Queen had not seen fit to open the town hall, there were nevertheless twenty-seven local mayors at the banquet who would doubtless have witnessed the enormous trades procession and gone home suitably impressed. Bradford, too, produced a particularly impressive procession with floats and companies of operatives representing every skilled trade in the town. They marched determinedly through the streets in spite of unbroken and torrential rain.

There is a frankness in the enjoyment of these festivities that drowns a good deal of our later criticism. Significantly, there is seldom any record of objections to spending on the festivities, though financing the town hall which was the occasion for them was always opposed and sometimes fought at every stage. The opening festivities were merely the first and grandest celebrations set against a theatrical backdrop that had been created as an individual palace for each town. The buildings were created in part to provide a suitable setting[11] and in so doing to advertise their town. Their vulgarity is itself a measure of the importance attached to this and the continuance of the rather endearing local pomp in spite of reorganisation is a sign that the function has a real value in building and maintaining a sense of corporate identity. Indeed as recently as 1972 John Boynton, then Clerk to the Cheshire County Council, saw the provision of a physical background as necessary to the sustained attempt to get rid of old names and identities and create new. Writing in advance of the last local government reorganisation he urged that old loyalties must be made to die and foresaw the sale of £80 million worth of redundant town halls.

Today we still do not know precisely how big a community can be and yet retain any sense of identity. In the great period of town hall building towns really were tightly knit and more or less within the bounds of comprehension. Had they not been it is doubtful whether such extensive celebrations could have been organised or drawn such crowds, or at least not within that existing political framework. It is this sense of unity that ultimately gave the corporations and their town hall committees the consensus that allowed the building of town halls. Without it the buildings would be meaningless husks.

The full meaning of a town hall is only realised on ceremonial occasions such as I have described, and such occasions can only be enjoyed to the full if one surrenders to the emotional pull of this municipal religion. Such a ceremonial function may seem hard to justify in the modern world, but it remains a fact that the buildings were erected to serve that function. In the buildings of the 1850s, 1860s and 1870s it ranked high in the minds of both patrons and architects and led to some of the best buildings. It is fashionable now to concentrate on the faintly ridiculous aspects of local ceremonial and to dismiss the whole thing in a mood of impatience at our too distant local government. In doing so we forget that in the nineteenth century the actual achievement of properly local government was something to celebrate. Its novelty and potential were valued more than its shortcomings were criticised. The constant refrain of town hall builders was that they were not only housing the municipal bureaucracy but building dignified figureheads, and the buildings demand to be seen as such. Their symbolic value was accepted at the time without question, and it was only towards the end of the century that urbanisation was widely seen as the juggernaut we have been brought up to fear. The successful concentration of population in the nineteenth century was generally seen as a matter for congratulation. Although romantics feared and decried the process, the confident tone of books such as Head's *Tour* was much more widely heard and accepted. Taken in this sense the buildings make a triumphant statement of successful progress achieved with a confidence that we may well envy even while we sneer at its naïveté.

Notes

Introduction

1 W. Cobbett, *Rural Rides* (1830), Everyman edn, 1912, vol. I, p. 16.

2 Some titles were specifically local and can be ignored, while not all the titles always refer to buildings that can properly be considered town halls. It is also worth noting that certain titles, such as Municipal Buildings or Civic Hall, are creations of the second generation, and describe a slightly different function, particularly in towns where more than one building for civic use survives. The most common titles are: Assembly Room, Burgh Hall (Scotland), Civic Hall, Council House, Council Offices, Corn Exchange, Exchange, Guildhall, Mansion House, Market Hall, Moot Hall, Municipal Buildings, Public Hall, Public Rooms, Public Offices, Town Hall and Vestry Hall. In many cases two or more titles are used in conjunction for a single building.

3 One can hardly think of Manchester town hall without being aware of Waterhouse's assize courts as well. In fact in Manchester there was an even closer connection with the exactly contemporary magistrates' courts. At Birmingham the council house and assize courts are similarly linked and were originally intended for the same building.

4 The town hall was the last major work of E. W. Mountford, and was completed by his assistant F. D. Clapham. It seems likely that the fire station was entirely Clapham's work.

5 E. W. Godwin, for example, provided an awkward but quiet flat for the hall keeper in the roof of Northampton town hall. In spite of its most inconvenient access through the base of the tower, it remained in use until the late 1950s. The problem was not always easy to solve, and an unbuilt design by Alfred Waterhouse for Middlesbrough town hall shows a basement bedroom whose ceiling cannot have been more than four feet high!

1 The emergence of municipal democracy and the need for a town hall

1 The original intention was to house offices and assize courts in one council house. This idea was abandoned as the formal rooms were expanded to fill almost the whole of the first floor. The development of the complete site was delayed, presumably on the grounds of economy. The council house was completed in 1879 and the assize courts separately housed in a sumptuous building by Sir Aston Webb and Ingress Bell

(1887–91) at the far end of Corporation Street.

2 F. H. Spencer, *Municipal Origins*, Constable, 1911, p. 141. His view is quoted as of someone looking back from close to the end of the Victorian era, when the achievement of the 'modern' municipal pattern was a fresh memory.

3 Report of the Royal Commission on Municipal Corporations, 1835, BPP vol. XXIII, p. 32.

4 See Appendix I.

5 The property rights did not, of course, vanish immediately; and various other privileges, some antiquated and some important, survived and are still in force. At Berwick-on-Tweed, for instance, freemen had certain privileges in education until quite recently which must have been of real importance before 1870. Freemen of Berwick also have the right to graze geese on the common ground, and the oldest resident freeman is entitled to the use of a gold-topped walking stick. They also undertake not to feed their apprentices salmon more than twice a week!

6 There were, of course, exceptions. The Hundred Court of the Wirral controlled Birkenhead until about 1850, and the Earl of Sefton had power in Manchester through its Court Leet until 1846. In some towns like Morpeth and Alnwick the lord's control was more nearly absolute for much longer.

7 Rochdale paid a probably unconscious tribute to the power of the symbol as late as 1972 by citing its town hall and civic centre as among the most imposing in the country in only the third sentence of the brief description of the town in the *Municipal Year Book*.

8 See Appendix I.

9 There was even an attempt at Bolton to finance the new town hall by drawing on the funds of the Poor Law Board on the grounds that the work would provide extra local employment. This was not in fact allowed, but it is an indication of the wide range of possibilities open to the corporations in funding their buildings.

10 Gothic or Elizabethan designs were specifically debarred from the Kensington vestry hall competition even in 1877.

11 Lanchester, Stewart & Rickards built the town hall at Deptford on a cramped site with only a single frontage to the street, but the street is entirely composed of modest shops and houses. The town hall stands on the inside of a slight curve at the foot of a hill, both factors which make it difficult for the building to tell. Holborn town hall was equally an in-fill building, but set in a major thoroughfare.

12 At Leeds the School Board offices formed a separate block, but they are by the same architect and in a similar style to the adjacent municipal buildings.

13 The actual town hall extension was not built until 1925. However, there was already considerable pressure on space by the end of the nineteenth century which led to a major competition (1911) for an art gallery and library on the site of the old infirmary at Piccadilly (one of the sites originally proposed for the town hall). The competition was abortive, but with it was associated a proposal, also abortive, for a £700,000 extension to the town hall (*Builder*, vol. CV, 1913, 2, pp. 239 and 335).

14 *Building News*, vol. LXII, 1892, 1, p. 2.

15 The only intrusion into the courtyards has been the recent provision of a new kitchen to serve functions in the hall. At Bradford, in contrast, similar spaces have been filled, and there are even a number of offices concealed in extra additions at rooftop level added at various dates in this century. Intrusions into the courtyard of the London County Hall are even more extensive if more formally planned.

16 There was usually particularly strong

opposition to the removal of old buildings. At Worcester proposals to demolish the guildhall of 1721 and rebuild (1878) were bitterly resented by the ratepayers; and Hereford's demolition of a particularly handsome half-timbered town hall (by John Abel, c. 1620) provoked a national furore in 1862.

17 At Leigh, as in many other small towns, there is only one major stair. Thus the segregation begins at first floor level after the public have climbed the imposing grand staircase. There is a separate lobby for councillors with access to the council chamber, mayor's apartments and committee rooms and with a door to the office section. To reach the public gallery of the council chamber one has to climb on into the attics.

18 It is interesting to note that even in town halls such as Leeds or Huddersfield, where the stage was designed to accommodate the huge orchestras and huger choruses that were popular, the architects did not design large enough retiring rooms for all the performers except with considerable overcrowding.

19 There were several complaints that the bedroom windows were only dormers, and thus unsuited to the dignity of the superintendent.

20 At first both ring and spine corridors were badly lit. A ring corridor could however be given natural light from courtyards which was seldom possible with spine corridors. At Northampton the spine corridor is at two levels, and the lower corridor can only be lit by a row of floor lights in the side of the upper floor corridor.

2 The growth of municipal patronage

1 The figures ignore the many market halls, courthouses and other buildings which more than double the total but which may not be regarded strictly as town halls. The reckoning also, with two exceptions, ignores the quite numerous and extensive alterations to existing buildings. The reconstruction of the London guildhall in the period after 1854, and Poynter's restoration of the Maison Dieu at Dover (1852–61) both seem to qualify as major commissions. In addition some towns had already built in the previous decades.

2 Exact figures are hard to come by and have not been available in all cases. Though some expensive proposals were abandoned, in general costs exceeded estimates by a considerable margin, so that, while I put forward these figures with some diffidence, they should be regarded as under- rather than over-estimates.

3 The oak roof was the gift of the local MP.

4 *Builder*, vol. IX, 1851, p. 377. The actual sum is disclaimed as erroneous, but they could hardly have expected to buy such eminence cheaply.

5 *Leeds Intelligencer*, 20 August 1853.

6 Quoted in T. W. Reid, *A Memoir of John Deakin Heaton M.D. of Leeds*, Longman, 1883, pp. 147–8.

7 These went through several stages of design before reaching their present form. One detail drawing (in the Leeds City Archives) shows three alternative shapes for the vases on the corners of the tower, and there are a good many other drawings in the series.

8 Mayor's speech at the foundation laying, quoted in *Wakefield Echo Supplement*, 19 October 1877.

9 Reid, op. cit., p. 142.

10 *Leeds Intelligencer*, 11 September 1858.

11 The organ was installed for the opening of the town hall in 1834, but the managers of the General Hospital requested it be set back in a recess (probably to the detriment of its tone) in 1835. The first design for this

change was made in 1839, an extremely hamfisted protrusion through the colonnade. The fully extended colonnade of fifteen columns instead of thirteen dates from 1846. The designs are by Charles Edge.

The organ, costing some £3,000, was by W. Hill who had recently completed the York Minster organ. It was a monstrous affair, said to surpass York, Rotterdam and Haarlem. Among its more extraordinary features was a carillon of hand bells played from the keys of the swell organ, and a Tuba Mirabilis, the first of its kind in the world, made after Hill's experiments in high pressure whistles for his friend Hudson, the railway king. Mendelssohn was one of the earliest celebrities to play on the instrument, but he complained that the mechanical action was very heavy and doubted his ability to play Bach's Toccata and Fugue on it satisfactorily without completely exhausting himself.

12 The problem of combining classical and Gothic motifs, particularly with regard to spires, preoccupied a number of architects at about this time. Brodrick had tried a classical spire in his design for Bolton town hall and again in his design for Manchester town hall. There is a fairly close copy of the Halifax spire on the Liverpool municipal buildings (J. Weightman and E. R. Robson) where there is a further marriage of Gothic and classical aims in the treatment of detail.

13 Assessor's report quoted in *Builder*, vol. XXVI, 1868, p. 190.

14 The ruling was given in answer to a query from T. H. Wyatt. The correspondence is preserved in the Manchester City Archives. All the other competitors were kept informed of all the questions raised and the rulings given. The printed instructions were not specific, though they indicated that projecting steps would be allowed.

15 The list of extras is preserved in the Manchester City Council Proceedings, 1873–4. The extras are listed under six heads. One whole section is of works designed to make the building more monumental, another section involves improvements in the quality of the stairs, fireplaces and door frames. The, now famous, passages will have been much improved by the substituting of terracotta ribs for plaster and by breaking up their length with seating bays. The upper corridors which were to have been completely plain, and thus unbearably long, were broken up at intervals by the insertion of solid piers and pointed arches (see also p. 226).

16 His fee of £173 5*s*. (Manchester City Council, Town Hall Sub-Committee Minutes, 23 February and 16 March 1868) shows that there was a good deal of work involved.

17 He was soon himself to serve on the council and attended the opening of the town hall as an alderman.

18 *Builder*, vol. V, 1847, pp. 90, 112, 163, 289–90; vol. VIII, 1850, p. 473; and vol. IX, 1852, p. 62.

19 Not only the general style of the tower, but the side façade and the unusual octagonal corner turrets with their steeply pitched roofs are closely anticipated in a design for a municipal mansion by A. B. Mitchell which won the Soane medallion for 1884 and was published in the *Builder* the following year (vol. XLVII, 1885, 1, p. 412). It is tempting to see Mountford's design as directly derivative.

3 Size and splendour

1 Minutes of the Royal Commission on Local Government 1888, Part II, pp. 213–33, quoted in H. Finer, *English Local Government*, Methuen, 1950.

2 The building was surfaced with a cement rendering at some point in this century which effectively destroyed the elegance of the original detail.
3 *Builder* (vol. XXXVI, 1878, p. 822–3) claims that a town hall was built in 1868. The reference can only be to C. J. Adams' royal exchange of that year which does not fulfil the conditions of public accessibility required by a real town hall. However, the confusion of terminology is interesting.
4 He did, however, provide direct financial help in the extremes of the 1875 slump.
5 The effect of severity is considerably increased by the recent unfortunate removal of most of the carved decoration. The soft red sandstone had not weathered well and much of the ornament was in a poor state, but its loss is to be regretted.
6 The competition drawing published in the *Building News* (vol. XXXIV, 1878, p. 316) shows a grand entry by stairs under the tower rising to first floor level as at Bradford. These do not appear on the plans published with the drawing and must have been abandoned before the design was finalised rather than in any rearrangement.

4 The workings of patronage: individuals

1 The site was purchased with the intention of building a town hall as far back as 1796.
2 They visited Halifax, Leeds, Blackburn and Preston which were respectively reported to have cost £40,000 (or £28 per sq. yd), £100,000 (or £18 per sq. yd), £23,000 (or £11 per sq. yd) and £40,000 (or £20 per sq. yd).
3 *Rochdale Observer*, 9 January 1864.
4 As a former pupil of G. G. Scott his pedigree was, of course, excellent, and another possibility is that he may have been involved to some extent as Scott's assistant at Preston. The question has not so far been researched.
5 Letter from Lord Ashton to Lancaster Corporation, recorded in Lancaster Council Minutes, 9 November 1904, Council in Committee. There may have been special personal reasons why Lord Ashton made the offer, for his second wife had died a month before and he was planning to erect in her memory the extraordinary Ashton Memorial which John Belcher designed. This would be, he claimed, 'a useful and ornamental structure . . . in place of the Queen's memorial', which the council had arranged should stand in Dalton Square. In fact Ashton paid for that too, and it now faces the town hall. It is interesting that during the whole of this period, and in spite of an invitation to the mayoralty, Ashton was never personally involved as a member of the council.
6 There was no competition at Lancaster and one can assume that Lord Ashton was involved in the selection of the architect. Thereafter the whole scheme was left to the council and managed by a town hall committee exactly as in any other town.
7 The designs were drawn by Elkington, but submitted to Waterhouse before the plate was made. The gift was valued at £7,000, but an entry in the corporation accounts for 1878 of £3,282 14*s.* 1*d.* for the purchase of plate suggests that the donors may have overreached themselves and that the ratepayers had to fill the gap.

5 The workings of patronage: committees

1 *Builder*, vol. XIV, 1856, p. 210.
2 There was more than a hint of jobbery in this competition, for Lainson was employed by the council to examine the competitive designs that were all rejected. He was not technically an assessor, but was required to measure the plans, and thus it will have been on his recommendation that they were

rejected as unsuitable or too expensive. It appears that his own plans were for a modification of the original requirements, and it is likely that the modifications came from his own suggestion. His connection with the Reading town council has not been researched, and his practice was in Brighton. It is possible even that he was in a position to liaise with Waterhouse who was building the town hall at Hove at the time. A further hint of jobbery comes in a letter, one of several letters of complaint, published in the *Building News* (vol. XXXIV, 1878, 1, p. 26) claiming that the public subscription that was organised to fund the building was in fact launched by one of the competing architects. The first decision is reported as a vote of five to three in favour in a meeting of a committee that should have numbered fourteen. The selected design did not comply with the published instructions, but the result of complaints made to the council was that only six plans short-listed by the council were submitted to the assessor, instead of the forty designs sent in for the competition.

Letter from the architect quoted in the Minutes of the Municipal Buildings and High Level Bridge Committee, 21 May 1883, Barrow-in-Furness Corporation Records. This letter was sent two years before the failure of the tower.

Diary of E. Hopkinson, 29 July and 31 July 1885, MS, Barrow-in-Furness Reference Libary.

This was not expensive even for market buildings. The market at Bolton (1851–5) cost £50,000. Waterhouse certainly could build economically if he wanted. The Reading municipal buildings cost only £10,000 (for the Waterhouse block) in 1877, while his town hall at Hove, complete with hall, banqueting hall and offices, cost only around £40,000 in 1881. One of the published figures for Hove town hall was in fact only £32,000.

7 T. E. Collcutt was obviously well aware of this danger in preparing his design for Barrow-in-Furness town hall. His competition design was for an elaborate structure in the Queen Anne style with a grand arcaded loggia across the front. It was essential that the whole façade be built, yet the corporation were preparing to build only the municipal accommodation. Collcutt arranged his plan so that the whole of the court accommodation could be detached without affecting his façade. W. H. Lynn's winning design had to be completely rearranged in order to preserve most of its façade.

8 Mayor's speech at the opening ceremony, *Oldham Chronicle*, 18 October 1879.

6 The strong architect and the corporation

1 Mayor's speech at the opening of Leigh town hall, *Leigh Journal and Times*, 26 July 1907.

2 Quoted in Asa Briggs, *Victorian Cities*, Penguin, 1968, p. 159.

3 'Civicus', 'Scheme for a new large public hall, and other halls; also for a new town hall', Blackburn n.d. (Blackburn Central Library).

4 Quoted in *Leeds Intelligencer*, 11 September 1858.

5 Ibid.

6 John Donaldson, clerk of works, log book, 15 September 1854, MS, Leeds City Archives.

7 Ibid., 28 January 1854; see also 6 February 1854 and 14 February 1854.

8 Ibid., 16 March 1855.

9 Ibid., 26 October 1854.

10 Ibid., 25 June 1856.

11 Leeds Corporation, Town Hall Committee Minutes, 1 February 1854 and Council Minutes, 6 February 1854.

12 Brodrick read a paper on the structure to the

British Association at their meeting in Leeds town hall in 1858. He did not say where he had got the idea from, but claimed to know of only one other example in England—that at King's Cross. The invention he credited to a French engineer working on a bridge over the Rhine in 1811. Some connection with the Crystal Palace might be hinted at by the visit of Paxton to the site (clerk of works' log book, 4 December 1855) which makes it at least unlikely that Brodrick was unaware of his use of the method though Brodrick may possibly have modified it. He used eight sets of laminated principals each consisting of twelve layers of 9 in. by 1½ in. planks held by wrought iron bolts and ties. These had a clear span of 71 ft and were sufficiently true to be used directly as the centering for the elaborate plaster ceiling. The bolts needed tightening under the architect's supervision in 1865, but otherwise they have remained untouched to this day.

13 Clerk of works' log book, 14 April 1855 and 20 April 1855.

14 *Builder*, vol. V, 1847, p. 91. One disastrous effect was that a workman, mistaking the door into a new ventilating shaft for one of the lavatories, entered and fell to his death.

15 Leeds town hall was one of their first major commissions, but was so successful that they were later commissioned to design heating systems for many major town halls including Bolton, Bradford, Manchester, Cardiff and Glasgow.

16 Clerk of works' log book, 2 March 1854.

17 It is interesting that his partner, S. Musgrave, was a native of Hull from where Brodrick came. It may be he or his son who later entered practice as an architect and won second prize in the Durban town hall competition of 1882.

18 The intention is recorded in the *Leeds Intelligencer*, 20 August 1853, and the plinths are shown on the contract drawings. They probably disappeared in the alterations to allow for a tower.

19 He made his bricks from the earth excavated on the site and fired them within the shell of the building so that the heat from the kilns dried the walls and provided warm working conditions. He also designed special scaffolding and a new crane that allowed the roof principals to be raised whole.

20 See *Builder*, vol. XXI, 1865, pp. 868–9.

21 Manchester Corporation Proceedings, 1873–4, pp. 381–3 (see also p. 223).

22 MS letter from W. H. Crossland, 12 September 1867, Rochdale Public Libraries, archives collection.

23 Reports commented that the men were afraid to work on it. It caught fire and burnt down on the night of 10 April 1883 destroying the tower as well. The insurance cover was sufficient to allow the commissioning of Waterhouse to build a replacement which still stands.

24 The Rochdale Jubilee Book (ed. Alderman Lt Col. Fishwick, Rochdale 1906) records the following loans up to 1886:

Gas	£137,000
Water	£826,480
Cemetery	£13,500
Baths	£8,500
Paving and Sewering	£42,631
Sewage Disposal	£61,160
Private Improvement	£17,369
General Purposes	£43,658
Improvements	£83,187
Town Hall	£155,000
Free Library	£6,500

7 Competitions

1 Presidential address to students at the RIBA, 1890, reprinted in the *Builder*, vol. LVIII, 25 January 1890, p. 57.

2 *Builder*, vol. I, 1843, p. 482.

3 *Builder*, vol. XLIII, 1882, p. 289; vol. LVII, 1889, p. 260 reports 125 designs.
4 See *Builder*, vol. XXI, 1863, p. 155. His survey was based on competitions advertised in the *Builder* and covers the four years 1857, 1858, 1861 and 1862. It was not, of course, restricted to civic buildings.
5 *Builder*, vol. XXVII, 1869, p. 840. Such a report may well be exaggerated, and the surviving correspondence does not fully bear out the suggestion, though as it is incomplete it cannot provide proof that the report is unjustified.
6 There is no question but that the tower bears a close resemblance to that designed by William Burges in his entry for the law courts competition. Lockwood & Mawson claimed an older prototype (the Bargello in Florence); but in any case Burges is generally supposed to have derived his tower from ideas of E. W. Godwin.
7 *Builder*, vol. XXVII, 1869, p. 840.
8 *Builder*, vol. XXXVI, 1878, p. 823.
9 *Building News*, vol. LXII, 1892, p. 1.
10 *Builder*, vol. XXVII, 1869, p. 840.
11 Bradford Central Library, local history collection, MS correspondence relating to Bradford town hall (uncatalogued) Several bundles of letters survive consisting of applications, acknowledgments, etc. The various lists do not precisely tally, and some letters are certainly missing. However, allowing for partnerships where one partner signed the application and another signed subsequent letters, the figures are substantially accurate.
12 Waterhouse had recently moved to London, but apart from his Manchester origins he still had connections there and there was an alderman Waterhouse on the council at the time of the competition.
13 There is some further confirmation in Waterhouse's behaviour at Middlesbrough where he is known to have had good connections with the Middlesbrough Owners. After being commissioned to produce complete designs for a town hall that was abandoned because of a slump he was apparently satisfied with a payment of $1\frac{1}{2}$ per cent on the estimates for all the design work, and later happily acted as assessor for the competition that superceded his design and clearly also gave a good deal of detailed advice about modifications to the selected design.
14 E.g. *Builder*, vol. XCVI, 1909, 1, p. 154 (Stanley council offices); *Builder*, vol. CII, 1912, 1, pp. 513, 544 (Padiham municipal buildings) or *Builder*, vol. CVI, 1914, 1, pp. 129, 164, 226, 256, 284, 386 (Barnsley town hall).

8 Developing styles

1 The Newcastle civic centre (1960–3) is still atypical in giving such direct prominence to the council chamber.
2 Francis Goodwin had previously built Macclesfield town hall (1823), also in a Roman classical idiom.
3 *Builder*, vol. LXXXII, 1902, 1, p. 40.
4 It is difficult to be sure how influential the Birmingham building was. Nash's fashionable building was certainly well known, and a delegation even went from Middlesbrough to view it when planning their first town hall. In any case Birmingham town hall was different from both the later examples mentioned in that the hall space extended down into the podium, a solecism for which the building was later much criticised.
5 The problem of combining a spire with a classical design was one which was exercising a number of architects at about this time. Brodrick tried one version in his rejected design for the Leeds tower. He tried again in his unsuccessful design for Bolton

town hall; and finally produced a truly fantastic columnar spire as the centrepiece of his design for Manchester town hall.

6 Godwin's method of construction also approximated to Ruskin's teachings about the virtues of the medieval guilds of masons. Godwin gathered round him a band of stonemasons and carvers, the best known being Richard Boulton of Cheltenham, and they later moved on to work for him again at Congleton.

7 These caused Godwin some trouble as he had done no figure drawing when he won the competition, and so could not easily furnish detailed sketches. He left the detailed design to Richard Boulton, and they are remarkably effective.

8 Godwin did not stick exclusively to symmetrical designs even in his Gothic phase. His later design for Winchester town hall retains a symmetrical façade, but both the design and the preparatory sketch for Leicester (the sketch is preserved in the Victoria & Albert Museum) are asymmetrical. His design for the Kensington vestry hall (1874), which is also preserved in sketch form in the V & A, reworks the basic theme of Northampton and Congleton, but the tower is moved to one side.

9 There is also a delightful sketch in one of his sketchbooks (Victoria & Albert Museum) for an imaginary town hall. Dated 1868–71, it shows a small asymmetrical building like a castle with a series of slit windows and a squat tower at one end.

10 This fine feature seems, in its municipal manifestations, to be best suited to Gothic. Its later translation into classical at Birmingham council house is lumpish and makes the lions look ridiculous.

11 In his original competition design Corson proposed to cap the municipal buildings with a series of ogee domes. These were later abandoned.

12 *Architect*, vol. XXIV, 1880, 2, p. 259.

13 The tower was not in fact built as designed but was somewhat shortened.

14 It is typical also of the close basis of these structures in local trade that the hall was fitted with a specially made carpet 15 yds across and woven as a single piece. This extravagant piece of manufacture was laid in 1909 and is still in use!

15 Another of his strange designs, for Edinburgh municipal buildings, also failed to get a premium. There he used some nearly Byzantine forms.

16 A. B. Thomas was more successful than Belcher. In addition to Belfast and Stockport town halls he was responsible for Woolwich town hall having won the competition for Plumstead municipal buildings. Generally his buildings lack the gaiety of those designed by Belcher, but the three that were built are all fine buildings.

9 Display: townscape and towers

1 Over a hundred architrave blocks were required, each about 15 ft long; and the cornice stones had to be deep enough to allow the projecting heads to be cut out of the solid stone.

2 At Cardiff (1847) Caen stone was used to face the whole upper floor.

3 In fact the ante-room at Manchester is a far from successful space since it is ill lit, and the projecting bow window in front of the tower is cut off from the room as a whole by the piers of the tower and now functions as a store for tables and chairs. At Bradford there was a similar problem and the space is now permanently divided by a partition.

4 The present open space formed by clearing the block in front of the municipal buildings is too long and narrow to be anything other than an overgrown thoroughfare.

5 A tower with a very similar cap appeared the year after this in William Scott's Soane

Medallion design for a free library and institute (see *Building News*, vol. XXVI, 1897, 1, p. 6). Collcutt uses the motif more effectively.

6 It was closely copied a decade later in a design for Darwen town hall by Smith & Heathcote.

10 Decoration: painting and sculpture

1 An earlier, more elaborate and more successful design is shown in a published perspective (*Builder*, vol. XCIII, 1907, 2, p. 496) but was apparently abandoned.

2 J. Ruskin, *The Seven Lamps of Architecture*, George Allen, 1880, pp. 246–7 (The Lamp of Beauty, section XXXIV).

3 The present decorative scheme with its elaborate plaster trophies dates only from the refurbishing of the interior in the 1930s.

4 The present arrangement of display cases unfortunately entirely destroys the effect of this space.

5 The fitted cupboards in the banqueting hall are part of the furnishings designed by Waterhouse, and they survive, as do many of the original chairs and settees. In the banqueting hall there are also the original curtains which were the work of the newly formed Royal School of Art Needlework.

6 At least one of the competition entries proposed galleries on three sides of the hall.

7 The organ itself is a three manual instrument by Cavaillé Coll of Paris. The case in oak was made by Farmer & Brindley.

8 There is a record that in the early years they were much dulled by the shoulders of people leaning against them and by officious dusting by the cleaning staff. They have, however, survived remarkably well.

9 Elmes had originally wanted the capitals of the columns to be solid bronze, but eventually settled for iron.

10 *Building News*, vol. IX, 1861, p. 399.

11 Rochdale was not simply a cotton town. The town directory for 1858 says the staple trade was baize and flannel though cotton and calico printing were extensively carried on. The Ordnance Survey map of 1851 shows nine cotton mills, three woollen mills and two cotton and woollen mills in the central area alone. Other allied industries were dyeing, bleaching, calico printing, carpet weaving, silk and velvet manufacture.

12 The stained glass cost a little over £10,000 altogether and the carving in the region of £5,000. Holliday's picture cost £450. This compares with an estimate of £50,000 for the decoration of Manchester in 1877. Ford Madox Brown was paid about £375 for each of his twelve panels.

13 The original conception (see *Builder*, vol. XCIII, 1907, 2, p. 496) was clearly for a richer composition with more figures. I have not been able to discover why Pomeroy abandoned this idea.

14 *Leeds Intelligencer*, 11 September 1858, p. 279.

15 These of course included the Biblical 'Except the Lord build the house; they labour in vain that build it', and such pithy sentiments as 'Trial by Jury', 'Labor Omnia Vincit', 'Magna Carta' and 'Forward'.

16 *Building News*, vol. IV, 1858, pp. 841–2.

17 Memorial booklet on the 'opening of the Bolton Town Hall and Visit of Their Royal Highnesses The Prince and Princess of Wales, Thursday, June 5th. 1873', p. 27. The memorial booklet is reprinted from the *Bolton Weekly Journal and District News*, 7 June 1873.

18 Ibid., p. 27.

19 Especially in a leading article in the *Builder* (vol. LXXVII, 1899, pp. 455ff.) which noted the monotony of the Paris *mairies* as architecture, but reckoned that they formed an important contribution to modern French art and had the effect of inducing painters to

'bring their art into closer relation with the spirit and circumstances of modern life'.

20 There are also external figure sculptures by H. C. Fehr.

21 The competition followed immediately after the completion of the extensions by Leonard Stokes, but the panels are in the hall of the original block by J. M. Brydon.

11 Town halls in use

1 The provision of refreshments as opposed to space was a different matter and was usually contracted out. Even so, the fact that the supplier was not responsible for the premises as well could mean that prices could be kept down without loss of quality. The Leeds refreshment room prices (1*s.* 3*d.* for breakfast with meat, 2*s.* for hot dinner with soup and pastry, 6*d.* for tea or coffee and a bun) compare well with prices charged eight years before at the Great Exhibition.

2 The sub-hall at Leeds was regularly set apart for rifle drill. Not surprisingly we find that within a few months of making the arrangements all the gas pendants in the room had to be raised (Town Hall Committee Minutes, 13 January 1860).

3 Ibid., 21 January 1859.

4 The two buildings are in fact separate and by separate architects, but were part of a single development from 1875 to 1881. The hall came first in 1875–6 by T. Wood and F. Wild and cost £57,000, while the offices were built by the borough surveyor from 1878 to 1881 at a cost of £19,000.

5 Other cities offered salaries ranging from £130 to £300.

6 Rochdale was fortunate in having Jacob Bright, a nationally known figure, as a former mayor of the town. At Rochdale the ceremonial at the foundation laying was nearly as extensive as at the opening.

7 It was later discovered that the mayor had ordered alterations to the architect's designs without consulting him so that safety limits were cut. The architect, J. Johnstone, was extremely well connected locally and avoided any censure.

8 This and the following quotations are from the account in the *Leeds Times*, 11 September 1858.

9 Ibid.

10 *Bolton Weekly Journal and District News*, 7 June 1873.

11 Birmingham city museum contains a painting of the decorations in the town hall for the Queen's visit to the town in the 1880s. The royal chair is surmounted by a colossal tent and baldacchino that would satisfy any stage designer.

APPENDIX I

Status of boroughs

The schedules of the major Acts of Parliament affecting the status of boroughs reflect the situation in the 1830s and at the close of our period. It has to be remembered, however, that the 1835 Municipal Reform Act was permissive in that individual boroughs had to apply for a charter of incorporation, and there might be a considerable delay before they assumed their full potential status.

Schedules of the 1832 Reform Act. 2 & 3 Wm IV C.45

(A) Boroughs to cease to send members to Parliament

Old Sarum, Newtown (IOW), St Michael's, Gatton, Bramber, Bossiney, Dunwich, Ludgershall, St Mawes, Beeralston, West Looe, St Germain's, Newport (Cornwall), Bletchingley, Aldborough, Camelford, Hindon, East Looe, Corfe Castle, Great Bedwin, Yarmouth (IOW), Queenborough, Castle Rising, East Grinstead, Higham Ferrers, Wendover, Weobley, Winchelsea, Tregony, Haslemere, Saltash, Orford, Callington, Newton, Ilchester, Boroughbridge, Stockbridge, Romney, Hedon, Plympton, Seaford, Heytesbury, Steyning, Whitchurch, Wootton Bassett, Downton, Fowey, Milborne Port, Aldeburgh, Minehead, Bishop's Castle, Okehampton, Appleby, Lostwithiel, Brackley, Amersham.

(B) Boroughs to return one member only

Petersfield, Ashburton, Eye, Westbury, Wareham, Midhurst, Woodstock, Wilton, Malmesbury, Liskeard, Reigate, Hythe, Droitwich, Lyme Regis, Launceston, Shaftesbury, Thirsk, Christchurch, Horsham, Great Grimsby, Calne, Arundel, St Ives, Rye, Clitheroe, Morpeth, Helston, North Allerton, Wallingford, Dartmouth.

(C) New boroughs to return two members to Parliament

Manchester, Birmingham, Leeds, Greenwich, Sheffield, Sunderland, Devonport, Wolverhampton, Tower Hamlets, Finsbury, Marylebone, Lambeth, Bolton, Bradford, Blackburn, Brighton, Halifax, Macclesfield, Oldham, Stockport, Stoke-upon-Trent, Stroud.

(D) New boroughs to return one member to Parliament

Ashton-under-Lyne, Bury, Chatham, Cheltenham, Dudley, Frome, Gateshead, Huddersfield, Kendal, Kidderminster, Merthyr Tydfil, Rochdale, Salford, South Shields, Tynemouth, Wakefield, Walsall, Warrington, Whitby, Whitehaven.

Schedules of the 1835 Municipal Reform Act. 5 & 6 Wm IV C.76

(A) Sections 1 and 2, lists of the boroughs which are to have a Commission of the Peace

Section 1. Aberystwyth, Abingdon, Barnstaple, Bath, Bedford, Berwick-upon-Tweed, Bridgwater, Bridport, Bristol, Bury St Edmunds, Cambridge, Canterbury, Cardiff, Carlisle, Caernarvon, Carmarthen, Chester, Chichester, Colchester, Dartmouth, Denby, Derby, Devizes, Dorchester, Dover, Durham, Evesham, Gateshead, Gloucester, Guildford, Harwich, Haverfordwest, Hereford, Hertford, Ipswich, Kendal, Kidderminster, Kingston-upon-Hull, King's Lynn, Leeds, Leicester, Leominster, Lichfield, Liverpool, Macclesfield, Monmouth, Neath, Newark, Newcastle-under-Lyme, Newcastle-upon-Tyne, Newport (Mon.), Newport (IOW), Northampton, Norwich, Nottingham, Oxford, Pembroke, Poole, Portsmouth, Preston, Reading, Ripon, Rochester, St Albans, Sarum, Scarborough, Shrewsbury, Southampton, Stafford, Stamford, Stockport, Sudbury, Sunderland, Swansea, Tiverton, Truro, Warwick, Wells, Weymouth, Wigan, Winchester, Windsor, Worcester, Yarmouth (Great).

Section 2. Andover, Banbury, Beverley, Bewdley, Bideford, Boston, Brecon, Bridgnorth, Chesterfield, Clitheroe, Congleton, Coventry, Deal, Doncaster, Exeter, Falmouth, Grantham, Gravesend, Grimsby, Hastings, Kingston-upon-Thames, Lancaster, Lincoln, Liskeard, Louth, Ludlow, Maidstone, Maldon, Newbury, Oswestry, Penzance, Plymouth, Pontefract, Richmond, Romsey, St Ives, Saffron Walden, Stockton, Tewkesbury, Walsall, Welshpool, Wenlock, Wisbech, York.

(B) Sections 1 and 2, lists of smaller boroughs which are not to have a Commission of the Peace unless on Petition and Grant

Section 1. Arundel, Beaumaris, Cardigan, Llanidloes, Pwllheli, Ruthin, Tenby, Thetford, Totnes.

Section 2. Basingstoke, Beccles, Blandford Forum, Bodmin, Buckingham, Calne, Chard, Chippenham, Chipping Norton, Daventry, Droitwich, Eye, Faversham, Flint, Folkestone, Glastonbury, Godalming, Godmanchester, Helston, Huntingdon, Hythe, Launceston, Llandovery, Lyme Regis, Lymington, Maidenhead, Marlborough, Morpeth, Penrhyn, Retford (East), Rye, Sandwich, Shaftesbury, South Molton, Southwold, Stratford-upon-Avon, Tamworth, Tenterden, Torrington, Wallingford, Wycombe (Chipping).

Third schedule of the 1888 Local Government Act. 51 & 52 Vic. C.41

A list of boroughs to be created county boroughs

Barrow, Bath, Birkenhead, Birmingham, Blackburn, Bolton, Bootle, Bradford, Brighton, Bristol, Burnley, Bury, Canterbury, Cardiff, Chester, Coventry, Croydon, Derby, Devonport, Dudley, Exeter, Gateshead, Gloucester, Great Yarmouth, Halifax, Hanley, Hastings, Huddersfield, Ipswich, Kingston-upon-Hull, Leeds, Leicester, Lincoln, Liverpool, Manchester, Middlesbrough, Newcastle-upon-Tyne, Northampton, Norwich, Nottingham, Oldham, Plymouth, Portsmouth, Preston, Reading, Rochdale, St Helens,

Salford, Sheffield, Southampton, South Shields, Stockport, Sunderland, Swansea, Walsall, West Bromwich, West Ham, Wigan, Wolverhampton, Worcester, York.

A list of county boroughs and municipal and metropolitan boroughs as at the time of the 1975 Local Government Act reflects the situation at the end of the period that was effectively codified in the 1929 Local Government Act

County boroughs (counties of cities in Scotland)

Aberdeen, Barnsley, Barrow, Bath, Belfast, Birkenhead, Birmingham, Blackburn, Blackpool, Bolton, Bootle, Bournemouth, Bradford, Brighton, Bristol, Burnley, Burton-upon-Trent, Bury, Canterbury, Cardiff, Carlisle, Chester, Coventry, Croydon, Darlington, Derby, Dewsbury, Doncaster, Dudley, Dundee, Eastbourne, East Ham, Edinburgh, Exeter, Gateshead, Glasgow, Gloucester, Grimsby, Halifax, Hastings, Huddersfield, Ipswich, Kingston-upon-Hull, Leeds, Leicester, Lincoln, Liverpool, London (City), Londonderry, Manchester, Merthyr Tydfil, Middlesbrough, Newcastle-upon-Tyne, Newport (Mon.), Northampton, Norwich, Nottingham, Oldham, Oxford, Plymouth, Portsmouth, Preston, Reading, Rochdale, Rotherham, St Helens, Salford, Sheffield, Smethwick, Southampton, Southend, Southport, South Shields, Stockport, Stoke-on-Trent, Sunderland, Swansea, Tynemouth, Wakefield, Wallasey, Walsall, Warrington, West Bromwich, West Ham, West Hartlepool, Wigan, Wolverhampton, Worcester, Yarmouth, York.

Municipal and metropolitan boroughs (large burghs in Scotland)

Abergavenny, Aberystwyth, Abingdon, Accrington, Acton, Airdrie, Aldeburgh, Aldershot, Altrincham, Andover, Appleby, Arbroath, Arundel, Ashton-under-Lyne, Aylesbury, Ayr, Bacup, Ballymena, Banbury, Bangor (Gwynedd), Bangor (Co. Down), Barking, Barnes, Barnstaple, Barry, Basingstoke, Batley, Battersea, Beaumaris, Bebington, Beccles, Beckenham, Beddington, Bedford, Bermondsey, Berwick-upon-Tweed, Bethnal Green, Beverley, Bewdley, Bexhill, Bexley, Bideford, Bilston, Bishop's Castle, Blyth, Bodmin, Boston, Brackley, Brecon, Brentford & Chiswick, Bridgwater, Bridgnorth, Bridlington, Bridport, Brighouse, Bromley, Buckingham, Bury St Edmunds, Buxton, Caernarvon, Calne, Camberwell, Cambridge, Cardigan, Carmarthen, Castleford, Chatham, Chard, Chelmsford, Chelsea, Cheltenham, Chesterfield, Chichester, Chippenham, Chipping Norton, Chorley, Cleethorpes, Clifton, Clitheroe, Clydebank, Coatbridge, Colchester, Coleraine, Colne, Colwyn Bay, Congleton, Conway, Cowdenbeath, Crewe, Crosby, Dagenham, Dartford, Darwen, Daventry, Deal, Denbigh, Deptford, Devizes, Dorchester, Dover, Droitwich, Dukinfield, Dumbarton, Dumfries, Dunstable, Durham, Ealing, East Leigh, East Retford, Eccles, Edmonton, Ellesmere Port, Enfield, Enniskillen, Epsom and Ewell, Erith, Evesham, Eye, Falkirk, Farnham, Farnworth, Faversham, Finchley, Finsbury, Fleetwood, Flint, Folkestone, Fowey, Fulham, Gillingham, Glastonbury, Glossop, Godmanchester, Gosport, Grantham, Gravesend, Great Torrington, Greenock, Greenwich, Guildford, Hackney, Halesowen, Hamilton, Hammersmith, Hampstead, Harrogate, Harrow, Harwich, Haslingden, Haverfordwest, Hayes and Harlington, Hemel Hempstead, Hendon, Hereford, Hertford, Heston and Isleworth, Heywood, Higham Ferrers, High Wycombe, Holborn, Honiton, Hornsey, Hove, Huntingdon, Hyde, Hythe, Ilford, Ilkeston,

Inverness, Islington, Jarrow, Keighley, Kendal, Kensington, Kettering, Kidderminster, Kidwelly, Kilmarnock, King's Lynn, Kingston, Kirkcaldy, Lambeth, Lampeter, Lancaster, Larne, Launceston, Leigh, Leominster, Lewisham, Leyton, Lichfield, Liskeard, Llandovery, Llanelli, Llanfyllin, Lostwithiel, Loughborough, Louth, Lowestoft, Ludlow, Lurgan, Luton, Lyme Regis, Lymington, Lytham St Anne's, Macclesfield, Maidenhead, Maidstone, Malden, Malden and Coombe, Malmesbury, Mansfield, Margate, Marlborough, Marylebone, Middleton, Mitcham, Monmouth, Montgomery, Morley, Morpeth, Mossley, Motherwell and Wishaw, Neath, Nelson, Newark, Newbury, Newcastle-under-Lyme, Newport (IOW), Newtownards, Nuneaton, Okehampton, Oldbury, Ossett, Oswestry, Paddington, Paisley, Pembroke, Penryn, Penzance, Perth, Peterborough, Pontefract, Poole, Poplar, Portadown, Port Talbot, Prestwich, Pudsey, Pwllheli, Radcliffe, Ramsgate, Rawtenstall, Redcar, Reigate, Rhondda, Richmond (Surrey), Richmond (Yorks), Ripon, Rochester, Romford, Romsey, Rowley Regis, Royal Leamington Spa, Royal Tunbridge Wells, Rugby, Rutherglen, Ruthin, Ryde, Rye, Saffron Walden, St Albans, St Ives (Cornwall), St Ives (Hunts), St Pancras, Sale, Salisbury, Saltash, Sandwich, Scarborough, Scunthorpe, Shaftesbury, Shoreditch, Shrewsbury, Slough, Solihull, Southport, South Molton, Southwark, Spenborough, Stafford, Stalybridge, Stamford, Stepney, Stirling, Stockton-on-Tees, Stoke Newington, Stourbridge, Stratford-upon-Avon, Stretford, Sudbury, Surbiton, Sutton and Cheam, Sutton Coldfield, Swindon, Swinton and Pendlebury, Tamworth, Taunton, Tenby, Tenterden, Tewkesbury, Thetford, Tipton, Tiverton, Todmorden, Totnes, Tottenham, Torquay, Truro, Twickenham, Uxbridge, Wallingford, Wallsend, Walthamstow, Wandsworth, Wanstead and Woodford, Wareham, Warwick, Watford, Wednesbury, Wells, Welshpool, Wembley, Wenlock, Westminster, Weston-super-Mare, Weymouth and Melcombe Regis, Whitehaven, Whitley Bay, Widnes, Willesden, Wilton, Wimbledon, Winchester, Windsor, Wisbech, Wokingham, Wood Green, Woolwich, Workington, Worksop, Worthington, Wrexham, Yeovil.

APPENDIX II

Competition statistics

This index presents the results of most of the competitions of major importance or other interest during the period. In that full information is less readily available for the period before about 1860 the list is probably unfairly weighted towards the end of the century. Where no assessor is shown it is likely that no professional assessor was employed. However the name of the corporation is only entered in cases where it is established that no independent qualified architect acted as assessor. Two-stage competitions are indicated †. Cases where the winning competitor was not appointed are indicated *. Where one of the other premiated designs was chosen for construction (sometimes jointly with the winner) the architect is marked @. The place of practice of the architect is shown where known except in the case of the better known practitioners.

Competition statistics

Name of town	Building	Date of competition	Date of building	Number of competitors	Allowance for cost (£) (E=estimate)
Aberdeen	Public buildings	1865	1867–8	3 by invitation	60,000
Acton	Town hall	1903	scheme abandoned 1907	—	52,946
Acton	Town hall	1907	—	40	18,000
Airdrie	Town hall	1910	—	—	10,000
Aldershot	Public offices	1902	—	26	9,000
Altrincham	Town hall	1898	1901	26	4,000
Annan	Town hall	1875	1875–8	7	2,500
Aston	Public offices	1879	1880–	—	18,000 E
Ayr	Town hall	1877	—	4	—
Barnsley	Town hall	1913	—	—	20,000
Barrow-in-Furness	Town hall	1877	1882–7	24	25,000
Barry	Municipal buildings	1902	1906–	—	—
Bath	Municipal buildings	1891	1893–5	19	22,500 E
Belfast	Town hall	1869	1869–	16	20,000 E
Belfast	City hall	1896†	1898–1906	51	1,000,000
Bethnal Green	Town hall	1907	1909–10	—	20,000
Bideford	Municipal buildings	1902	–1906	—	—
Birkdale	Town hall	1904	—	12	12,000
Birkenhead	Town hall	1881†	1883–7	138	42,000
Birmingham	Town hall	1831	1832–61	68	18,000
Birmingham	Council house	1871	1874–9	29	75,000 E
Birmingham	Municipal buildings	1907	1907–12	8 by invitation	137,000 E
Bishop Auckland	Town hall	1860	1860–2	23	3,500 E
Blackburn	Town hall (extension)	1900	1902	6 by invitation	40,180
Blackpool	Town hall	1895	1895–1900	—	8,000
Bolton	Town hall	1865	1866–73	38	70,000
Bootle	Town hall	1879	1800–2	9	6,000

Competition statistics

Result *First premium*	*Second premium*	*Third premium*	*Assessor*
Peddie & Kinnear (Aberdeen)	—	—	—
W. G. Hunt (London)	H. T. Hare	M. B. Adams (London)	J. MacIvar Anderson
—	@ Raffles & Gridley	—	R. N. Shaw
J. Thomson (Airdrie)	G. Arthur (Airdrie)	A. D. Aitkin (Airdrie)	—
C. E. Hutchinson (London)	T. Raffles Davison (London)	Coggin & Wallis (London)	F. T. Baggally
C. A. Hindle (Monton, Eccles)	J. Macnamara (Altrincham)	—	J. Ely (Liverpool)
R. Smith (Glasgow)	S. Shaw (Kendal)	—	—
Alexander & Henman (London & Stockton)	J. G. Dunn (Birmingham)	T. F. Proud (Wolverhampton)	A. Waterhouse
J. Murdoch (Ayr)	Clarke & Bell (Glasgow)	J. Campbell Douglas (Glasgow)	J. J. Burnet
P. H. Topham	—	—	Barnsley Corporation
W. H. Lynn (Belfast)	T. E. Collcutt	Perkin & Bulmer (Leeds)	A. Waterhouse
C. E. Hutchinson & E. Harding Payne (London)	W. H. Ashford (Birmingham)	G. Dickens Lewis (Shrewsbury)	T. E. Collcutt
J. M. Brydon	Burgess & Oliver (London)	T. B. Silcock (Bath)	W. Young
A. Jackson (Belfast)	—	—	—
A. Brumwell Thomas	Stark & Rowntree (Glasgow)	James Miller (Glasgow)	A. Waterhouse
P. Robinson & W. Alban-Jones (London)	Wills & Anderson (London)	—	H. T. Hare
A. J. Dunn (Birmingham)	J. E. Forbes (Birmingham)	Buckland & Farmer (Birmingham)	—
G. Brown (Birkdale)	T. W. Haigh (Birkdale & Liverpool)	R. Marmon	J. W. Beaumont (Manchester)
C. O. Ellison (Liverpool)	H. Hall & J. Eastwood (London)	E. P. Wright (Plymouth) & G. B. Rawcliffe (Barnsley)	C. Barry
J. A. Hansom & E. Welch	Fallows (Birmingham)	Rickman & Hutchinson	Birmingham Improvement Commissioners
1st award W. H. Lynn (Belfast)	R. Yeoville Thomason (Birmingham)	Ward (Birmingham)	A. Waterhouse
2nd award R. Yeoville Thomason (Birmingham)	Ward (Birmingham)	L. de Ville (London)	A. Waterhouse
Ashley & Newman (London)	H. T. Hare	A. N. Prentice	A. Webb & Ingress Bell (consultants)
*J. P. Jones	W. Hill (Leeds)	—	—
*H. T. Hare	Cheers & Smith (Twickenham)	J. G. Gibson (London)	A. N. Bromley (Nottingham)
Woodhouse & Potts (Bolton)	A. Gilbertson (Liverpool)	J. Lovell (London)	—
W. Hill (Leeds) jointly with Woodhouse (Bolton)—placed fifth	Turner (Glasgow)	C. Brodrick	T. L. Donaldson
J. Johnson (London)	J. Lowe (Manchester)	—	an Edinburgh architect

Name of town	*Building*	*Date of competition*	*Date of building*	*Number of competitors*	*Allowance for cost (£) (E=estimate)*
Boston	Athenaeum and exchange	1854	—	15	—
Bradford	St George's hall	1851	1851–3	21	16,000
Bradford	Town hall	1869	1870–3	31	40,000
Bristol	Assize courts	1865	1865–70	—	12,000 E
Bromley	Vestry hall	1904	1904–	43	20,000
Burnley	Town hall	1884	1885–8	—	—
Burslem	Town hall	1846	1852–7	34	—
Burslem	Municipal buildings	1909	1909–11	23	30,000
Bury	Municipal buildings	1891	—	37	60,000
Calne	Town hall	1883	1884–6	limited by invitation	—
Camberwell	Vestry hall	1871	1871–3	24	8,000
Cambridge	Guildhall	1859	1860–2	20	6,000
Cardiff	Town hall	1847	1851	—	8,000
Cardiff	Municipal buildings	1875	1878	3	—
Cardiff	City hall	1897	1900–4	56	125,000 +75,000 (Courts)
Chadderton	Town hall	1910	1912–13	4 limited to local	9,000
Chelsea	Vestry hall	1858	1858–61	15	5,000
Chelsea	Vestry hall	1884	scheme abandoned	3 by invitation	—
Chelsea	Vestry hall	1885	1885–7	52	15,000 E
Chester	Town hall	1864	1864–9	—	16–20,000
Chesterfield	Public hall	1874	—	27	—
Chorley	Town hall	1872	1875–9	63	10,000
Cleethorpes	Public hall	1894	—	—	—
Cleethorpes	Municipal buildings	1896	—	—	—
Colchester	Town hall	1897	1898–1902	6 invited + 2 local	35,560 E
Congleton	Town hall	1864	1864–6	—	5,600 E
Coventry	Municipal buildings	1895	—	8 invited +2 local	—
Coventry	Municipal buildings	1910	1912–20	—	—

Competition statistics

Result *First premium*	*Second premium*	*Third premium*	*Assessor*
Bellamy & Hardy (Lincoln)	Stanton (Boston)	W. Botterill (Hull)	—
Lockwood & Mawson (Bradford)	—	—	—
Lockwood & Mawson (Bradford)	Milnes & France (Bradford)	S. Jackson (Bradford)	Bradford Corporation
1st comp. *E. W. Godwin	E. W. Godwin	E. W. Godwin	A. Waterhouse
2nd comp. R. S. Pope & J. Bindon	E. W. Godwin	Hansom & Son	G. E. Street
R. F. Atkinson	Ashley & Newman (London)	C. H. Norton	J. G. Gibson (London)
H. Holtom (Dewsbury)	G. Corson (Leeds)	G. Nattress & F. Coward (London)	A. Waterhouse
G. T. Robinson (Wolverhampton)	R. W. Armstrong (London)	—	—
S. B. Russell & T. E. Cooper (London)	E. M. Thomas	Warwick & Hall (London)	H. T. Hare
A. N. Bromley (Nottingham)	H. T. Hare	Everard & Pick (Leicester)	Murgatroyd (Manchester)
C. B. Oliver (Bath)	—	—	—
E. Power (London)	Berryman (London)	—	—
Peck & Stephens (Maidstone)	J. & W. Papworth (London)	—	T. L. Donaldson
Horace Jones (Cardiff)	—	—	—
James Seward & Thomas (Cardiff)	James Seward & Thomas (Cardiff)	James Seward & Thomas (Cardiff)	—
Lanchester, Stewart & Rickards (London)	Gibson & Russell (London)	Cooksey & Cox (London)	A. Waterhouse
Taylor & Simister	—	—	Wills (London)
W. W. Pocock	—	—	—
E. Flint (London)	Zephaniah King (London)	J. T. Wimperis (London)	—
J. M. Brydon	W. Leck	Newman & Newman (London)	H. A. Hunt (surveyor)
W. H. Lynn (Belfast)	E. A. Heffer (Liverpool)	—	M. D. Wyatt
Smith & Woodhouse (Manchester)	Rollinson & Masters (Chesterfield)	J. C. Gilbert (Nottingham)	T. C. Hine
Ladds & Powell	—	J. J. Bradshaw (Bolton)	E. G. Paley
J. R. Withers (Shrewsbury)	S. Ford (London)	J. M. Bottomly (Middlesbrough)	—
G. A. Elphick (London)	A. R. Mayston (London)	Cooksey & Cox (London)	—
J. Belcher	Baker, Maye & Rickards (Colchester)	E. W. Mountford	R. N. Shaw
E. W. Godwin	—	—	—
H. Quick (Coventry)	H. T. Hare	H. W. Chattaway (Coventry)	C. Barry
Garrett & Simister with Buckland & Farmer (Birmingham)	W. E. Couch & H. T. B. Barnard (London)	H. J. Rowse (Liverpool)	E. G. Dawber

Name of town	Building	Date of competition	Date of building	Number of competitors	Allowance for cost (£) (E=estimate)
Crewe	Municipal buildings	1902	1903–5	44	14,000
Cromer	Town hall	1889	1890–	28	—
Crompton	Public offices	1892	—	52	—
Darlington	Market and public offices	1861	1863–4	13	—
Darlington	Municipal buildings	1894	1894–	84	—
Darwen	Town hall	1878	1881–2	by invitation	35,000 E
Denbigh	Municipal buildings	1910	—	32	10–15,000 E
Deptford	Town hall	1902	1903–5	45	30,000
Devizes	Corn exchange	1856	—	26	1,500 E
Devonport	Public hall	1879	1888–	18	10,000
Devonport	Guildhall	1913	—	27	95,000
Douglas	Municipal buildings	1896	—	17	10,000
Drogheda	Town hall	1864	—	5 by invitation	—
Dublin	Municipal buildings	1912	—	—	50,000
Dukinfield	Town hall	1898	—	22	10,000
Eastbourne	Town hall	1879	1884–6	22	5,000
East Ham	Public offices	1898	1898–1907	11	55,000
East Leigh	Town hall	1898	—	—	4,500 E
East Retford	Town hall	1864	–1868	18	6,057 E
Edinburgh	Municipal buildings	1886	scheme abandoned	55	66–280,000 (E range)
Enniskillen	Town hall	1897	1898–	—	—
Fulham	Vestry hall	1885	1887	63	20,000
Gateshead	Town hall	1863	1868–	11	12,000
Glasgow	City chambers	1880	scheme rejected	98	150,000
Glasgow	City chambers	1881†	1884–9	125	250,000
Gloucester	Guildhall	1889	1890–2	3 by invitation + 2 local	15,000
Godalming	Municipal buildings	1898	—	8	7,000
Gosport	Town hall	1883	—	7	8,800

Result *First premium*	*Second premium*	*Third premium*	*Assessor*
H. T. Hare	{ Banister Fletcher & Son / A. E. Dixon	Rodney & Denning	Woodhouse & Willoughby (Manchester)
G. J. Skipper (Norwich)	A. T. Scott (Norwich)	—	—
H. Cheetham (Oldham)	Woodhouse & Willoughby (Manchester)	J. Johnson (London)	J. Wild (Oldham)
A. Waterhouse	—	—	—
Clark & Moscrop (Darlington)	H. A. Cheers with J. Aspinall	G. G. Hoskins (Darlington)	J. MacIvar Anderson
C. Bell (London)	E. Salomons & R. S. Wornum (Manchester)	R. K. Freeman (Bolton)	A. Waterhouse
Porter & Elcock (Colwyn Bay)	A. Fairdale (York)	MacIntosh & Newman (London)	Leeming & Leeming (Halifax)
Lanchester, Stewart & Rickards	S. B. Russell & C. E. Mallows (London)	A. J. Gale	J. Belcher
*Phipps (Bath)	@ W. Hill (Leeds)	—	—
S. Knight (London)	Moorshead (Devonport)	—	Grüning
Ashley & Newman (London)	E. Vincent Harris & Moodie	R. Knott & Collins	E. Newton
A. Ardron (London)	(local)	(local)	Woolfall (Liverpool)
Barne (Belfast)	Caldbeck (Dublin)	—	—
McDonnell & Reid (Dublin)	F. G. Hicks (Dublin)	O'Callaghan & Webb (Dublin)	A. Murray
J. Eaton Sons & Cottrell (Ashton-under-Lyme)	Hindley & Marshall (Eccles)	—	—
W. T. Foulkes (Birmingham)	T. D. Barry & Son (Liverpool)	—	Eastbourne borough surveyor
Cheers & Smith (Twickenham)	Spalding & Cross	—	—
*Mitchell & Gutteridge (Southampton)	Colson, Farrow & Nisbett (London)	—	—
Bellamy & Hardy (Lincoln)	—	—	Retford Corporation
Leeming & Leeming (Halifax)	Malcolm Stark (Glasgow)	Simpson & Allen	A. Waterhouse
A. Scott & Son (Drogheda)	W. K. Perry (Dublin)	T. Rowe (Belfast)	T. Drew
*Newman & Newman (London)	—	—	H. Currey (Sutton)
J. Johnstone (Newcastle)	W. Watson (Newcastle)	—	—
G. Corson (Leeds)	Coe & Robinson (London)	E. Clarke (London)	C. Barry
W. Young (London)	Hall & Taylor (London)	W. H. Lynn (Belfast)	C. Barry and Glasgow City Engineer
G. H. Hunt (London)	Medland & Son (Gloucester)	J. F. Trew (Gloucester)	—
Lanchester, Stewart & Rickards	E. R. Robson (London)	Ardron & Dawson (London)	E. W. Mountford
Davis & Emmanuel (London)	W. Yeardye (Gosport)	A. H. Ford (Plymouth)	—

Name of town	*Building*	*Date of competition*	*Date of building*	*Number of competitors*	*Allowance for cost (£) (E=estimate)*
Govan	Town hall	1897	1898–	—	25,000 E
Grantham	Town hall	1866	1867–70	6	6,000 E
Greenock	Municipal buildings	1879	1881–	50	80,000
Greenwich	Public offices	1875	1875–7	21	—
Grimsby	Town hall	1861	1863–4	9	4,500
Grimsby	Town hall	1909	—	—	—
Hackney	Town hall	1864	1864–6	7 by invitation	—
Halifax	Public hall	1896	—	15	25,000
Hammersmith	Town hall	1894	1896–7	—	25,000
Hampstead	Vestry hall	1876	1876–	8	2,800
Handsworth	Public buildings	1876	1876–	29	10–11,000
Harrogate	Town hall	1902	—	75	40,000
Hastings	Town hall	1874	scheme abandoned	35	10,000
Hastings	Town hall	1875	1879–81	32	20,000
Hereford	Town hall	1901	1902–4	46	c. 18,000
Hertford	Municipal buildings	1908	—	98	3,500
High Wycombe	Town hall	1903	1904	—	9,500 E
Hindley	Public offices	1900	–1904	70–80	5,000
Hitchin	Town hall	1898	1898–1901	—	2,500 E
Hull	Town hall	1861	1862–6	40	20,000
Hull	City hall	1903	1906–14	32	100,000
Huyton with Roby	Public offices	1891	—	31	—
Ilkley	Town hall	1904	1906–8	—	10,053
Inverness	Town hall	1875	1878	—	—
Ipswich	Town hall	1864	1866–8	28	10,000
Ipswich	Corn exchange and public hall	1878	scheme rejected	7	3,400 E
Ipswich	Corn exchange and public hall	1879	—	15	24,000 E
Islington	Vestry hall	1856	1858	77	5,500 E
Keighley	Town hall	1865	1865	—	6,000 E

Result *First premium*	*Second premium*	*Third premium*	*Assessor*
J. Thomson & Sandilands (Glasgow)	Dykes & Robertson (Glasgow)	W. H. Howie (Glasgow)	—
W. Watkins (Lincoln)	—	—	E. G. Paley (with G. G. Scott as adviser)
H. & E. Barclay (Glasgow)	Beatson Habershon (Ealing)	Lambie, Moffat & Aitken (Edinburgh)	C. Barry
Wallen (architect to the Local Board)	Kersy & Garrett (London)	H. Roberts (London)	—
Bellamy & Fowler (Lincoln & Louth)	—	—	—
Eade, Johns & Browne	Withers & Meredith	Rigby, Oliver & Phipps	Sir A. Gelder
*Sancton Wood	—	—	—
Cheers & Smith (Twickenham)	H. & D. Barclay (Glasgow)	Farrow & Nisbett (London)	—
J. H. Richardson	E. W. Mountford	Isaacs & Florence	—
Kendall & Mew (London)	C. Bell (London)	F. W. Hunt	—
Alexander & Henman (Stockton)	R. Walker (London)	W. Wykes (Birmingham)	R. Yeoville Thomason (Birmingham)
H. T. Hare	Waddington, Sons & Dunkerley (London)	Heazell & Son (Nottingham)	J. MacIvar Anderson
Jeffery, Skiller & Wells (Hastings) (appointed for new scheme 1875)	E. A. Heffer (Liverpool)	Lee & Smith (London)	Sussex County Surveyor
—	—	—	Hastings Corporation
*MacIntosh & Newman (London)	H. T. Fowler (Barrow)	G. H. Stanger (Wolverhampton)	T. Blashill
—	—	—	J. P. Briggs
Bateman, Bateman & Hale (Birmingham)	F.H.— (London)	J. E. Forbes (London)	T. E. Collcutt
Heaton, Ralph & Heaton (Manchester)	—	—	—
@G. Lucas	—	—	@E. W. Mountford
C. Brodrick	Lockwood & Mawson (Bradford)	Green & Delville (London)	Sir William Tite
Russell, Cooper, Davis & Mallows (London)	Treadwell & Martin	A. Brumwell Thomas	T. Blashill
H. A. Cheers (Twickenham)	Boney & Wainwright (London)	Woolfall & Eccles (London)	—
W. Bakewell (Leeds)	R. T. Longden (Burslem)	Warwick & Hall (London)	G. B. Bulmer
A. Lawrie	—	—	D. Bryce (A. Lawrie to check quantities)
Bellamy & Hardy (Lincoln)	—	—	—
*H. Cheston	—	—	—
Brightwen Binyon (Ipswich)	—	—	—
*H. E. Cooper	@T. Allom	—	Islington Vestry
G. R. Green (London)	Bulmer & Holtom (Dewsbury)	—	—

Name of town	*Building*	*Date of competition*	*Date of building*	*Number of competitors*	*Allowance for cost (£) (E=estimate)*
Kensington	Vestry hall	1877	1878–80	62	18,000
King's Lynn	Municipal buildings	1894	1894	—	—
Lambeth	Municipal buildings	1904	1904–8	143	35,000
Leamington	Town hall	1881	1882–4	40	—
Leeds	Town hall	1850	1853–8	16	15,000
Leeds	Municipal buildings	1876	1877–	26	60,000
Leek	Town hall	1887	—	3	—
Leicester	Town hall	1871	scheme rejected	—	25,000
Leicester	Town hall	1873	1874–6	25	30,000
Leyton	Town hall	1880	–1882	10 by invitation	4,000
Liverpool	St George's hall	1839	1841–56	—	—
Liverpool	Assize courts	1839			
Llandudno	Town hall	1894	1898–1902	33	10,000
Llanelli	Town hall	1892	–1896	25	—
London	County hall	1906†	1911–	25 for second stage	1,706,000 E
Lowestoft	Town hall	1869	–1873	24	2,500
Manchester	Assize courts	1859	1859–64	—	—
Manchester	Exchange	1866	1869–74	52	250,000 E
Manchester	Town hall	1867†	1868–77	136	250,000 E
Manchester	Police courts	1868	1868–71	4 by invitation	25,000
Manchester	Library and art gallery	1911	scheme abandoned	—	70,000 E
Marylebone	Town hall	1911	1912–18	181	70,000
Middlesbrough	Town hall	1882	1883–8	10	70,000
Middleton	Town hall	1914	—	107	—
Morley	Town hall	1891	1892–5	—	15,000
Motherwell	Town hall	1886	1886	14	6,000 E
Newbury	Town hall	1875	1876	—	4,000 E
Newcastle-under-Lyme	Public buildings	1885	1885–9	—	10,000
Newport (Mon.)	Town hall	1882	—	38	—

Result *First premium*	*Second premium*	*Third premium*	*Assessor*
R. Walker (London)	J. J. Thomson & F. Davis	E. C. Robins	J. Whichcord
P. Tree & I. Price (London)	G. Sedger (London)	—	—
Warwick & Hall (London)	H. P. Burke-Downing	Crouch, Butler & Savage (Birmingham)	H. T. Hare
J. Cundall	R. K. Freeman (Bolton)	Scrivener & Son (Hanley)	—
C. Brodrick	Lockwood & Mawson (Bradford)	Young & Lovatt (Wolverhampton)	Sir Charles Barry
G. Corson (Leeds)	D. Brade (Kendal)	Hill & Swann (Leeds)	F. P. Cockerell
*A. Waterhouse	J. W. Critchlow (Leek)	@Sugden & Son (Leek)	—
*Barnard & Smith (Leicester)	Goddard & Spiers (Leicester)	Innocent & Brown (Sheffield)	G. E. Street
F. J. Hames (London)	Ordish & Traylen (Leicester)	J. O. & G. G. Scott	T. H. Wyatt
*T. E. Knightley (London)	Wilson, Son & Aldwinckle (London)	C. W. Wimperis (London)	—
		—	—
H. L. Elmes			
T. B. Silcock (Bath)	J. H. Currey (Sutton, Surrey)	—	T. M. Lockwood
—			
*Simon & Tweedie (Edinburgh & Manchester)	@W. Griffiths (Llanelly)	—	C. Barry
R. Knott (London)	—	—	R. N. Shaw and London County Architect
*W. H. Spaull (Oswestry)	@W. O. Chambers (London)	—	—
A. Waterhouse	Robinson	—	—
Mills & Murgatroyd (Manchester)	Mills & Murgatroyd (Manchester)	Lowe (Manchester)	—
A. Waterhouse	Speakman & Charlesworth (Manchester)	J. O. Scott	G. Godwin (first stage) T. L. Donaldson and G. E. Street (second stage)
T. Worthington (others Speakman & Charlesworth, Clegg & Knowles and E. Salomons all of Manchester			Manchester Corporation
—	—	—	—
T. E. Cooper (London)	Wallis & Bowden	North & Robin (London)	H. T. Hare
G. G. Hoskins (Darlington)	G. Nichols (London)	Lacy W. Ridge (London)	A. Waterhouse
A. G. Hornsell (London)	Briggs, Wolstenholme & Thorneley (Liverpool)	F. D. Clapham & Symons Jeune (London)	—
Holtom & Fox (Dewsbury)	Morley & Woodhouse (Bradford)	W. Hanstock (Batley)	—
J. B. Wilson (Glasgow)	H. B. Steel (Glasgow)	Wilson & Stewart (Glasgow)	—
J. H. Money (Newbury)	—	—	—
@Sugden, Blood & Sugden (Leek)	@Chapman & Snape	—	T. M. Lockwood
@E. A. Lansdowne (Newport)	@T. M. Lockwood (Chester)	—	Newport Corporation

Name of town	*Building*	*Date of competition*	*Date of building*	*Number of competitors*	*Allowance for cost (£) (E=estimate)*
Northampton	Town hall	1860	1861–4	—	12,000
Nottingham	Guildhall	1883	1883–8	7	100,000
Ormskirk	Municipal buildings	1897	1897–9	24	—
Ossett	Town hall	1904	1906–8	33	12,000
Oxford	Town hall	1892	1893–	135	50,000
Paisley	Town hall	1875	1879–82	60	20,000
Pendleton	Town hall	1865	1865–8	6 by invitation	9,000
Penzance	Town hall	1836	1836–7	2	—
Perth	City hall	1907	1909–	136	25,000
Pitlochry	Public hall	1898	1900	16	2,366 E
Plumstead (Woolwich)	Municipal buildings	1899	1903–6	40	35,000
Plymouth	Guildhall	1869	1869–74	26	25,000
Pontefract	Town hall	1880	1881–3	59	7,000
Pontypridd	Public offices	1903	—	55	—
Poplar	Public offices	1867	1869–	43	6,080 E
Preston	Town hall	1854	1862–7	—	30,000
Radcliffe	Town hall	1907	1911	54 (Lancs only)	12,000
Reading	Town hall	1877	1879–82	—	—
Rhyl	Town hall	1874	1874–	5 by invitation	—
Richmond (Yorks)	Town hall	1889	1891–3	8 by invitation	10,000
Rochdale	Town hall	1863	1866–71	27	20,000
Rotherhithe	Town hall	1895	1895–7	6 by invitation	15,000
Rugby	Municipal buildings	1897	—	39	—
Rugeley	Town hall	1876	1878–9	9	6,500
St Helens	Town hall	1871	1873–9	7	28,000 E
St Mary Abbot's	Public offices	1876	—	3	1,200 E
St Pancras	Town hall	1892	—	60	—
Saltcoats	Town hall	1891	1892	17	—
Seacombe	Public offices	1905	—	96	—
Sheffield	Town hall	1890†	1890–7	179	80,000

Result First premium	Second premium	Third premium	Assessor
* —	@E. W. Godwin	—	Sir William Tite
{Verity & Hunt (London)@ F. Holden (Manchester)*	—	G. Corson (Leeds)	A. Waterhouse
Willinck & Thicknesse (Liverpool)	H. E. Peach (Southport)	R. J. M'Beath (Sale)	J. Dodd (Liverpool)
W. Hanstock (Batley)	—	—	J. Kirk (Huddersfield)
H. T. Hare	E. Runtz	—	—
*Rennison & Scott (Paisley)	J. Robertson (Inverness)	H. Higgins (Glasgow)	Mathieson
A. Darbyshire (Manchester)	—	—	—
W. Harris (Bristol)	Inman	—	—
H. E. Clifford (Glasgow)	Stewart & Paterson (Glasgow)	J. Campbell Douglas & A. N. Paterson (Glasgow)	J. J. Burnet
Alexander & Ness (Dundee)	J. Menzies (Pitlochry)	J. Leonard (Pitlochry)	Prof. Gourlay
Hall, Cooper & Davis (London)	H. I. Potter (London)	@A. Brumwell Thomas	—
Norman & Hine (Devonport) (appointed with E. W. Godwin as consultant)	C. F. Hayward (Exeter)	—	A. Waterhouse
Perkin & Bulmer (Leeds)	Roper & Brown (Manchester)	—	G. Corson (Leeds)
H. T. Hare	S. D. Adshead (London)	A. Colbourne Little (London)	J. S. Gibson
@W. A. Hills & Fletcher (late Local Board Surveyor)	@Harston & Harston	G. A. Wilson (London)	Sancton Wood
*W. Hill (Leeds)	W. B. Gingell (Bristol)	—	Stewart (Liverpool)
W. M. Gillow (Manchester)	D. Bird (Manchester)	H. Lord (Manchester)	F. Willoughby (Manchester)
*W. T. Sams	—	—	@T. Lainson (Brighton) adviser on competition plans
Wood & Turner (Barrow)	—	—	—
Elkington & Son (London)	T. Verity (London)	—	J. Edmeston
W. H. Crossland (Leeds)	J. W. Best (Bolton)	J. W. Maxwell (Bury)	Rochdale Corporation
Murray & Foster	C. Bell (London)	—	Rotherhithe Corporation
North & Hawke (London)	D. Bird (Manchester)	—	Rugby Corporation
W. T. Foulkes (Birmingham)	W. A. Benney (Rugeley)	Dodd (Reading)	—
H. Sumners (Liverpool)	—	—	—
E. Power & Wheeler (London)	others A. Williams and Harston		—
W. Harrison (London)	M. Stark & Robinson (Glasgow)	Gibson & Russell (London)	PRIBA
all designs rejected—design from plan by corporation			—
Briggs, Wolstenholme & Thorneley (Liverpool)	A. R. Jemmett & G. T. M'Combie (London)	W. Ashford & Gladding (Birmingham)	Emerson
E. W. Mountford	6 premiated from sketch competition		A. Waterhouse

Name of town	*Building*	*Date of competition*	*Date of building*	*Number of competitors*	*Allowance for cost (£) (E=estimate)*
Shipley	Municipal buildings	1914	—	—	20,000 E
Shoreditch	Town hall	1899	1901	4	—
Sligo	Town hall	1864	—	—	5,000 E
Slough	Public buildings	1885	scheme abandoned	26	—
Slough	Public buildings	1886	1886	—	—
Smethwick	Municipal offices	1904	—	5 local	15,000 E
Southend	Municipal buildings	1898	—	6 by invitation	40,000
South Shields	Town hall	1869	—	24	—
South Shields	Municipal buildings	1890	scheme abandoned	33	10,000
South Shields	Municipal buildings	1900	scheme abandoned	72	20,000
South Shields	Municipal buildings	1903	1905–10	6 by invitation	35,000
Staines	Town hall	1876	scheme abandoned	25	2,500
Staines	Town hall	1879	1880–1	c. 50	3,500
Stockport	Town hall	1903	1904–8	—	60,000
Stoke-on-Trent	Town hall	1909	1910	80	30,000
Stratford (London)	Vestry hall	1867	1867–9	30	12,000
Stretford	Public offices	1886	—	—	—
Sunderland	Town hall	1874	scheme abandoned	—	—
Sunderland	Town hall	1874	–1879	—	—
Sunderland	Municipal buildings	1886	1890	23	27,000 E
Sunderland	Town hall extension	1904	—	30	30,000
Surbiton	Municipal buildings	1897	—	26	5,000
Sutton	Public offices	1895	—	—	—
Sutton Coldfield	Town hall	1903	1905–6	40	8,000 E
Taunton	Town hall	1898	—	13	—
Tiverton	Town hall	1861	1862–4	60	3,000
Wakefield	Town hall	1877	1877–80	—	35,000
Walsall	Council house	1892	scheme abandoned	—	—
Walsall	Council house	1900	1905	5	55,000
Walton-on-Thames	Municipal buildings	1901	1902	9	—

Result *First premium*	*Second premium*	*Third premium*	*Assessor*
Anderton & Bailey (Shipley)	Clark & Moscrop (Darlington)	R. T. Wilson (Bradford)	F. E. P. Edwards
W. G. Hunt (London)	Spalding & Cross	—	—
W. Hague (Dublin)	W. J. Barr (Belfast)	Lanyon, Lynn & Lanyon (Belfast)	Sir J. Benson
H. A. Cheers (Twickenham)	T. R. Richards (London)	F. Hemings (London)	F. W. Albany (Reading)
F. W. Albany (Reading)	—	—	T. R. Richards (London)
F. J. Gill	—	—	T. E. Collcutt
*J. M. Brydon	H. T. Hare	—	—
J. Johnstone (Newcastle)	J. Johnson (London)	—	—
Perkin & Bulmer (Leeds)	Clark & Moscrop (Darlington)	J. H. Morton (South Shields)	G. G. Hoskins
E. E. Fetch (London)	R. Savage (London)	Louis Ambler	—
E. E. Fetch (London)	—	—	J. Belcher
Byrne (Windsor)	—	—	—
J. Johnson (London)	—	—	—
A. Brumwell Thomas	Willoughby & Langham (Manchester)	H. T. Hare	T. E. Collcutt
*Garrett & Simister	Warwick & Hall (London)	W. Heywood (Birmingham)	L. Stokes
L. Angell (Local Board Surveyor) and J. Giles	G. A. Wilson	H. S. Legg	—
*J. Gibbons (Magnall & Littlewood appointed to build Gibbons' design)	C. McLeod	—	—
J. Johnstone (Newcastle)	E. H. Godwin	J. King James (Hull) & F. Caws (Sunderland)	—
*E. H. Godwin	J. P. Pritchard (Darlington)	E. M. Gibbs (Sheffield)	—
B. Binyon (Ipswich)	Grayson & Ould (Liverpool)	Doubleday & Caws (Wolverhampton)	A. Waterhouse
Wills & Anderson (London)	R. Hemingway & A. W. Bradshaw (Nottingham)	S. G. Goss & H. Burgess (London)	J. MacIvar Anderson
*C. W. Wimperis & H. S. East (London)	@Forsyth & Maule (London)	W. E. Hewitt & S. Ryan Tenison	E. W. Mountford
Currey & Tatlock (Sutton)	H. T. Hare	—	R. P. Spiers
Mayston & Eddison (London)	H. A. Hall (London)	W. F. Edwards (Birmingham)	J. A. Cossins
Sansom & Cottam (Taunton)	J. M. Brydon	H. T. Hare	E. W. Mountford
H. Lloyd (Bristol)	Hayward (Exeter)	—	—
T. E. Collcutt	F. Simpson	Austin, Johnson & Hicks	G. E. Street
J. R. Withers (Shrewsbury)	D. Arkell (Birmingham)	—	—
J. S. Gibson (London)	W. A. Pite & R. S. Balfour (London)	Cranfield & Potter (London)	J. MacIvar Anderson
MacIntosh & Newman (London)	G. Sedger (London)	S. Tatchell (London)	—

Name of town	*Building*	*Date of competition*	*Date of building*	*Number of competitors*	*Allowance for cost (£) (E=estimate)*
Wednesbury	Town hall	1870	1872	25	—
West Bromwich	Town hall	1871	1874–5	—	40,000
West Bromwich	Market	1871	1874–5	—	—
West Bromwich	Library	1871	1874–5	—	—
West Bromwich	Baths	1871	1874–5	—	—
Westminster (St James)	Vestry hall	1880	1882–3	11	15,000
Willesden	Public offices	1886	1887	54	6,000
Winchester	Guildhall	1870	1872–3	46	11,000
Wolverhampton	Town hall	1866	1869–71	19	25,000 E
Yardley	Public offices	1898	1899	—	—
Yarmouth	Town hall	1878	1878–82	40	17–20,000
Yeovil	Town hall	1847	1849	—	—

Result *First premium*	*Second premium*	*Third premium*	*Assessor*
J. Loxton (Wednesbury) (member of Local Board)	S. Horton (Wednesbury)	G. B. Nicholls (West Bromwich)	—
Alexander & Henman (Stockton)	W. Hale (Birmingham)	—	Ewan Christian
Weller & Proud (Wolverhampton)	—	—	Ewan Christian
Weller & Proud (Wolverhampton)	J. Hewitt (London)	—	Ewan Christian
Pincher	W. Hale (Birmingham)	—	Ewan Christian
Lee & Smith (London)	J. E. Trollope	Hunt & Steward	C. Barry
*E. Harnor (London)	Newman & Newman (London)	—	Ewan Christian
Jeffery & Skiller (Hastings)	J. Newman, Ross & Minns (London)	J. J. O'Callaghan (Dublin)	—
*G. Bidlake (Wolverhampton)	@E. Bates (Manchester)	—	A. Waterhouse
A. Harrison (Birmingham)	J. R. Nicholls (Birmingham) Ingall & Son (Birmingham)	—	W. Martin
J. B. Pearce (Norwich)	G. Nattress & Sedger (London)	B. Binyon (Ipswich)	E. Boardman (Norwich)
T. Stent (Yeovil)	—	—	—

APPENDIX III

A chronological list of town halls, 1820–1914

This list includes all the major buildings of the period and the majority of other typical buildings; however, it cannot be considered exhaustive. I have also included certain other buildings such as Manchester assize courts (1859–64) and Liverpool cotton exchange (1904) that are closely related to the concept of a town hall in either their purpose or their clients.

Dates: The first given is that of the commencement of the building wherever possible. This may be a year or even several years after the relevant competition (see Appendix II). Where a second date is given it is that of the opening of the building.

Building name: I have used the original name of the building, though in a number of cases the titles are now changed or absorbed in another building.

Dates of extensions: The majority of town halls have been modified or altered to some extent. Dates are included here only when major alterations by named architects are known to have taken place within the period.

Dimensions: The variation in the shape of city centre sites all too frequently renders a comparison of overall dimensions unhelpful; yet precise figures for the total superficial area are equally hard to come by. I have therefore isolated the dimensions that relate most closely to the effort to display civic pride, and given those where they are known. Where only one figure is given in the overall column it is that of the main frontage. Although the measurements of the hall provide a surer basis for the comparison of civic magnificence, it should be remembered that the buildings listed range from those containing merely a hall to those in which the hall is a relatively minor feature. Where there is more than one hall the measurements are those of the larger hall.

Cost: It is possible to distinguish several types of figure among those given for the cost of these buildings. I have noted the allowance set by the corporation, estimates of the cost of particular designs (usually supplied by the architect) and the final cost. Since allowances were frequently increased, I have entered the first firm figure mentioned wherever more than one figure is known. The estimates given are either those of the architect or the contractor's tender, which frequently did not include the cost of fittings and furnishing. The final cost is given precisely wherever possible, but I have had to rely heavily on published figures which are frequently underestimates.

Population: The raw population figures are given as a rough indication of the size of the town at the time of building, though in many cases the rate of growth is a more significant factor. Figures are for the preceding census with the exception of 1820 when the figures are for the census of 1821.

Architects: With the exception of the better known names I have indicated the place of practice of the architect wherever possible.
* denotes an architect known to have been employed as the local borough surveyor or in some similar capacity.

A chronological list of town halls, 1820–1914

Dates	Towns	Building name	Dates of extensions	Dimensions in ft overall	Main hall
1820	Aberdeen	Town house			
1820	Aberystwyth	Assembly rooms			
1820	Kington	Town hall	1845		
c. 1820–5	Ryde	Town hall			
1820–1	Wakefield	Public rooms			
1821	Bourne	Town hall			
1821–3	Devonport	Town hall			
1821	Guisborough	Town hall	1870		
1821	Margate	Town hall and market			
1822–7	Bristol	Council house	1828		
1822–3	Cullen (Banff)	Town hall and post office			
1822–5	Manchester	Town hall	–1843		
1822–4	Preston	Corn exchange and public hall	1882		
1823–4	London St Andrew Holborn	Vestry hall			
1823–4	Macclesfield	Town hall and assembly rooms	1869–71		
1823–6	Newcastle-upon-Tyne	Guildhall			
1824	Market Drayton	Market			
1824	Spilsby	Sessions house			
1825	Abergavenny	Market			
1825	Andover	Guildhall			
1825–9	Bolton	Exchange			
1825–7	Kendal	Assembly rooms			
1825–7	Salford	Town hall and market	1849, '62, '75, 1908		58 × 28 × 23
1825–7	Swansea	Town hall	1852		
1826	Alnwick	Northumberland hall			
1826–8	Barnstaple	Guildhall			
1826	Bolton (Little)	Town hall			
1826	Boston	Assembly rooms			
1826	Bridgwater	Market			
1826	Droitwich	Town hall			
1826–32	Kirkcaldy	Town hall			
1826	Oundle	Town hall			
1827	Leith	Town hall			
1828–30	Ayr	Municipal buildings	1880		
1828	Bradford	Public rooms			
1828–30	Derby	Town hall and market			
1828	Sudbury	Town hall			
1829–33	St Albans	Town hall and courts			
1830–2	Brighton	Town hall			
1830–1	Chorlton-on-Medlock	Town hall			
1830–1	Haddington	Town hall (spire)			
c. 1830	London St Martin in the Fields	Vestry hall			
1830–1	Stalybridge	Town hall	1882		
1830	Warminster	Town hall			
1831–2	Caernarvon	Market			

Height of tower	*Cost in £*				
	Allowance	*Estimate*	*Total*	*Architect*	*Population*
				J. Smith (Aberdeen)	26,484
				G. S. Repton (London)	3,556
				B. Wishlade (Kington)	1,980
				J. Sanderson (London)	3,945
				—	10,764
				Bryan Browning (Thurlby)	2,029
				J. Foulston (Plymouth)	39,621
				—	1,912
				E. White (Margate)	7,843
				Sir Robert Smirke	52,889
				W. Robertson (Elgin)	1,452
			40,000	Francis Goodwin (Manchester)	133,788
				—	24,575
				J. H. Good*	26,492
				Francis Goodwin (Manchester)	17,746
				J. Dobson (Newcastle)	35,181
				—	4,426
				H. E. Kendall (London)	1,234
				J. Westcott (Ailburton, Glos)	3,244
				J. Langdon (London)	25,142
				R. Lane (Manchester)	31,295
				G. Webster (Kendal)	8,984
			13,000	R. Lane (Manchester)	25,772
				J. Collingwood (Gloucester)	10,255
				—	5,927
				T. Lee (Barnstaple)	5,097
			3,000	—	9,258
				—	10,373
				J. Bowen (Bridgwater)	6,155
				—	2,176
				W. Burn (Edinburgh)	4,452
				—	2,150
				R. & R. Dickson (Edinburgh)	25,990
				T. Hamilton (Edinburgh)	7,455
				Francis Goodwin (Manchester)	13,064
				M. Habershon (London)	17,423
				T. Ginn (Sudbury)	3,956
				G. Smith (London)	4,472
				T. Cooper (Brighton)	24,429
				R. Lane (Manchester)	8,209
				—	—
				John Nash	5,255
			4,100	Fairbairn & Lillie	1,609
				E. Blore	5,612
				J. Lloyd (Caernarvon)	7,642

A chronological list of town halls, 1820–1914

Dates	Towns	Building name	Dates of extensions	Dimensions in ft overall	Main hall
1831	Leamington	Town hall			
1832	Beverley	Guildhall (façade)			
1832–61	Birmingham	Town hall	1846–61		92 × 65 × 65 extended to 145 1846
1832	Settle	Town hall			
1832–3	Sheffield	Town hall (extensions)			
1832	Upton-upon-Severn	Town hall			
1833	Basingstoke	Town hall			
1833	Ellesmere	Town hall			
1833–4	Evesham	Town hall (extensions)	1884–5		
1834	Bradford	Court house			
1834	Helston	Guildhall			
1834	Leeds	Court house			
1834	Ripon	Public rooms			
1834	Stoke-on-Trent	Town hall	1842, '50, 1910		
1835–6	Mansfield	Town hall			
1836	Arundel	Town hall			
1836	Gravesend	Town hall (altered)			
1836	Lutterworth	Town hall			
1836	Middlesbrough	Exchange			
1836–7	Penzance	Town hall			
1837–8	Bodmin	Court house			
1837–9	Flint	Town hall			
1837	Helston	Market house			
1838	Bampton	Town hall			
1838–9	Forres	Town hall			
1838	Glossop	Town hall			
1838	Newcastle-upon-Tyne	Town hall	1858–63		
1838	Oakham	Agricultural hall			
1839	Bodmin	Market house			
1839–41	Bristol	Victoria rooms			
1839	Hitchin	Town hall			
1839–40	Plymouth	Town hall			
1839–40	St Helens	Town hall			
1839	Stamford	Corn exchange			
1840	Ashton-under-Lyne	Town hall	1878		
1840	Church Stretton	Market house			
1840	Cirencester	Town hall (rebuilt)		38 × 50 (high)	
1840	Hoyland Nether	Town hall			
1840	Shrewsbury	Music hall			
1840	Tewkesbury	Town hall (extensions)	1891		
1841–3	Boston	Sessions house			
1841–2	Derby	Town hall			
1841–56	Liverpool	St George's hall	1879		169 × 74 × 75
1841	Oldham	Town hall	1909	68 × 66	32 × 64

A chronological list of town halls, 1820–1914

Height of tower	Cost in £ Allowance	Estimate	Total	Architect	Population
				—	6,209
				C. Mountain (Hull)	8,302
		18,000	25,000 (40,000—1861)	J. A. Hansom & E. Welch	146,986
				G. Webster (Kendal)	1,627
				W. Hurst (Doncaster)	91,692
				—	2,343
				L. W. Wyatt (London)	3,581
				—	7,057
				—	3,991
				J. Richardby (Bradford)	23,223
				G. Wightwick (Plymouth)	3,293
				R. D. Chantrell (Leeds)	123,393
				—	12,882
				H. Ward (Stafford)	37,220
			8,000		
				J. & W. A. Nicholson	9,426
				R. Abraham (London)	2,803
				A. H. Wilds (Brighton)	5,097
				J. A. Hansom	2,262
				G. Burlison (Darlington)	154
				W. Harris (Bristol)	6,563
				H. Burt	3,782
				J. Welch (St Asaph)	2,216
				W. Harris (Bristol)	3,293
				G. Wilkinson (Witney)	2,514
				W. Robertson (Elgin)	3,424
				Weightman & Hadfield (Liverpool)	18,080
				J. & B. Green (Newcastle)	42,760
				—	2,390
				W. Harris (Bristol)	3,782
				C. Dyer (London)	103,886
				T. Bellamy	5,211
				G. Wightwick (Plymouth)	75,534
				A. Y. & G. Williams (Liverpool)	14,199
				Rev. H. de Foe Baker	5,837
				Young & Lee	33,597
				—	1,302
				P. F. Robinson (London)	5,420
				—	1,670
				E. H. Haycock (Shrewsbury)	23,492
				—	5,780
			10,000	C. Kirk (Sleaford)	12,942
				M. H. Habershon (London)	32,741
	80,000	90,000	300,000	H. L. Elmes	286,487
			6,500	J. Butterworth (Manchester)	42,595

A chronological list of town halls, 1820–1914

Dates	*Towns*	*Building name*	*Dates of extensions*	*Dimensions in ft overall*	*Main hall*
1842	Chipping Norton	Town hall			
1842	Holmfirth	Town hall			
1842	Spalding	Sessions house			
1843–6	Bristol	Guildhall			
1843–5	Colchester	Town hall			26 × —
1844	Arbroath	Town hall (extensions)			
c. 1844	Birkenhead	Town hall and market			
1844–5	Colchester	Corn exchange			78 × 47
1844	London	Mansion house (alterations)			90 × 60
1844	Middlewich	Town hall			
1844–5	North Shields	Town hall	1894		
1845	Belfast	Assembly room (alterations)	1895		
1845	Coventry	Market			
1845	Kington	Town hall			
1845	Perth	City hall			seat 1400
1845	Romford	Corn exchange		51 × 168	60 × 34
1845	Tynemouth	Town hall			
1845	Wetherby	Town hall			
1846 (proposed)	Bristol	Town hall			
1846	Bury St Edmunds	Guildhall (alterations)			
1846	Carmarthen	Market			
1846	Dorchester	Guildhall (extensions)			
1846	Ely	Market and corn exchange			
1846 (proposed)	Hull	Markets	scheme abandoned		
1846 (proposed)	Leominster	Town hall and assembly rooms			
1846–8	Lichfield	Guildhall			
1846	Liverpool	Town hall (alterations)			
1846	Luton	Town hall	1893		
1846	Middlesbrough	Town hall and market		100 × 60	55 × 24
c. 1846	St Austell	Town hall			
1846	Saxmundham	Town hall			
1846–7	Truro	Public hall and market		90 × 105	
1846	Wickham Market	Public building			
1847	Birkenhead	Market			
1847	Birmingham	Corn exchange		172 × 40	110 × 40 × 50
1847–51	Cardiff	Town hall		130 × 55 (high)	70 × 36 × 25
1847	Darlington	Public buildings			
1847–8	Doncaster	Guildhall		152 × 63 × 46	
1847–9	Doncaster	Markets			
1847	Dudley	Court house			
1847–8	Lincoln	Corn exchange	1878		
1847–8	Lytham St Anne's	Market house	1872	100 × 36 × 24	
1847	Melksham	Market house and town hall			

A chronological list of town halls, 1820–1914

Height of tower	*Cost in £ Allowance*	*Estimate*	*Total*	*Architect*	*Population*
				G. S. Repton (London)	3,031
				—	13,400
				C. Kirk (Sleaford)	7,721
				R. S. Pope (Bristol)	122,296
			6,000	R. Brandon & J. Blore	17,790
				D. Smith (Dundee)	7,218
			10,000	C. Rampling (Birkenhead)	8,223
			2,400	—	17,532
				J. B. Bunning*	347,061
				—	4,755
				J. Dobson (Newcastle)	7,509
				C. Lanyon (Belfast)	—
				—	30,179
				B. Wishlade (Kington)	3,131
				W. M. McKenzie*	20,167
				—	5,317
				J. Dobson (Newcastle)	11,890
				—	1,433
				—	123,188
				—	12,168
				F. E. H. Fowler	9,526
				—	5,402
				—	6,825
			10–20,000	(C. Brodrick and Lockwood & Mawson among competitors)	65,670
				J. Clayton (Hereford)	4,846
				J. Potter II (Lichfield)	6,587
				Ingram	286,656
			4,000	—	5,827
			2,000	W. Lambie Moffat (Doncaster)	5,463
				C. Eales (London)	10,320
				—	1,097
				C. Eales (London)	9,901
				—	1,400
			26,000	—	8,223
		5,000		S. Hemming	182,922
	8,000	11,690		Sir Horace Jones* and Johnson (Cardiff)	9,714
				—	11,033
		17,000		J. Butterfield*	10,455
	16,000			—	10,455
				—	31,157
				W. A. Nicholson	13,411
30				C. Reed (Liverpool)	2,082
				—	6,236

A chronological list of town halls, 1820–1914

Dates	*Towns*	*Building name*	*Dates of extensions*	*Dimensions in ft overall*	*Main hall*
1847	Merthyr Tydfil	Town hall			
1847	Newark	Corn exchange			
1847 (proposed)	Sheffield	Town hall	1891		seat 10,000
1847 (proposed)	Sheffield	Corn exchange	1870 (proposed)		
1847	Sheffield	Markets			
1847–9	Yeovil	Town hall			58 × 35 × 25
1848	Botley	Market hall		40 × 25 × 17	
1848	Bridlington	Public rooms			
1848–9	Edinburgh	Corn exchange		152 × 96	
1848	Lewes	Corn exchange		156 × 33 × 36	
1848	Malmesbury	Market and assembly rooms			
1848	Peterborough	Corn exchange			
1848 (proposed)	St Ives	Assembly rooms			
1848	Saffron Walden	Corn exchange			
1848	Swansea	Town hall			
1848	Tavistock	Guildhall			
1848	Worcester	Corn exchange (Angel St)		75 × 60 × 48	
1849	Altrincham	Town hall	1879		
1849	Brentford	Town hall and market			
1849–50	Brigg	Corn exchange			
1849	Carlisle	Town hall (alterations)			
1849	Gainsborough	Corn exchange			
1849	Hereford	Corn exchange		66 × 43 × 15	
1849 (proposed)	Knighton	Buttercross			seat 200–300
1849–50	Lichfield	Corn exchange			
1849–50	Manchester	Royal exchange	1866		
1849	Northampton	Corn exchange			
1849	Stourbridge	Corn exchange			
1849	Worcester	Corn exchange (St Martin's)			
1850	Birmingham	Exhibition hall			
1850	Bury	Athenaeum and public buildings			102 × 43 × 28
1850	Chippenham	Market and public hall			
1850	Heywood	Municipal buildings			
1850	Ipswich	Corn exchange and public hall			66 × 78 × 22
1850	Kidderminster	Guildhall (alterations)			
1850 (proposed)	Leicester	Market			
1850	Leighton Buzzard	Town hall		68 × 20	
1850–1	Liverpool	Corn exchange			
c. 1850	Mansfield	Court house			

A chronological list of town halls, 1820–1914

Height of tower	*Cost in £* *Allowance*	*Estimate*	*Total*	*Architect*	*Population*
				—	42,917
			7,000	Duesbury	10,220
				Flockton, Lee & Flockton (Sheffield)	109,597
				—	109,597
				—	109,597
		3,500		T. Stent (Yeovil)	6,302
			500	C. Pink (Hambleton)	904
			7,000	Worth (Sheffield)	5,162
			7,800	Cousin*	132,977
				W. Dunk	9,282
				—	6,674
				S. Hemming	6,991
				G. G. Day	8,645
			2,500	R. Tress	5,111
				T. Taylor	22,982
				G. H. Jones	6,075
				H. Rowe (Worcester)	26,306
				—	3,399
				—	5,058
		1,227		Lockwood & Mawson (Hull)	1,822
				—	20,815
	4,000			—	7,860
			391	Hollingsworth*	11,367
				—	1,183
				Johnson & Son	6,587
	250,000		86,000	A. Mills	240,367
	8,000	7,800		S. Alexander & Hall	20,637
		465	550	E. Smith	7,481
				—	26,306
				S. Hemming	182,922
		4,000		Sidney Smirke	—
			12,000	—	6,606
				—	1,545
		1,070		Woolnough (Ipswich)	24,660
				Nettleship (Kidderminster)	15,427
				Flint & Wicks (Leicester)	50,365
				—	3,965
				J. A. Picton (Liverpool)	286,487
				—	9,388

A chronological list of town halls, 1820–1914

Dates	*Towns*	*Building name*	*Dates of extensions*	*Dimensions in ft overall*	*Main hall*
1850	Newby	Assembly rooms			
c. 1850	Pontypool	Town hall			
1850	St Neots	Corn exchange			
1850	Southampton	Town hall (extensions)			
1850–1	Thrapston	Corn exchange		50 × 35	
1850–2	Wolverhampton	Corn exchange and market			100 × 50 × 50
1851–2	Barnsley	Corn exchange			
1851	Bideford	Town hall		47 × 45	45 × 29 × 23
1851–5	Bolton	Market		215 × 294	
1851–3	Bradford	St George's hall			152 × 76 × 54
1851	Colchester	Public hall			
1851	Devonport	St George's hall			
1851	Durham	Town hall			
1851	Elgin	Market and public offices			
1851	Hadleigh	Town hall			
1851–2	Haslingden	Public hall			
1851	Hastings	Town hall			
1851–2	Hemel Hempstead	Town hall	1861	83	50 × 25 × 25
1851 (proposed)	Reading	Market			
1851	Stockport	Market		36	
1851–2	Stockton-on-Tees	Borough hall			80 × 36
1851	Stroud	Town hall (extensions)			
1851 (proposed)	Teignnouth	Town hall			
1851	Whitehaven	Town hall			
1851	Windsor	Guildhall			
1851–2	Wisbech	Assembly rooms			
1851	Worksop	Town hall and public rooms			58 × 29 × 19
1852	Bethnal Green	Town hall			
1852	Blackburn	Town hall		120 × 62 (high)	114 × 50 × 34
1852	Broughton	Town offices		45 × 21	
1852–7	Burslem	Town hall			50 × 80
1852	Chertsey	Town hall and market		54 × 48	51 × 30
1852	Devonport	Market			
1852	Halstead	Town hall			60 × 33 × 22
1852	Hitchin	Corn exchange			
1852	Leicester	Temperance hall		105 × 58	seat 1,600
1852–5	Loughborough	Town hall			
1852	Rotherham	Public rooms			61 × 42
1852–3	Southport	Town hall		120 × 52	71 × 33
1852–4	Swindon	Market and town hall		75	47 × 27
1852	Wenlock	Corn exchange		70 × 44	
1852	Wigan	Public hall		53 × 121	
1853	Bradford-on-Avon	Town hall			
1853–5	Cheetham Hill	Town hall			

Height of tower	*Cost in £*				
	Allowance	*Estimate*	*Total*	*Architect*	*Population*
	1,000			—	890
				Bidlake & Lovatt (Wolverhampton)	12,077
				—	3,123
			700	Elliott	27,490
				—	1,131
		4,045	8,815	G. T. Robinson (Wolverhampton)	92,943
				Whitworth	13,437
50			1,400	R. D. Gould (Barnstaple)	5,775
	28,000	16,500	50,000	G. T. Robinson (Wolverhampton)	61,171
	16,000		13,000	Lockwood & Mawson (Bradford)	103,778
			900	F. Barnes (Ipswich)	19,443
			6,000	—	38,180
				P. C. Hardwick	13,188
				MacKenzie & Matthews (Elgin)	5,383
				—	3,338
			1,500	—	6,154
				—	16,966
				G. Low (London)	2,727
				Hawkes*	21,456
		800	4,000	J. Stevens & Park (Macclesfield)	53,835
				Clephan	9,808
		339		F. Niblett	8,798
				—	5,013
				W. Barnes (London)	18,916
		899		P. C. Hardwick	9,596
				—	10,594
				Gilbert (Nottingham)	3,138
proposed			3,200	Simmonds	90,193
80		22,119	35,000	Patterson (Blackburn)	46,536
		1,090		Pennington & Jarvis	—
				G. T. Robinson (Wolverhampton)	15,954
			1,600	G. Briand (London)	2,743
				J. P. St Aubyn	38,180
			2,000	E. Horner	5,658
				W. Beck (London)	5,258
	7,500			J. Medland (Gloucester)	60,584
				W. Slater	10,900
		1,700		—	6,325
		2,249		T. Whitnell (Southport)	4,765
		1,200		S. Sage & E. Robertson (Swindon)	4,876
				S. Pountney Smith (Shrewsbury)	18,728
		2,500		R. Lane (Manchester)	31,941
				T. Fuller (Bath)	4,240
				T. Bird	11,175

A chronological list of town halls, 1820–1914

Dates	*Towns*	*Building name*	*Dates of extensions*	*Dimensions in ft overall*	*Main hall*
1853–5	Kidderminster	Corn exchange and public rooms	1875		85 × 46 × 33
1853–8	Leeds	Town hall		250 × 200	162 × 75 × 75
1853	London Paddington	Vestry hall			46 × 26 × 27
1853	Louth	Corn exchange			
1853	Runcorn	Town hall			
1853–4	Uttoxeter	Town hall			
1853	Winchcombe	Town hall	1871		
1854	Banbury	Town hall			60 × 34
1854	Boston	Athenaeum and exchange			
1854	Crewe	Market hall	1871	200 × 76 × 25	
1854	Louth	Town hall			
1854–6	Manchester	Free trade hall			
1854–6	Spalding	Corn exchange			
1854	West Hartlepool	Market			
1855–7	Bridgnorth	Markets			80 × 32
1855	Malton	Town hall (extensions)			
c. 1856	Basingstoke	Town hall			
1856	Castle Cary	Market hall		64 × 24 × 25	51 × 20
1856	Chelmsford	Corn exchange			100 × 45 × 40
1856	Coventry	Corn exchange			110 × 55
1856	Devizes	Corn exchange			
1856–7	Eye	Town hall			74 × 27
1856	Leyburn	Town hall			
1856–8	London Islington	Vestry hall	1878	77 × 112	58 × 40 × 27
1857–8	Accrington	Town hall/ Peel institute			
1857–8	Alston	Town hall			54 × 25 × 30
1857	Ashby-de-la-Zouch	Market hall			
1857	Cambridge	Public rooms			
1857	Chesterfield	Market hall			
1857	Kendal	Public hall			
1857–9	Lichfield	Library and museum			
1857	London Clerkenwell	Vestry hall (extensions)			
1857–8	Preston	Court house	1901		
1857–8	Rugby	Town hall and corn exchange			78 × 32 × 26
1857	Sleaford	Corn exchange			
1858	Cardigan	Market and guildhall			
1858	Cranbrook	Vestry hall			
1858	Droylsden	Council offices			
1858	Dundee	Public hall and corn exchange			
1858	Folkestone	Town hall		100 × 50	
1858	Hounslow	Town hall	1888	50 × 120	seat 600
1858–9	Leominster	Corn exchange			
1858	London Battersea	Public hall			
1858–61	London Chelsea	Vestry hall	1887		56 × 40 × 30

Height of tower	*Cost in £*				
	Allowance	*Estimate*	*Total*	*Architect*	*Population*
60				Bidlake & Lovatt (Wolverhampton)	18,462
225	20,000	30,000	124,000	C. Brodrick	172,270
			5,300	J. Lockyer	46,305
		2,000		—	10,467
				C. Verelst	8,049
				T. Fradgley	3,468
				W. H. Knight	2,052
				Bruton (Oxford)	4,026
				Bellamy & Hardy (Lincoln)	14,733
				C. Meason	4,491
		4,000		P. Bellamy (Lincoln)	10,467
		20,000		E. Walters	303,382
				Bellamy & Hardy (Lincoln)	7,627
		3,000		—	—
				Griffiths (Stafford)	6,172
				—	7,661
				—	4,263
			2,300	F. C. Penrose	1,860
			4,923	Chancellor	6,033
			7,600	J. Murray	36,208
		1,500		W. Hill (Leeds)	6,554
74				E. B. Lamb	2,587
				—	800
		5,500		T. Allom (London)	95,329
			11,000	J. Green & T. Birtwhistle	7,481
			2,199	A. B. Higham (Newcastle)	2,005
				—	3,762
				—	27,815
				Davies & Sons	7,101
				—	5,604
				Bidlake & Lovatt (Wolverhampton)	7,012
		412		—	64,778
				J. H. Pack	69,542
		2,889		Murray (Coventry)	6,317
				C. Kirk (Sleaford)	3,729
		4,741		R. J. Withers	3,876
		1,747		M. Bulmer	1,652
				A. Waterhouse	6,280
				C. Edwards	61,449
	3,000			Whichcord & Blandford	6,726
	1,800	1,787	3,000	Nelson & Innes	3,514
				Cranston	5,214
				T. W. Horn (London)	11,729
	5,000	4,500	11,929	W. Wilmer Pocock	56,538

A chronological list of town halls, 1820–1914

Dates	*Towns*	*Building name*	*Dates of extensions*	*Dimensions in ft overall*	*Main hall*
1858 (proposed)	London West Ham	Town hall			
1858	Market Harborough	Exchange buildings			
1858–63	Newcastle-upon-Tyne	Town hall		300 × 100	147 × 60 × 46
1858	Tunstall	Town hall			
c. 1859	Ardrossan	Town hall			
1859–62	Halifax	Town hall			51 × 41 × 42
1859	Irvine	Town hall		90 × 70	
1859–60	Lowestoft	Town hall			68 × 26 × 26
1859–64	Manchester	Assize courts			
1859	Manchester Cheetham Hill	Assembly rooms			87 × 50
1859–60	Newport (Salop)	Town hall			
1859–60	Pontefract	Market hall			
1859	Sutton Coldfield	Town hall		72 × 38	50 × 35
1860	Aldershot	Assembly rooms and market			
1860–1	Blackburn	Exchange			120 × 50 × 34
1860	Bo'ness	Town hall (tower)			
1860–2	Cambridge	Guildhall	1884		110 × 52 × 40
1860	Carmarthen	Town hall and shire hall			
1860	Landport	Public offices and hall			
1860–3	Leeds	Corn exchange			
1860	Leith	Corn exchange			110 × 70
1860–2	London Mile End	Vestry hall			54 × 36 × 22
1860–2	London St George in the East	Vestry hall		57 × 60	54 × 33 × 24
1860	London St James Westminster	Vestry hall			38 × 28 × 18
1860	London St Mary Abbot's Kensington	Vestry hall (alterations)			
1860	London Southwark	Vestry hall			
1860	Lytham St Anne's	Public buildings			
1860	Newcastle-under-Lyme	Town hall			
1860	New Mills	Public hall			
1860	Ross	Corn exchange and public rooms			
c. 1860–5	Salford	Court house			
1860	Shotley Bridge	Town hall			
1861	Ashbourne	Town hall		33	
1861	Alnwick	Public hall		100 × 50	
1861	Allonby	Library and newsroom			
1861	Barnsley	Court house			
1861–2	Bury St Edmunds	Corn exchange			
1861	Carlisle	Town hall			
1861	Croydon	Town hall (alterations)			
1861	Dover	Town hall (alterations)	1880–3		79 × 57 × 36
1861–4	Grimsby	Town hall	1909	117	80 × 40 × 30
1861	Ilfracombe	Market and public hall			
1861–2	Knaresborough	Town hall			

A chronological list of town halls, 1820–1914

Height of tower	Cost in £ Allowance	Estimate	Total	Architect	Population
				—	—
				—	2,325
120		17,000	30,000	J. Johnstone (Newcastle)	87,784
		660		G. T. Robinson (Wolverhampton)	9,566
				—	2,071
160	1,700	23,525	50,126	Sir Charles & E. M. Barry	33,582
120					4,790
			1,400	J. L. Clemence	6,580
	70,000			A. Waterhouse	303,382
			14,000	Mills & Murgatroyd (Manchester)	11,175
				J. Cobb	2,906
				J. Wilson	5,106
64		3,300		G. Bidlake (Wolverhampton)	4,574
		963		T. Goodchild (London)	875
		20,000		W. H. Brackspear (Manchester)	46,536
75				—	—
	6,000	25,000		Peck & Stevens (Maidstone)	27,815
				Lindsay	10,524
				C. M. Houghton	26,798
		12,529		C. Brodrick	172,270
		4,000		Peddie & Kinnear (Aberdeen)	30,919
			3,700	J. Knight	56,600
		4,675		G. A. Wilson	48,376
		6,000		A. P. Howell* with E. Pierce (façade)	36,406
				—	44,053
				H. Jarvis	172,863
				C. Holt	2,698
				—	10,569
				C. Yates	4,366
	2,750			T. Nicholson (Hereford)	2,674
				—	63,850
				Oliver & Lamb (Newcastle)	1,227
				B. Wilson (Derby)	2,120
				T. Robertson (Alnwick)	5,670
				A. Waterhouse	1,002
				C. Reeves	17,890
				Ellis & Woodward	13,318
				J. Gordon*	29,417
		2,087		E. C. Robins	20,325
				Poynter	25,325
	4,500	7,000		Bellamy (Lincoln) and Fowler (Louth)	11,067
	2,500			—	3,034
				J. Child (Knaresborough)	11,277

A chronological list of town halls, 1820–1914

Dates	*Towns*	*Building name*	*Dates of extensions*	*Dimensions in ft overall*	*Main hall*
1861–9	Liverpool	Municipal buildings	1896		
1861	London Lambeth	Vestry hall (extensions)	1872		
1861	Malvern (Great)	Municipal offices			
1861	Manchester Prestwich	Public buildings			
1861–4	Northampton	Town hall	1889	80 × 180	94 × 36
1861	Reigate	Public hall			
1861–4	Swansea	Public hall			seat 2,400
1861	Torrington	Town hall			
1861–2	Warrington	Public hall			seat 1,500
1861	Wolsingham	Town hall			
1862	Birmingham	Exchange and library		186 × 63	
1862	Bishop Auckland	Town hall and market			86 × 40
1862	Budleigh Salterton	Assembly rooms			50 × 28 × 18
1862	Cirencester	Corn hall			
1862–6	Hull	Town hall		105 × 220	
1862–3	Inveraray	Town hall			
1862–5	Manchester Hulme	Town hall		184	90 × 45 × 40
1862	Norwich	Corn exchange		125 × 81	
1862–3	Portobello	Town hall		62	58 × 30 × 25
1862–7	Preston	Town hall			82 × 54 × 48
1862	Rutherglen	Town hall			
1862	Skipton	Town hall	1903		
1862–4	Tiverton	Town hall			50 × 32 × 27
1862	Waterloo (Crosby)	Town hall	1893		
1863	Ambleside	Market hall			
1863	Berkhamsted	Market hall			
1863 (proposed)	Bromley	Town hall			
1863	Chester	Market		120 × 50	
1863–4	Darlington	Market and public offices			
1863	Deal	Assembly rooms			
1863	Kilmarnock	Corn exchange and public hall			81 × 51
1863	Liverpool	Exchange			
1863	London Wapping	Vestry hall			
1863	Longton	Town hall and market	1912		90 × 36
1863–4	Reading	Town hall (alterations)			
1863	South Molton	Market hall		320 × 120	
1863	Tunbridge Wells	Public hall		150 × 300	seat 800
1864–5	Aylesbury	Corn exchange and market		90 × 45	42 × 33
1864	Bradford	Exchange			
1864–6	Congleton	Town hall			seat 1,000
1864	Derby	Market hall		220 × 110	
1864	Drogheda	Town hall			
1864	Easingwold	Town hall			54 × 35
1864–8	East Retford	Town hall			90 × 40 × 26
1864	Eccleshall	Corn exchange		53 × 36	52 × 22

A chronological list of town halls, 1820–1914

Height of tower	*Cost in £ Allowance*	*Estimate*	*Total*	*Architect*	*Population*
200		100,000	142,410	J. Weightman* & E. R. Robson*	443,938
				R. Parris	294,883
				H. Rowe (Worcester)	4,484
				E. Bates (Manchester)	117,961
110	12,000	12,000	20,917	E. W. Godwin	32,813
		3,127		J. Lees (London)	9,975
			4,000	W. Richards	33,972
				R. D. Gould (Barnstaple)	3,298
		3,000	4,000	—	26,431
				—	5,531
100		19,300		E. Holmes	296,076
100	3,500	6,000	9,000	J. Johnstone (Newcastle)	6,480
				W. T. Cross (Exeter)	2,496
				Medland, Maberly & Medland (Gloucester)	6,336
135		20,200	28,000	C. Brodrick	97,661
		2,500	3,000	J. R. McKenzie (Aberdeen)	1,075
			12,000	J. C. Lynde*	68,433
			8,000	T. D. Barry & H. Butcher (Liverpool)	74,891
		3,000		I. Bryce (Edinburgh)	4,366
	30,000	36,000	70,000	Sir G. G. Scott	82,985
				—	8,071
				—	4,533
100	3,000	3,600	8,000	H. Lloyd (Bristol)	10,447
				F. S. Yates*	2,046
				—	1,603
				E. B. Lamb	3,631
				T. C. Sorby	5,505
				W. & J. Hay (Liverpool)	31,110
			14,000	A. Waterhouse	15,781
	2,000			—	7,531
110			6,000	J. Ingram	20,703
				T. H. Wyatt	443,938
		1,297		C. Dunch	4,038
			14,500	J. Burrell (Longton)	16,690
	700	1,461		W. H. Woodman*	25,045
		6,677		W. T. Cross (Exeter)	3,830
	6,000			Hooker & Wheeler (Bromley)	13,807
		7,040	10,000	D. Brandon	6,168
		27,000		Lockwood & Mawson (Bradford)	106,218
110		5,430	7,500	E. W. Godwin	12,344
				J. C. Thorburn*	43,091
				Barne (Belfast)	—
			1,500	Taylor (York)	2,147
100		6,057		Bellamy & Hardy (Lincoln)	2,982
			1,100	Barrett & Son	1,491

A chronological list of town halls, 1820–1914

Dates	Towns	Building name	Dates of extensions	Dimensions in ft overall	Main hall
1864	London	Guildhall (restoration)	1877, '81, '89		153 × 50 × 80
1864–6	London Hackney	Town hall			
1864	Romsey	Corn exchange			39 × 38 × 25
1864	Ruthin	Town hall			
1864	Saltburn	Assembly rooms			50 × 30 × 27
1864	Sligo	Town hall			
1864	Witney	Corn exchange			
1865–8	Aberdeen	Public buildings	1895–1900	200 × 115	76 × 46 × 48
1865 (proposed)	Arbroath	Public hall			
1865–70	Bristol	Assize courts			
1865–9	Chester	Town hall			
1865–9	Chester	Guildhall			
1865	Dorchester	Corn exchange			
1865	Dumbarton	Burgh hall			
1865–6	Elgin	Court house			
1865–6	Farnham	Town hall and corn exchange			48 × 32 × 30
1865–6	Hartlepool	Town hall and market			
1865–6	Hexham	Town hall and corn exchange			75 × 34 × 30
1865	Horncastle	Courthouse			
1865	Hull	Corn exchange		150 × 100	70 × 40
1865	Keighley	Town hall			50 × 95
1865	London St Luke Chelsea	Vestry hall			50 × 25 × 25
1865–8	Pendleton	Town hall			
1865	Romsey	Town hall			
1865 (proposed)	Stockport	Town hall			
1865	Towcester	Town hall and corn exchange			58 × 36
1865–6	Toxteth	Public offices			
1865–7	Walsall	Guildhall			
1866 (proposed)	Auchterarder	Town hall			
1866–73	Bolton	Town hall		204 × 177	112 × 56 × 56
1866	Brighouse	Town hall			90 × 40 × 26
1866	Burnley	Market			
1866–8	Guiseley	Town hall		108 × 99	65 × 36 × 27
1866	Headcorn	Public hall			58 × 22
1866	London Newington	Vestry hall		110 × 90	
1866 (proposed)	London Southwark	Town hall			
1866	Louth	Market hall		100 × 60	
1866–74	Manchester	Exchange			
1866–71	Rochdale	Town hall	1883	303 × 123	90 × 56
1866 × 7	Smethwick	Public hall			

Height of tower	*Cost in £ Allowance*	*Estimate*	*Total*	*Architect*	*Population*
		23,000		J. B. Bunning*	112,063
			15,000	Hammack & Lambert (London)	76,687
		1,423		B. Oakley (Rochester)	2,116
		3,300		Poundley & Walker	3,372
100		9,000	8,000	J. Ross	509
		5,000		W. Hague (Dublin)	—
			2,000	Bartlett	3,458
190		60,000	50,000	Peddie & Kinnear (Aberdeen)	12,514
				—	8,143
		12,000		R. S. Pope & J. Bindon (Bristol)	154,093
	16,500	22,590		W. H. Lynn (Belfast)	31,110
				J. Harrison	31,110
				H. Hall (London)	6,823
		7,000		Melvin & Lieper (Glasgow)	6,283
			4,110	Reid (Elgin)	6,403
88			3,500	W. Tarn (London)	3,926
100	3,500		5,000	C. J. Adams (Stockton)	12,245
	8,000			J. Johnstone (Newcastle)	4,655
				C. Reeves	4,846
	3,500	6,560		W. Botterill (Hull)	97,661
		6,000		G. R. Green (London)	15,005
				Christie* and F. W. Stent	57,073
	9,000	9,245	10,000	A. Darbyshire (Manchester)	20,900
				Hinves & Bedborough (Southampton)	2,116
				—	54,681
			3,000	T. H. Vernon	2,417
		5,788		Layland	62,284
	5,000	5,083		G. B. Nichols (W. Bromwich)	37,760
				—	2,844
200	70,000		167,000	W. Hill (Leeds)	70,395
		7,000		Mallinson & Barber (Halifax)	4,562
90		10,000		J. Grear (Todmorden)	28,700
		3,000	3,000	Knowles & Wilcock (Bradford)	2,226
	500			A. Chambers	1,339
		6,240	10,000	H. Jarvis	82,220
				—	193,593
		5,967		Rogers & Marsden (Louth)	10,560
				Mills & Murgatroyd (Manchester)	338,722
240	30,000	26,510	154,755	W. H. Crossland (Leeds)	38,114
				R. Yeoville Thomason (Birmingham)	13,379

A chronological list of town halls, 1820–1914

Dates	*Towns*	*Building name*	*Dates of extensions*	*Dimensions in ft overall*	*Main hall*
1866	Stourport	Town hall (extensions)			60 × 23
1866–8	Wigan	Town hall			
1867–9	Accrington	Market			
1867–9	Bristol	Colston hall			150 × 80 × 72
1867	Frome	Public hall			
1867–70	Grantham	Town hall			60 × 30 × 21
1867	Hadlow	Public hall			
1867–8	Ipswich	Town hall			
1867	Johnstone	Town hall			62 × 46
1867	Kinross	Town hall (extensions)			
1867–8	London Shoreditch	Vestry hall			
1867–77	Manchester	Town hall		328 × 350	100 × 50 × 58
1867	Runcorn	Public hall			seat 800
1867–71	Saltaire	Institute			
1867	Walthamstow	Public hall			60 × 40
1868	Antrim	Public hall			63 × 42 × 35
1868	Exeter	Public hall		150 × 100	seat 4,000
1868	Gateshead	Town hall			
1868	Helensburgh	Town hall (restoration)			
1868	Ipswich	Public hall			50 × 50 × 98
1868	London Stoke Newington	Assembly rooms			seat 500
1868–71	Manchester	Police courts			
1868	Middlesbrough	Exchange			120 × 60
1868	Mirfield	Town hall			90 × 40
1868	Nantwich	Market hall			
1868–9	Rawtenstall	Public hall			90 × 55
1868	St John's Chapel	Town hall			90 × 55
1869–71	Barrow-in-Furness	Town hall and market			
1869–70	Belfast	Town hall			
1869	Bideford	Public hall			90 × 36 × 27
1869	Bradford	Markets			
1869–71	Brighton	Town hall (alteration)			
1869	Burnham	Town hall and market			
1869	Hanley	Town hall			
1869	Insch	Public hall			
1869	London Hackney	Public offices			
1869	London Poplar	Public offices		60 × 112	70 × 40
1869–73	Lowestoft	Public hall			seat 800
1869	Luton	Corn exchange			
1869	Oswestry	Market and corn exchange			
1869–74	Plymouth	Guildhall			58 × 146
1869	Sheerness	Assembly rooms			
1869	South Shields	Town hall			
1869	Truro	Public hall			seat 800
1869–70	Wareham	Town hall			
1869	Welshpool	Courthouse and town hall			80 × 36
1869–71	Wolverhampton	Town hall			

A chronological list of town halls, 1820–1914

Height of tower	Cost in £ Allowance	Estimate	Total	Architect	Population
			650	—	9,659
			17,000	Nuttall & Cook	37,658
		6,500		J. F. Doyle	13,872
				Foster & Wood (Bristol)	154,093
		2,100		J. Hine (Plymouth)	11,200
100		6,000	11,000	W. Watkins (Lincoln)	4,954
		800		Friend	2,568
120	10,000	11,750	16,000	Bellamy & Hardy (Lincoln)	37,950
				J. L. Lamb (Paisley)	6,404
				—	—
			33,000	C. A. Long	129,364
235	250,000	250,000	1,000,000	A. Waterhouse	338,722
				Culshaw (Liverpool)	10,434
				Lockwood & Mawson (Bradford)	2,083
			1,500	F. Wallen (Greenwich)	7,137
				Young & McKenzie	—
	5,500	3,000		Whitaker (Taunton)	33,738
	30,000			J. Johnstone (Newcastle)	33,587
				Honeyman (Glasgow)	4,613
			14,000	—	37,950
				—	82,220
	25,000	28,410	68,982	T. Worthington (Manchester)	338,722
				C. J. Adams (Stockton)	18,992
			4,000	Kirk & Sons (Huddersfield)	9,263
				G. Latham	6,225
		6,000	7,000	Maxwell & Tuke (Bury)	7,823
				—	—
			3,750	Paley & Austin	3,135
		16,000	20,000	A. T. Jackson (Belfast)	—
		3,000		Gould & Son (Barnstaple)	5,742
		20,000		Lockwood & Mawson (Bradford)	106,218
				—	77,693
				Edwin Down (Weston-super-Mare)	2,233
				R. Scrivener (Hanley)	31,953
				Matthews (Aberdeen)	1,565
				W. Lee (London)	83,295
	6,080	7,550		Harston & Harston	79,196
	2,500		4,000	W. O. Chambers (Lowestoft)	10,663
			15,000	—	15,329
				—	5,414
200	25,000	35,000	43,833	A. Norman & J. Hine (Plymouth) with E. W. Godwin	62,599
				—	79,196
				J. Johnstone (Newcastle)	35,239
			900	Habershon & Pite (London)	11,337
		1,700	1,830	G. R. Crickmay (Weymouth)	6,230
90		10,000		B. Lay (Welshpool)	7,304
		17,000	20,000	E. Bates (Manchester)	60,860

A chronological list of town halls, 1820–1914

Dates	Towns	Building name	Dates of extensions	Dimensions in ft overall	Main hall
1870	Abergavenny	Market and town hall			75 × 45 × 35
1870 (proposed)	Anstruther	Town hall			
1870–3	Bradford	Town hall	1903–9, 1911		
1870 (proposed)	Cuckfield	Town hall			
1870	Dolgellau	Market and public hall			seat 600
1870	Doncaster	Corn exchange and market			91 × 84
1870–1	Hungerford	Town hall			
1870–2	Knutsford	Town hall			
1870	Larne	Town hall and corn exchange			
1870	Pendlebury	Public hall			
1870	Rochester	Corn exchange			
1870	Scarborough	Town hall			
1870	Stone	Town hall and mechanics' institute			
1870	Swansea	Guildhall (extensions)			
1870–5	Todmorden	Town hall		54 × 140	44 × 79
1871	Barnsley	Court house			
1871	Glasgow	Municipal buildings		100 × 130	
1871–3	London Camberwell	Vestry hall			47 × 42
1871–3	Renfrew	Town hall			
1871	Thurso	Town hall			
1871	Winsford	Town hall			
1871	Wirksworth	Town hall			60 × 30 × 25
1872–3	Bilston	Town hall	1880	95 × 74	70 × 43
1872 (proposed)	Carlisle	Public hall and corn exchange			seat 2,000
1872	Dorking	Public hall			
1872–5	Harrow	Public hall			56 × 37 × 36
1872 (proposed)	Stockton	Exchange			seat 1,700
1872 (proposed)	Tonbridge	Public hall			
1872	Wavertree	Town hall			
1872	Wednesbury	Town hall	1913		75 × 46 × 37
1872	Whitchurch	Town hall			65 × 41
1872–3	Winchester	Guildhall			85 × 45
1872	Wotton under Edge	Town hall			
1873	Lewes	Town hall and market			
1873	Northallerton	Town hall			
1873–9	St Helens	Town hall		200	96 × 45 × 40
1873–4	Southport	Cambridge hall		130 × 72	126 × 49
1874 × 9	Birmingham	Council house	1884	120 × 35	
1874	Caernarvon	Guildhall			

A chronological list of town halls, 1820–1914

Height of tower	*Cost in £*				
	Allowance	*Estimate*	*Total*	*Architect*	*Population*
112			7,000	Wilson & Wilcox (London & Bath)	4,621
		1,100		Harris	1,521
217	40,000	43,730	100,000	Lockwood & Mawson (Bradford)	106,218
				—	3,539
			2,200	W. H. Spaull (Oswestry)	2,217
				W. Watkins (Lincoln)	16,406
				J. H. Money (Newbury)	2,031
				A. Waterhouse	3,575
			5,500	A. Tate	—
				W. Williamson	3,548
		5,000		Flockton & Abbott (Sheffield)	16,862
		2,300		Stewart	18,377
		2,500		W. Bakewell (Nottingham)	4,509
		2,500		C. J. Phipps (London)	41,606
			40,000	J. Gibson	11,797
				T. C. Sorby	23,021
		30,000		—	181,492
	8,000		11,000	—	111,306
				J. L. Lamb (Paisley)	4,600
			2,200	R. McKenzie (Aberdeen)	3,604
				J. Redford (Manchester) & J. A. Davenport (Over)	—
71		4,000		Picton, Chambers & Bradley (Liverpool)	3,338
		2,000	5,000	Bidlake (Wolverhampton)	24,188
	4,500			—	31,049
				Driver & Rew (London)	8,567
		8,000	3,000	C. F. Hayward (Exeter)	4,997
	9,000			Alexander & Henman (Stockton)	27,738
				—	8,209
				J. E. Reeve	7,810
		2,325		J. Loxton (Wednesbury)	25,030
	5,000	5,910	6,100	T. Lockwood (Chester)	3,696
120	11,000	10,496	12,000	Jeffery & Skiller (Hastings)	16,366
				—	2,314
				W. E. Baxter*	6,010
				Ross (Darlington)	3,164
130		28,000	28,000	H. Sumners (Liverpool)	45,134
132	7,000			Maxwell & Tuke (Bury)	18,086
162	120,000	84,120		R. Yeoville Thomason (Birmingham)	343,787
			3,000	J. Thomas*	9,449

A chronological list of town halls, 1820–1914

Dates	Towns	Building name	Dates of extensions	Dimensions in ft overall	Main hall
1874	Carshalton	Public hall			
1874 (proposed)	Chesterfield	Public hall			
1874	Clitheroe	Public hall			80 × 42
1874 (proposed)	Heywood	Town hall and market			
1874	Houghton-le-Spring	Market and town hall			
1874–6	Huntly	Public hall			80 × 45 × 40
1874–6	Leicester	Town hall		216 × 118	
1874–6	Lewisham	Vestry hall			
1874–5	London St Clement Danes	Vestry hall			
1874	London St Pancras	Vestry hall			70 × 40
1874 (proposed)	London Woolwich	Public hall			seat 1,200
1874–80	Maidenhead	Town hall			73 × 40 × 25
1874	Oxton	Public offices			
1874	Rhyl	Town hall			79 × 40 × 30
1874	Stranraer	Town hall			
1874	Sunderland	Town hall			
1874–5	West Bromwich	Town hall	1891		81 × 48
1875–8	Annan	Town hall			45 × 25
1875–	Barnstaple	Town hall			
1875	Boroughbridge	Market cross			
1875–7	Builth	Public hall			70 × 30 × 28
1875–9	Chorley	Town hall			100 × 58 × 36
1875–7	Glasgow	Public hall		200 × 160	75 × 186
1875	Holyhead	Town hall			seat 900
1875–81	Huddersfield	Town hall and municipal offices		154 × 72	78 × 60 × 55
1875–8	Inverness	Town hall	1904		
1875–7	Kidderminster	Town hall			
1875–7	London Greenwich	Public offices			
1875	London New Cross	Public hall			100 × 45 × 28
1875	Otley	Town hall			
1875–7	Stafford	Borough hall			103 × 50 × 39
1875	Tregaron	Town hall and market			
1875	Wallasey	Public hall			75 × 45 × 36
1876–8	Barnsley	Public hall			114 × 58 × 40
1876	Dartmouth	Guildhall			60 × 30
1876–8	Dunfermline	Corporation buildings		144 × 64	
1876	Handsworth	Public buildings			
1876	Hartlepool	Exchange			
1876	Lincoln	Town hall			
1876	London Hampstead	Vestry hall	1886 1902	90 × 64	61 × 41
1876–9	London Penge	Vestry hall			57 × 27 × 22
1876	Newbury	Town hall and public offices			

Height of tower	Cost in £ Allowance	Estimate	Total	Architect	Population
	2,500			J. D. Hayton	3,668
				Smith & Woodhouse (Manchester)	11,427
80			3,000	W. S. Varley (Blackburn)	8,208
		10,000		Maxwell & Tuke (Bury)	21,248
				Leighton	5,276
			3,000	J. Anderson (Huntly)	3,570
145	25,000	31,285	50,000	F. J. Hames (London)	95,220
		12,000		Elkington (London)	36,525
		7,000	9,700	Cadogan & Butler (London)	11,503
				H. H. Bridgman (London)	221,465
				—	35,557
			4,000	C. Cooper & Davy	6,173
			1,630	J. Brattan	2,610
160			6,000	Wood & Turner (Barrow)	4,229
				Brown & Wardnop (Edinburgh)	3,615
				J. Johnstone (Newcastle)	98,242
130		40,000		Alexander & Henman (Stockton)	47,918
105		2,500	3,000	R. Smith (Glasgow)	4,174
				Gould (Barnstaple)	11,659
				—	857
			3,500	Haddon (Hereford)	1,059
	10,000		24,000	Ladds & Powell	16,864
	80,000	62,500		J. Cunningham (Liverpool) & J. Campbell Douglas (Glasgow)	181,492
				J. Thomas*	5,916
			76,000	J. H. Abbey* and T. Wood & F. Wild	70,253
	12,000	15,000		A. Lawrie (Inverness)	10,451
		7,546		J. T. Meredith*	19,473
			1,500	Wallen & Paxon*	169,361
				A. B. Hutchings	—
			2,000	B. Hartley	5,855
		7,300		H. Ward*	14,437
				R. Williams	1,788
			4,000	G. E. Grayson (Liverpool)	1,826
136		12,000	25,000	Hill & Swann (Leeds)	23,021
				E. Appleton (Kingswear)	5,338
116	20,000			J. C. Walker (Edinburgh)	10,804
		10,000		Alexander & Henman (Stockton)	16,042
				G. G. Hoskins (Darlington)	13,166
	13,000			—	26,766
		10,000	11,000	H. E. Kendall & F. Mew (London)	32,281
		5,500	4,341	G. Elkington*	13,202
		4,000		H. Money (Newbury)	6,602

A chronological list of town halls, 1820–1914

Dates	*Towns*	*Building name*	*Dates of extensions*	*Dimensions in ft overall*	*Main hall*
1876	Okehampton	Town hall and market			
1876–8	Wantage	Municipal buildings and town hall			
1876	Wimbledon	Public offices			
1877	Ayr	Town hall			
1877	Dunfermline	Public hall			80 × 60 × 43
1877	East Looe	Town hall		120 × 75	
1877	Falkirk	Municipal buildings			
1877	Grangemouth	Public hall			
1877–84	Leeds	Municipal buildings			
1877–83	London	Guildhall (extensions)			
1877	London Kilburn	Public hall			
1877	Portobello	Municipal buildings			
1877	Reading	Municipal buildings	1878–82		
1877—9	Saffron Walden	Town hall			
1877	Smethwick	Public hall			seat 400
1877	Southport	Markets			
1877	Stonehaven	Town hall			63 × 37 × 28
1877	Stow-on-the-Wold	Town hall			50 × 26
1877	Tipperary	Town hall			
1877–80	Wakefield	Town hall		176 × 106	
1878	Aston	Assembly rooms			220 × 87 × 50
1878–9	Burslem	Market hall			
1878	Burton-upon-Trent	Town hall	1894		
1878	Cardiff	Municipal buildings			
1878	Grantown	Public hall			64 × 40
1878	Horwich	Public hall			
1878	Huddersfield	Market			
1878–80	Lincoln	Corn exchange (extensions)			
1878 (proposed)	London Battersea	Vestry hall		191 × 115	seat 1,000
1878–80	London Holborn	Town hall		100 × 124	96 × 45 × 32
1878–80	London Kensington	Vestry hall	1899		91 × 46 × 32
1878–82	London Wandsworth	Vestry hall	1897	100 × 60	85 × 38 × 26
1878 (proposed)	Luton	Public hall			
1878	Newburgh	Town hall			seat 250
1878–9	Rugeley	Town hall and market			
1878	Stow-on-the-Wold	St Edward's hall			
1878 (proposed)	Sutton	Public hall			seat 400
1878	Truro	Corn exchange			
1878–80	Worcester	Guildhall (reconstruction)			
1878–82	Yarmouth	Town hall		115 × 115	100 × 45
1878–80	Yeadon	Town hall		140 × 80	72 × 48 × 31
1879	Alton	Public buildings			

A chronological list of town halls, 1820–1914

Height of tower	*Cost in £* *Allowance*	*Estimate*	*Total*	*Architect*	*Population*
				E. Harbottle & J. Crocker (Exeter)	1,900
				W. Tasker (London)	3,295
	2,750			T. Goodchild (London)	9,087
				—	8,279
			9,000	J. Starforth (Edinburgh)	10,804
90				J. F. Gould (Barnstaple)	1,396
		3,000		A. & W. Black (Falkirk)	11,712
				D. Smart (Perth)	2,569
	60,000			G. Corson (Leeds)	259,212
	106,000			Sir H. Jones*	74,897
				F. W. Hunt	19,544
		5,000		Paterson (Edinburgh)	5,486
100			10,000	A. Waterhouse	32,324
		3,500		E. Burgess (London)	5,718
			1,800	F. Lloyd (Birmingham)	17,158
				Mellor & Sutton (Southport)	18,086
		3,000		Matthew & Lawrie (Inverness)	3,396
		4,000		Saunders	2,040
				T. G. Jackson	—
190	35,000	43,700	80,000	T. E. Collcutt	28,069
90				T. Naden (Birmingham)	33,948
				Richards*	25,562
				—	20,378
		13,000		James Seward & Thomas (Cardiff)	39,536
			1,500	Matthews & McKenzie (Elgin)	1,322
				—	3,671
		23,900		E. Hughes (Huddersfield)	70,253
				Bellamy & Hardy (Lincoln)	26,766
		18,000		—	67,218
129	25,000	25,987	32,000	Isaacs & Florence	33,493
	18,000	20,000	40,000	R. Walker (London)	120,299
135	7,000	9,000		G. Patrick	19,783
		1,000		Pearson & Sons (London)	17,317
			3,000	Thompson & Dunn (Newcastle)	781
90	6,500	7,000	7,000	W. T. Foulkes (Birmingham)	3,375
				Medland (Gloucester)	2,040
	2,000			E. Lowe (London)	6,558
				S. Trevail (Truro)	11,049
		11,543		H. Rowe* and Sir G. G. Scott	33,226
110	17,000	24,000	30,000	J. B. Pearce (Norwich)	41,819
			7,000	W. Hill (Leeds)	5,246
				—	4,092

A chronological list of town halls, 1820–1914

Dates	Towns	Building name	Dates of extensions	Dimensions in ft overall	Main hall
1879	Bromley	Vestry hall	1904	53	48 × 32
1879	Crosshill	Town hall			
1879	Govanhill	Municipal buildings			100 × 45
1879–81	Hastings	Town hall			
1879–80	Kingstown (Dunlaoghaire)	Municipal buildings		130	76 × 41 × 22
1879–81	Limehouse	Town hall			70 × 40 × 26
1879	Loftus-in-Cleveland	Town hall			
1879–82	London Bermondsey	Vestry hall			80 × 52 × 37
1879	London Kensal Town	Vestry hall			
1879–80	Oldham	Town hall (extensions)	1909	68 × 108	
1879–82	Paisley	Town hall			130 × 60 × 62
1879	Pembroke	Town hall			45 × 21
1879–80	Perth	Municipal buildings	1895		75 × 57
1879–82	Reading	Town hall			97 × 60 × 50
1879	Rothesay	Town hall			83 × 48 × 46
1879	Southampton	Public offices			
1879–81	Staines	Town hall			seat 500
1879	Stretford	Town hall			
1879–81	Withington	Public buildings			50 × 25
1880	Aston	Public offices			
1880–2	Bootle	Town hall			
1880	Cardiff, Canton	Public hall		100	seat 2,000
1880	Charlton	Assembly rooms			seat 300
1880	Devonport	Public hall			100 × 67 × 47
1880–3	Dover	Town hall		63 × 102	
1880	Dunstable	Town hall			seat 500
1880	Ealing	Vestry hall			seat 300
1880–1	Eccles	Town hall			90 × 40
1880–1	Hove	Town hall		190 × 142	91 × 60
1880	Ipswich	Public offices			
1880	Ipswich	Corn exchange and public hall			131 × 60
1880–2	Leyton	Town hall			70 × 70
c. 1880	Lincoln	Exchange			
1880	Thornliebank	Public hall			70 × 35
1881	Belper	Public hall			
1881 (proposed)	Cork	Town hall			
1881–2	Darwen	Town hall			seat 1,000
1881–9	Glasgow	City chambers		240 × 240	103 × 54 × 50
1881	Greenock	Municipal buildings			
1881	Hastings	Municipal buildings			
1881	Launceston	Municipal buildings			
1881–7	London St George's	Vestry hall			
1881	Nelson	Town hall			
1881–3	Pontefract	Town hall (extensions)			81 × 37
1881 (proposed)	Ramsgate	Town hall			

A chronological list of town halls, 1820–1914

Height of tower	*Cost in £ Allowance*	*Estimate*	*Total*	*Architect*	*Population*
		5,300		A. & C. Harston	10,674
				—	2,265
				F. Stirratt (Glasgow)	19,200
	10,000	20,000		Jeffery, Skiller & Wells (Hastings)	29,291
120	8,000	13,000	16,000	J. L. Robinson (Dublin)	—
		8,000	10,000	A. & C. Harston	29,919
			5,000	E. R. Robson (London)	2,580
	20,000	21,200		G. Elkington (London)	80,429
				—	—
			24,000	G. Woodhouse (Bolton) and E. Potts (Oldham)	82,629
	20,000	40,000	100,000	W. H. Lynn (Belfast)	48,240
		3,300		E. H. Carson (Dublin)	13,704
		12,000	11,000	A. A. Heiton (Perth)	22,274
	25,000	44,000	60,000	T. Lainson (Brighton)	32,324
		11,000	20,000	J. Hamilton (Glasgow)	7,760
				J. Lemon	53,741
	2,500	4,792		J. Johnson (London)	3,464
100				W. A. Lofthouse (Stretford)	11,945
				L. Booth (Manchester)	6,291
		22,000		Alexander & Henman (Stockton)	33,948
	6,000	6,593		J. Johnson (London)	3,464
	10,000			—	7,061
			2,175	J. Rowland (Plumstead)	7,699
	10,000	12,000		S. Knight (London)	49,449
93		17,540		W. Burges	28,506
			1,690	H. Elliott (London)	4,558
				Harnor & Walters	18,189
		4,500	4,600	J. Lowe (Manchester)	67,770
120		32,000		A. Waterhouse	11,277
				J. Johnson (London)	42,947
		24,000		B. Binyon (Ipswich)	42,947
80	4,000		6,500	J. M. Knight	10,394
				Bellamy & Hardy (Lincoln)	26,766
			4,000	Thomson & Turnbull (Glasgow)	2,123
				J. Johnson (London)	22,247
				J. L. Robinson (Dublin)	80,124
		50,000		C. Bell (London)	29,744
190	250,000		540,000	W. Young (London)	166,078
245	80,000	88,000		H. & E. Barclay (Glasgow)	65,884
			20,000	H. Ward & Andrews*	42,258
60				Hine & Odgers (Plymouth) and O. B. Peter (Launceston)	3,217
	12,000		15,326	R. W. Jearrad*	89,573
				—	—
	7,000	7,000	10,000	Perkin & Bulmer (Leeds)	8,798
	18,000			Barley*	9,816

A chronological list of town halls, 1820–1914

Dates	Towns	Building name	Dates of extensions	Dimensions in ft overall	Main hall
1881–3	St Mary Church	Town hall			
1882–7	Barrow-in-Furness	Town hall		240	
1882	Bideford	Library and museum			
1882 (proposed)	Bideford	Market			
1882	Blaina	Town hall and market			
1882	Consett	Town hall			
1882 (proposed)	Hawick	Public hall			
1882	Kilkenny	Town hall		75 × 40	50 × 30
1882	Lampeter	Town hall			
1882–4	Leamington	Town hall			
1882	Lerwick	Town hall			
1882–3	London Battersea	Public hall	scheme abandoned 1884		106 × 40 × 32
1882–3	London St James Westminster	Vestry hall			81 × 42
1882	Midhurst	Public hall			80 × 45
1882	Newport	Town hall			
1882	Preston	Public hall			147 × 95
1882–93	Preston	Harris Library and Museum			
1882 (proposed)	Teddington	Public offices			
1882	Stalybridge	Town hall (extensions)			
1883–7	Birkenhead	Town hall	1903		seat 700
1883	Birkenhead	Sessions court			
1883	Brechin	Town hall			70 × 40 × 27
1883	Epsom	Market and town hall			68 × 40 × 26
1883 (proposed)	Gosport	Town hall			
1883	Haverhill	Town hall			
1883–5	Hyde	Town hall			
1883	Jersey St Helier	Town hall			
1883–8	Middlesbrough	Town hall		295 × 180	118 × 60
1883–5	Tunstall	Town hall			
1884	Birkenhead	Public hall			61 × 34
1884	Burnley	Assembly rooms			seat 2,000
1884–6	Calne	Town hall			
1884	Dublin	Public offices			
1884–6	Eastbourne	Town hall		200	83 × 45 × 26
1884–5	Evesham	Town hall (alterations)			
1884	Edgbaston	Vestry hall			70 × 40
1884–8	Nottingham	Guildhall			
1884	Peckham	Public hall			90 × 42 × 22
1885–8	Burnley	Town hall		100	

A chronological list of town halls, 1820–1914

Height of tower	*Cost in £ Allowance*	*Estimate*	*Total*	*Architect*	*Population*
				G. S. Bridgman	5,970
170	25,000	31,000	60,000	W. H. Lynn (Belfast)	47,100
			4,000	Bryden	6,512
				—	6,512
				Wing & Johnson (Abergavenny)	—
				W. Lister (Newcastle)	27,075
				—	16,184
			3,060	Hall & Henry (St Andrews)	2,759
			3,000	J. R. Withers (Shrewsbury)	1,897
130		14,000	20,000	J. Cundall	22,979
				Ross (Inverness)	3,854
		10,000		Morris & Stallwood (Reading)	107,262
	15,000	25,000		Lee & Smith (London)	29,941
				W. Buck (Horsham)	12,103
150		range 6,000–30,000		T. M. Lockwood (Chester) and E. M. Lansdowne (Newport)	35,313
			11,000	B. Sykes (Preston)	96,537
			80,000	J. Hibbert	96,537
				W. Taylor	6,599
				—	22,785
200	42,000			C. O. Ellison (Liverpool)	84,006
		30,000		T. D. Barry (Liverpool)	84,006
			2,500	A. Ross (Inverness)	9,031
				Traherne*	34,155
	8,800			Davis & Emmanuel (London)	6,581
				E. Sherman	3,696
				J. W. Beaumont (Manchester)	28,603
				J. M. Bignell (London)	—
	70,000		130,000	G. G. Hoskins (Darlington)	55,934
				A. R. Wood	29,675
74			5,000	G. Vigers	84,006
		6,000		G. B. Rawcliffe (Barnsley)	58,751
				C. B. Oliver (Bath)	2,474
				—	249,602
130	13,000	25,000	33,000	W. T. Foulkes (Birmingham)	21,595
				G. H. Hunt (London)	7,019
			11,200	Osborne & Reading (Birmingham)	22,760
	100,000	161,257		G. Verity & Hunt (London)	186,575
				J. Wilkins (Peckham)	71,089
90			50,000	Holtom & Fox (Dewsbury)	58,751

A chronological list of town halls, 1820–1914

Dates	*Towns*	*Building name*	*Dates of extensions*	*Dimensions in ft overall*	*Main hall*
1885	Edmonton	Town hall			94 × 38 × 24
1885–7	London Chelsea	Vestry hall	1904		81 × 45 × 35
1885–6	London Fulham	Vestry hall			
1885–6	London Mile End	Public hall			130 × 70 × 44
1885–9	Newcastle-under-Lyme	Public buildings			90 × 50
1886	Alyth	Town hall			
1886	Darlaston	Public buildings			
1886 (proposed)	Edinburgh	Municipal buildings	(scheme abandoned)		
1886	Lewes	Public hall			
1886 (proposed)	London Bethnal Green	Town hall			
1886–7	London Willesden	Public offices			
1886	Motherwell	Town hall			seat 1,200
1886	Slough	Public buildings			85 × 35
1886	Stretford	Public offices			
1886–9	West Hartlepool	Municipal buildings			
1887–8	Alloa	Town hall		165 × 87	95 × 49
1887	Corbridge	Town hall			
1887–9	Helston	Public hall			
1887	Leek	Town hall			
1887 (proposed)	London Lewisham	Town hall			seat 1,000
1887	London Streatham	Town hall		120	85 × 45
1887	Ludlow	Market hall			
1887	Moreton-in-Marsh	Redesdale Hall			
1887 (proposed)	New Barnet	Public buildings			75 × 55
1887–90	Portsmouth	Town hall		206 × 194	72 × 45 × 60
1887	Stourbridge	Town hall			76 × 46 × 38
1887–90	Sunderland	Municipal buildings		151 × 100	
1887	Widnes	Town hall			
1888–9	Dewsbury	Town hall			seat 1,500
1888	Elland	Town hall			seat 1,050
1888	Exeter	Guildhall (restoration)	1899		
1888–9	Fenton	Town hall			
1888	Isleworth	Jubilee hall			58 × 31
1888	Lydney	Town hall			
1888 (proposed)	Surbiton	Public hall			50 × 30
1888	Tamworth	Municipal buildings			
1888	Trowbridge	Town hall			
1888–9	Tunstall	Jubilee building			
1889	Buxton	Town hall			
1889	Northampton	Town hall (extensions)			
1889	Sandbach	Town hall			

Height of tower	*Cost in £ Allowance*	*Estimate*	*Total*	*Architect*	*Population*
			9,000	E. A. Eachus*	111,804
		15,000		J. M. Brydon	88,128
	20,000			H. Cheston & J. Perkin	42,900
				Bulnois & Warner	116,286
	10,000	12,000		Sugden, Blood & Sugden (Leek)	17,508
				A. Heiton (Perth)	2,377
	4,500	5,125		J. A. Cossins (Birmingham)	13,563
		range 66,000–280,000		—	228,357
		2,000		S. Denman (Brighton)	11,199
				—	126,961
	6,000			A. Ardron (London)	27,453
	6,000	5,500		J. B. Wilson (Glasgow)	12,904
				F. W. Albany (Reading)	5,095
				J. Gibbons and Magnall & Littlewood (Manchester)	19,018
			7,000	R. K. Freeman (Bolton)	36,252
		30,000		A. Waterhouse	8,812
				F. Emily	1,593
				C. E. Dyer (Portsmouth)	3,432
				Sugden & Son (Leek)	33,077
	8,000			A. L. Guy	53,065
		8,000		W. J. Holland	21,611
				H. A. Cheers (Twickenham)	5,035
				Sir Ernest George	2,359
	5,000			F. Miller (London)	10,092
205				W. Hill (Leeds)	127,989
100		3,500	4,500	T. G. Robinson (Stourbridge)	35,225
	27,000	25,000	50,000	B. Binyon (Ipswich)	116,542
				F. & G. Holme	24,935
135	20,000	28,300	50,000	Holtom & Fox (Dewsbury)	29,637
			7,000	C. F. L. Horsfall (Leeds)	8,278
				E. L. Parsons (Exeter)	37,665
				R. Scrivener (Hanley)	13,830
			1,500	S. Woodbridge	12,973
				Seth-Smith	6,364
		6,000		—	9,406
				T. W. F. Newton (Birmingham)	4,891
				A. S. Goodridge (Bath)	18,230
				A. R. Wood	29,675
				Pollard	10,054
		25,000		M.W. Holding and A. W. Jeffery (Hastings)	51,881
				T. Bower (Nantwich)	5,493

A chronological list of town halls, 1820–1914

Dates	*Towns*	*Building name*	*Dates of extensions*	*Dimensions in ft overall*	*Main hall*
1889–91	Swindon	Public offices			seat 600
1889–91	York	Guildhall and council offices			
1890–2	Cleckheaton	Town hall			seat 1,000
1890	Cromer	Town hall			seat 900
1890	Ealing	Public hall and offices			100 × 45 × 40
1890	Eton	Public offices			
1890	Gloucester	Guildhall			78 × 40
1890	London St Martin in the Fields	Vestry hall			40 × 77
1890–1	Oldbury	Municipal buildings			
1890	Selby	Town hall			
1890	Stockton-on-Tees	Public offices			
1890	Thornaby-on-Tees	Town hall			
1890–2	York	Law courts			
1891–2	Bodmin	Public buildings			80 × 40
1891 (proposed)	Brighton	Public offices			
1891 (proposed)	Bury	Municipal buildings			
1891	Camborne	Public hall			112 × 57
c. 1891–6	Croydon	Municipal buildings		285 × 170	64 × 36 × 43
1891 (proposed)	Drighlington	Town hall			
1891–2	Gainsborough	Town hall	1908		
1891	Huyton with Roby	Public offices			
1891	Lockerbie	Town hall			75 × 43 × 30
1891 (proposed)	Newton in Makerfield	Public buildings			seat 1,600
1891	Oswaldtwhistle	Town hall			
1891–3	Richmond (Yorks)	Town hall			
1891 (proposed)	Rochester	Municipal buildings			
1891–2	Saltcoats	Town hall			83 × 41
1891–7	Sheffield	Town hall		205 × 140	155 × 35 × 22
1891	Tewkesbury	Town hall (alterations)			
1892	Ambleside	Assembly rooms			
1892	Bexley	Public offices			
1892	Cheetham Hill	Public hall			
1892	Crompton	Public offices			
1892	Goole	Bank chambers			
1892	Ledbury	Browning memorial building			
1892–6	Llanelli	Town hall			
1892	London Battersea	Town hall and parochial offices		110	117 × 55
1892–6	London Leyton	Public offices and institute		100 × 200	78 × 47 × 30
1892	London St Pancras	Town hall	1914		

A chronological list of town halls, 1820–1914

Height of tower	*Cost in £ allowance*	*Estimate*	*Total*	*Architect*	*Population*
			9,000	B. Binyon (Ipswich)	41,152
			16,000	E. G. Mawbey*	49,530
100				Mawson & Hudson (Bradford)	10,653
				G. J. Skipper (Norwich)	1,597
135			22,000	— *	25,436
				R. Aborn (Eton)	3,984
	12,000	30,000	31,000	G. H. Hunt (London)	36,521
	25,000	26,352		R. Walker (London)	17,508
				Wood & Kendrick (W. Bromwich)	20,501
				H. Thorp (Leeds)	6,046
	2,500	3,327		J. M. Garry (W. Hartlepool)	41,015
				J. M. Garry (W. Hartlepool)	10,795
				E. Kirkby (Liverpool)	49,530
				O. Ralling & L. Tonar	5,151
	5,000			—	115,873
	60,000			A. N. Bromley (Nottingham)	57,212
		3,500		S. Trevail (Truro)	14,700
170	70,000	80,000		C. Henman (Croydon)	102,695
		1,150		—	4,322
				—	14,372
				H. A. Cheers (Twickenham)	4,625
115			7,000	F. J. C. Carruthers (Lockerbie)	1,143
	4,500			—	12,861
				R. N. Hunter	13,296
	10,000		24,000	W. J. Ancell (London)	4,216
				F. T. W. Goldsmith & E. J. Gosling	26,290
				W. D. Howie & H. D. Walton (Glasgow)	2,755
200	80,000		200,000	E. W. Mountford	324,243
				Medland & Son (Gloucester)	5,269
				R. Walker (Windermere)	2,360
				H. Ward (Hastings)	10,605
				Booth & Chadwick	29,590
				H. Cheetham (Oldham)	12,901
				H. B. Thorpe (Goole)	4,853
				B. Binyon (Ipswich)	4,303
98				W. Griffiths (Llanelli)	32,034
		26,000	30,000	E. W. Mountford	150,558
				J. Johnson (London)	63,056
	30,000			W. Harrison (London)	234,379

A chronological list of town halls, 1820–1914

Dates	Towns	Building name	Dates of extensions	Dimensions in ft overall	Main hall
1892–5	Morley	Town hall		140 × 146	90 × 46 × 36
1892	Newton le Willows	Town hall			
1892–3	Oswestry	Municipal buildings			
1892 (proposed)	Shepton Mallet	Town hall			
1893–5	Bath	Municipal buildings			
1893	Cheadle	Town hall (alterations)			
1893	Ilford	Public offices			
1893	Kendal	Town hall			
1893	Law Lanark	Public hall			seat 400
1893	Luton	Town hall (extensions)			
1893 (proposed)	Otley	Public offices			
1893	Oxford	Town hall		210 × 225	180 × 55
1893	Pontypridd	Town hall and market			seat 1,500
1893–5	Stafford	Town hall			
1893–7	West Hartlepool	Town hall			seat 550
1894	Bath	Pump room (extensions)			
1894	Bexhill	Town hall	1907		
1894	Burton-upon-Trent	Town hall (extensions)			
1894	Cleethorpes	Public hall			
1894	Clontarf	Town hall			65 × 35
1894	Coatbridge	Town hall			
1894	Colne	Town hall			
1894	Dalbeattie	Town hall			seat 400
1894	Darlington	Municipal buildings			
1894	Kilkenny	Town hall			
1894	King's Lynn	Municipal buildings			
1894	North Shields	Town hall (extensions)			
1894	Openshaw & Clayton	Municipal buildings			
1894	Rotherham	Town hall (extensions)			
1894	Shaw	Town hall			
1894	Warrington	Public hall			90 × 48
1895 (proposed)	Aberdeen	Municipal buildings	1900, '05		
1895–1900	Blackpool	Town hall		72 × 70	
1895	Brodick	Public hall			
1895	Coventry	Municipal buildings			
1895	Cowbridge	Town hall (restoration)			
1895	Hanbury	Town hall			
1895–7	Hyson Green	Municipal buildings		320	
1895	London Clerkenwell	Town hall			60 × 42
1895–7	London Rotherhithe	Town hall	1904	53 × 161	52 × 38
1895	Sutton	Public offices			
1895	Thurles	Town hall and market			
1895	Woking	Public hall			
1896	Bovey Tracey	Town hall			
1896	Chatham	Town hall			90 × 45

A chronological list of town halls, 1820–1914

Height of tower	*Cost in £ Allowance*	*Estimate*	*Total*	*Architect*	*Population*
	15,000	18,126	36,000	Holtom & Fox (Dewsbury)	21,068
				T. Beesley	478
				H. A. Cheers (Twickenham)	8,496
				G. J. & F. W. Skipper (Norwich)	5,500
		22,500		J. M. Brydon	51,844
				G. F. Armitage	16,830
				Clark & Hutchinson (London)	10,913
		16,000		S. Shaw (Kendal)	14,430
				J. L. Murray	4,605
				T. Roscoe*	30,006
	2,500			—	7,838
	50,000	56,876		H. T. Hare	45,742
			6,000	T. Rowlands (Pontypridd)	19,969
				H. T. Hare	20,270
				H. A. Cheers (Twickenham)	42,710
				J. M. Brydon	51,844
				T. R. Davison (London)	5,206
				R. Churchill (Burton)	46,047
				J. R. Withers (Shrewsbury)	4,306
				W. G. Perrott	—
				A. M. Mitchell*	29,996
				J. W. & R. F. Beaumont (Manchester)	4,023
				A. B. Crombie (Dumfries)	1,493
				Clark & Moscrop (Darlington)	38,060
				J. K. Freeman (Dublin)	—
				P. Tree & I. Price (London)	18,360
				J. F. Smillie*	21,920
				—	23,927
				R. J. Lovell (London)	42,061
				H. Cheetham (Oldham)	4,466
				W. Owen (Warrington)	52,743
				J. Souttar (Aberdeen)	50,587
	8,000			Potts, Son & Hemmings (Bolton)	23,846
				J. J. Burnet (Glasgow)	1,055
				H. Quick (Coventry)	52,724
				C. B. Fowler (Cardiff)	1,377
				—	1,122
			7,000	A. Brown*	16,086
				C. Evans Vaughan	66,216
	15,000			Murray & Foster (London)	39,255
				Currey & Tatlock (Sutton)	13,977
				J. K. Freeman (Dublin)	4,411
				Homer & Ridler (London)	9,776
			300	Segar	2,422
126		20,000		G. E. Bond	31,657

Dates	Town	Building name	Dates of extensions	Dimensions in ft overall	Main Hall
1896	Cleethorpes	Municipal buildings			
1896–8	Cork	Municipal buildings			
1896	Douglas	Municipal buildings			
1896	Halifax	Public hall			
1896	Holywell	Town hall			
1896–8	Hoylake	Town hall			seat 500
1896	Hunstanton	Town hall			77 × 37
1896	Ledbury	Public hall			80 × 30 × 24
1896	Liverpool	Municipal buildings (extensions)			
1896–7	London Hammersmith	Town hall			76 × 52
1896–8	Merthyr Tydfil	Town hall			
1896	Pollokshaws	Town hall			seat 800
1896	Rathmines	Town hall			74 × 44 × 44
1896	St Austell	Public hall			80 × 40 × 33
1897	Aberdare	Town hall (extensions)			
1897	Baldock	Town hall			40 × 31
1897	Brechin	Council offices			
1897	Conway	Municipal buildings			
1897	East Cowes	Town hall		42 × 102	70 × 35
1897	East Dereham	Town hall			
1897	Featherstone	Assembly rooms			
1897	Heacham	Public hall			
1897–8	Kidsgrove	Victoria hall			
1897	Kirton-in-Lindsay	Town hall			47 × 33 × 22
1897–1902	Llandudno	Town hall			
1897–9	Markinch	Municipal buildings			
1897	Mytholmroyd	Council offices			
1897	Newport (IOW)	Public hall			60 × 30 × 22
1897–9	Ormskirk	Municipal buildings			
1897	Prestonpans	Town hall			60 × 35
1897	Rugby	Municipal buildings			
1897	Selkirk	Public hall			
1897	Surbiton	Municipal buildings			
1897 (proposed)	Teignmouth	Public hall			92 × 43 × 36
1897	Waddesdon	Public hall			seat 450
1897	Worksop	Public buildings			
1898	Atherton	Council offices			
1898–1906	Belfast	City hall		300 × 250	70 × 38
1898	Bristol	Municipal buildings			
1898 (proposed)	Cambridge	Guildhall	(scheme abandoned)		
1898–1902	Colchester	Town hall			84 × 33
1898	Dukinfield	Town hall			
1898	East Leigh	Town hall			

Height of tower	*Cost in £* *Allowance*	*Estimate*	*Total*	*Architect*	*Population*
				G. A. Elphick (London)	4,306
		2,000	2,000	H. A. Cutler*	75,345
				A. Ardron (London)	—
	25,000			Cheers & Smith (Twickenham & Blackburn)	89,832
				J. Lloyd-Williams (Denbigh)	9,471
		5,500	6,500	T. W. Cubbon (Birkenhead)	6,545
				G. J. & F. W. Skipper (Norwich)	1,725
				G. H. Godsell (Hereford)	4,303
				E. W. Mountford	517,980
	25,000		25,000	J. H. Richardson	97,239
		12,000		E. A. Johnson & Williams	58,080
				R. Anderson (Edinburgh)	10,228
				T. Drew (Dublin)	32,602
				S. Trevail (Truro)	11,377
				O. Williams*	40,917
			2,000	T. Brown & Fisher (Wellingborough)	2,301
				D. W. Galloway*	5,139
		2,500		Farrington*	3,442
				J. Newman (Sandown)	2,872
				G. J. & F. W. Skipper (Norwich)	5,524
				Garside & Keyworth (Pontefract)	4,132
				Milne & Hall (London)	989
		2,046		Woods & Hutchings (Tunstall)	3,841
		1,200		J. K. Broughton	1,623
	10,000	16,000	23,000	Silcock & Reay (Bath)	6,065
		1,200		J. Gillespie & Scott (St Andrews)	1,350
				S. Sutcliffe*	4,388
				E. A. Swann & Clark	10,216
			2,500	Willinck & Thicknesse (Liverpool)	6,298
				P. Whitecross (Prestonpans)	1,606
				North & Hawke (London)	11,262
			7,000	H. J. Blanes (Edinburgh)	5,788
	5,000			W. A. Forsyth & Maule (London)	10,052
				J. Watson (Teignmouth)	8,292
				W. F. Taylor (Aylesbury)	1,610
				T. Kidd*	12,734
				J. C. Prestwich (Leigh)	15,833
173	1,000,000		300,000	A. B. Thomas	273,184
	80,000	2,500		T. H. Yabbicom*	221,578
				J. Belcher	36,983
162	36,000	35,960	53,000	J. Belcher	34,559
	10,000			J. Eaton Sons & Cottrell (Ashton-under-Lyme)	29,239
		4,500		J. Evans*	—

A chronological list of town halls, 1820–1914

Dates	*Town*	*Building name*	*Dates of extensions*	*Dimensions in ft overall*	*Main hall*
1898	Enniskillen	Town hall			
1898	Godalming	Municipal buildings			
1898	Govan	Town hall			seat 2,000
1898	Hitchin	Town hall			seat 750
1898	Kingston	Municipal buildings			96 × 42
1898–9	Levenshulme	Town hall		75	72 × 40
1898–1903	London East Ham	Public offices			100 × 50
1898	Lonmay	Public hall			seat 500
1898	Lynton	Town hall			
1898	Margate	Municipal buildings			
1898	Oakham	Town hall			
1898	Oundle	Town hall			
1898–1900	Pitlochry	Public hall			60 × 33 × 24
1898 (proposed)	Reigate	Municipal buildings			
1898	Rothes	Town hall			70 × 30
1898–1903	Scarborough	Town hall (by conversion)			
1898	Southend	Municipal buildings			
1898 (proposed)	Taunton	Town hall			
1898	Windermere	Municipal buildings			
1898	Yardley	Municipal buildings			
1899	Aberdeen	Council offices		64 × 36	38 × 30 × 20
1899–1902	Blantyre	Municipal buildings		122 × 224	100 × 50
1899	Dorchester	Municipal buildings (extensions)			
1889–1903	Dumbarton	Municipal buildings			
1899 (proposed)	Hendon	Public offices			
1899	Henley	Municipal buildings		100 × 44	
1899	London Edmonton	Public buildings			
1899	London Kensington	Vestry hall (extensions)			
1899 (proposed)	London Plumstead	Municipal buildings		(scheme abandoned: v. London Woolwich 1903)	
1899 (proposed)	London Wandsworth	Public offices			
1899 (proposed)	Lymm	Public offices			
1899	Maindee	Municipal buildings			
1899	Workington	Town hall			
1900–5	Aberdeen	Municipal buildings (reconstruction)			
1900–4	Cardiff	Municipal buildings			100 × 50
1900	Clitheroe	Town hall			
1900	Great Harwood	Town hall			
1900	Halesowen	Public offices			
1900–1	Helmsley	Town hall		54 × 62	

Height of tower	*Cost in £ Allowance*	*Estimate*	*Total*	*Architect*	*Population*
				A. Scott & Son (Drogheda)	5,412
	7,000			Lanchester, Stewart & Rickards	2,797
		25,000		Thomson & Sandilands (Glasgow)	61,364
		2,500		G. Lucas & E. W. Mountford	9,510
100	14,000	6,600		Macaulay & Berry*	41,886
			6,000	J. Jepson*	5,500
150	55,000		78,000	Cheers & Smith (Twickenham & Blackburn)	28,741
				F. Gillie	—
		14,000		Macdonald	1,547
				A. Latham*	18,417
				E. Jeeves (Melton Mowbray)	1,146
		1,725		J. B. Corby (Stamford)	2,667
		2,366	3,000	A. Ness (Dundee)	1,136
	15,000			—	22,646
		2,000		Pratt (Elgin)	1,548
			19,500	W. H. Smith*	33,776
	40,000	45,000		F. T. Baggally	12,333
				Sansom & Cottam (Taunton)	18,026
		1,700		R. Walker (Windermere)	1,504
				A. Harrison (Birmingham)	17,141
			15,000	A. H. MacKenzie (Aberdeen)	50,587
120	30,000		55,000	J. Millar (Glasgow)	2,255
				G. J. Hunt*	7,946
		15,000		J. Thomson (Glasgow)	13,118
	12,000			—	15,483
		10,132		M. E. Fitt (Reading)	14,669
				W. G. Scott	36,351
				W. G. Hunt (London)	166,308
	35,000	46,500		A. B. Thomas	52,436
	18,000			—	156,942
				—	4,995
			5,900	R. Haynes*	12,744
				Oliver & Dodgshun (Carlisle & Leeds)	23,490
				J. Rust* and A. M. MacKenzie (Aberdeen)	50,587
180	200,000			Lanchester, Stewart & Rickards	128,915
				Briggs & Wolstenholme (Liverpool)	10,815
				Briggs & Wolstenholme (Liverpool)	9,073
			10,000	H. Rowe (Worcester)	3,603
				T. L. Moore	1,508

A chronological list of town halls, 1820–1914

Dates	Town	Building name	Dates of extensions	Dimensions in ft overall	Main Hall
1900–4	Hindley	Public offices			
1900	Musselburgh	Municipal buildings			seat 1,000
1900–5	Walsall	Council house			
1901	Altrincham	Town hall			
1901	Ayr	Town hall			seat 1,078
1901–2	Cheltenham	Town hall			112 × 82 × 43
1901	London Shoreditch	Town hall			
1901–2	Walton-on-Thames	Municipal buildings		104 × 77	
1902	Aldershot	Public offices			
1902–5	Batley	Town hall			
1902–6	Bideford	Municipal buildings			
1902–4	Boston	Municipal buildings			
1902	Colne	Municipal buildings			seat 1,000
1902	Harrogate	Municipal buildings			
1902–4	Hereford	Town hall		99 × 180	
1902–4	Jarrow	Municipal buildings			
1902	Marlborough	Town hall			
1902	Mountain Ash	Municipal buildings			
1902	Thetford	Town hall			52 × 27 × 24
1902–3	Wolverhampton	Mansion house			
1903	Brading	Town hall			55 × 25 × 20
1903–5	Crewe	Municipal buildings			
1903–5	Deptford	Town hall			72 × 33
1903	Galashiels	Municipal buildings (extensions)			
1903 (proposed)	Hamilton	Municipal buildings			
1903–4	High Wycombe	Town hall			
1903	Horbury	Town hall			
1903	Leith	Municipal buildings (extensions)			
1903 (proposed)	London Acton	Town hall	(scheme abandoned v. 1907)		
1903–6	London Woolwich	Town hall		114 × 230	seat 750
1903	Pontypridd	Public offices			
1903	Prestatyn	Public offices			
1903 (proposed)	Rawtenstall	Municipal buildings			
1903	Shipley	Municipal buildings			
1903	Skipton	Town hall (extensions)			
1903	Stanhope	Town hall			
1903–5	Wem	Town hall			
1903 (proposed)	Yeovil	Town hall			
1904	Abram	Public offices			
1904	Abercarn	UDC offices			
1904	Birkdale	Town hall			
1904	Bo'ness	Town hall			

Height of tower	*Cost in £ Allowance*	*Estimate*	*Total*	*Architect*	*Population*
	5,000	7,000	7,318	Heaton, Ralph & Heaton (Wigan)	18,973
				W. Constable (Musselburgh)	8,885
	55,000	55,000	101,000	J. S. Gibson (London)	71,789
	4,000			C. H. Hindle (Monton, Eccles)	16,831
		9,515		Kennedy & Hunter (Ayr)	31,537
		35,000		F. W. Waller (Gloucester)	47,955
				W. G. Hunt (London)	118,637
				MacIntosh & Newman (London)	10,329
	9,000			C. E. Hutchinson (London)	30,974
		6,500		W. Hanstock (Batley)	30,321
			5,492	A. J. Dunn (Birmingham)	8,754
	16,500		20,000	J. Rowell	15,667
			10,000	Woodhouse & Willoughby (Manchester)	23,000
	40,000	39,750		H. T. Hare	28,423
		18,450	25,000	H. A. Cheers (Twickenham)	21,382
		8,955	12,000	F. Rennoldson (S. Shields)	34,295
				C. E. Ponting	3,046
				J. H. Phillips (Cardiff)	31,093
			10,000	H. J. Green (Norwich)	4,613
				J. W. Bradley*	94,187
				Newman (Sandown)	1,732
	14,000	18,000		H. T. Hare	42,074
	30,000	28,433	50,000	Lanchester, Stewart & Rickards	110,398
		4,250		J. Hall	13,969
		42,714		A. Cullen	40,372
		9,500	13,838	Bateman, Bateman & Hale (Birmingham)	15,542
			6,100	W. Hanstock (Batley)	6,736
			12,000	G. Simpson*	78,895
	52,946	35,000		W. G. Hunt (London)	37,744
140		51,000		A. B. Thomas	117,178
				H. T. Hare	32,316
				Bell*	1,261
	30,000			—	31,053
		20,000		W. H. Beevers	25,573
				Butler, Wilson & Oglesby (Leeds)	11,896
			3,000	Clark & Moscrop (Darlington)	1,964
				J. Brown (Shrewsbury)	2,149
				—	9,861
			3,400	Heaton, Ralph & Heaton (Wigan)	6,306
			1,500	J. Williams*	12,607
	12,000			G. Brown (Birkdale)	14,197
			12,000	G. Washington Brown (Edinburgh)	—

A chronological list of town halls, 1820–1914

Dates	*Town*	*Building name*	*Dates of extensions*	*Dimensions in ft overall*	*Main hall*
1904	Bromley	Vestry hall (extensions)			
1904	Cleethorpes	Council house			
1904	Darnall	Public hall			100 × 42
1904	Darvel	Town hall			seat 1,000
1904	Ince	Municipal buildings			67 × 36 × 25
1904	Kempston	UDC offices			
1904–7	Leigh	Town hall		150 × 100	
1904	Liverpool	Cotton exchange			
1904	London Chelsea	Vestry hall (extensions)			
1904–8	London Lambeth	Municipal buildings			
1904–6	London Tottenham	Public offices			
1904	Smethwick	Municipal offices			
1904 (proposed)	Southampton	Town hall			
1904–8	Stockport	Town hall			seat 2,000
1904	Sunderland	Town hall			
1904	Tipton	Town hall			
1904	Inverness	Town hall (extensions)			
1904	Woking	UDC offices			
1905 (proposed)	Bournemouth	Municipal buildings	(scheme abandoned)		
1905–6	Kirkintilloch	Town hall			seat 1,200
1905	New Malden	Public offices			seat 500
1905	London St Anne Limehouse	Vestry hall			
1905–6	Penrith	Town hall			
1905	Seacombe	Public offices			70 × 94
1905–10	South Shields	Municipal buildings			
1905–6	Sutton Coldfield	Town hall			78 × 42 × 30
1906	Barry	Municipal buildings			
1906	Bodmin	Municipal offices			
1906	Cowdenbeath	Municipal buildings		52	
1906 (proposed)	Dartmouth	Town hall			
1906	Harwich	Town hall			
1906–14	Hull	City hall		600	
1906–8	Ilkley	Town hall			
1906–9	Lancaster	Town hall		132 × 220	128 × 30
1906–8	London Holborn	Town hall			
1906–8	Ossett	Town hall			seat 1,300
1907	Bargoed	Town hall			
1907	Bexhill	Town hall (extensions)			
1907–12	Birmingham	Municipal buildings			
1907 (proposed)	Cheltenham	Municipal buildings			
1907	London Acton	Town hall			
1907–8	Wallsend	Town hall			

Height of tower	*Cost in £ allowance allowance*	*Estimate*	*Total*	*Architect*	*Population*
	20,000			R. F. Atkinson	27,354
				H. C. Scaping	12,578
				A. C. Turnbull	51,807
			4,000	T. H. Smith (London)	—
		30,000		Heaton, Ralph & Heaton (Wigan)	21,262
				E. H. C. Inskip*	4,729
		30,000	c. 45,000	J. C. Prestwich (Leigh)	40,001
				Matear & Simon (Liverpool)	684,958
				Leonard Stokes	73,842
134	35,000		40,000	Warwick & Hall (London)	301,895
				Taylor & Jemmett	102,541
	15,000	17,000		F. J. Gill	54,539
	75,000			—	104,824
110	60,000	70,000	100,000	A. B. Thomas	78,897
	30,000	27,600		Wills & Anderson (London)	146,077
				A. G. Latham (Birmingham)	30,543
				J. H. Rhind (Edinburgh)	27,046
	5,000			Wooldridge*	16,244
		126,000		C. E. Mallows and F. W. Lacey*	47,003
		8,000	9,000	Walker & Ramsay (Glasgow)	14,401
			5,000	W. H. Hope	5,565
				Sir Banister Fletcher	32,369
				J. J. Knewstubb (Penrith)	9,182
				Briggs, Wolstenholme & Thorneley (Liverpool)	20,749
154	20,000	35,000	70,000	E. E. Fetch (London)	97,263
		8,000	12,000	A. R. Mayston (London)	14,264
		7,488		C. E. Hutchinson & E. H. Payne (London)	27,030
				R. T. Buscombe*	5,353
				T. H. Ure (Dunfermline)	7,467
				E. Vincent Harris	6,579
		4,714		H. H. Packe	10,070
	100,000	114,300	150,000	Russell, Cooper & Davis and C. E. Mallows (London)	240,259
	10,053		20,000	W. Bakewell (Leeds)	7,455
146		110,000	155,000	E. W. Mountford & F. D. Clapham	40,329
	19,205	21,375	25,000	Warwick & Hall (London)	59,405
	12,000	20,000	22,000	W. Hanstock (Batley)	12,903
		2,000		P. V. Jones	—
				H. Ward (Hastings)	12,213
		137,000		Ashley & Newman (London)	522,204
		16,000		Pearson & Milburn (London) and T. Malvern (Cheltenham)	49,439
	18,000			Raffles & Gridley	37,744
		14,000	14,000	Liddle & Brown (Newcastle)	20,918

A chronological list of town halls, 1820–1914

Dates	*Town*	*Building name*	*Dates of extensions*	*Dimensions in ft overall*	*Main hall*
1908	Cavan	Town hall			66 × 35
1908	Farnworth	Town hall			
1908 (proposed)	Hertford	Municipal buildings			
1908	Londonderry	Guildhall (restoration)			
1908	Reddish	Municipal buildings			
1908 (proposed)	Stirling	Municipal buildings			
1908	Turriff	Municipal buildings			
1909–11	Burslem	Municipal buildings			
1909	Grimsby	Town hall			
1909–10	London Bethnal Green	Town hall			
1909	Newbury	Municipal buildings			
1909–11	Oldham	Town hall (extensions)			
1909	Perth	City hall (reconstruction)			
1909	Torquay	Town hall			
1909	Walkden	Municipal buildings			
1910	Armagh	Town hall			80 × 35
1910	Airdrie	Town hall			seat 1,300
1910	Denbigh	Municipal buildings			seat 200
1910	Pudsey	Town hall			
1910	Sheringham	Council offices			
1910	Stoke-on-Trent	Town hall (extensions)			
1911	Kirton-in-Holland	Town hall			
1911	London	County hall		730 × 300	
1911 (proposed)	Manchester	Library and art gallery	(scheme abandoned)		
1911	Radcliffe	Town hall			
1912–13	Chadderton	Town hall			
1912–20	Coventry	Municipal buildings			
1912	Dublin	Municipal buildings			
1912 (proposed)	Goole	Municipal buildings			
1912–18	London Marylebone	Town hall			
1912	Masham	Town hall			
1912	Portobello	Town hall			80 × 58 × 38
1913 (proposed)	Barnet	Municipal offices			
1913 (proposed)	Barnsley	Town hall			
1913	Blackburn	King George's hall			
1913 (proposed)	Devonport	Municipal buildings			seat 1,500
1914 (proposed)	Middleton	Town hall			
1914	Newburn-on-Tyne	Council offices			
1914–15	Sale	Town hall			
1914–20	Wallasey	Town hall			

A chronological list of town halls, 1820–1914

Height of tower	*Cost in £* *Allowance*	*Estimate*	*Total*	*Architect*	*Population*
		3,500		W. Scott (Dublin)	2,822
			10,000	W. J. Lomax (Bolton)	25,925
	3,500			—	9,322
	17,300	24,000		M. A. Robinson*	39,892
				Dixon & Potter (Manchester)	8,668
		21,000		Salmon, Son & Gillespie (Glasgow)	18,609
				W. L. Duncan	2,273
	30,000	24,918		S. B. Russell & T. E. Cooper (London)	38,766
				Eade Johns & Browne	63,138
	20,000	25,000		P. Robinson & W. Alban Jones	129,680
		2,406		S. J. L. Vincent*	11,061
	25,000	26,000		Taylor & Simister	137,246
	25,000	30,000		E. Clifford (Glasgow)	29,793
	30,000			T. R. Davison (London)	33,625
		11,000		J. T. Proffitt	—
				M'Caffrey	7,588
		10,000		J. Thomson (Glasgow)	22,288
		15,000		Porter & Elcock (Colwyn Bay)	6,438
				Jowett & Kendall (Pudsey)	14,907
				S. Simons (Sheringham)	2,359
	30,000			Wallis & Bowden	30,458
				—	—
	1,706,000	1,412,000		R. Knott	4,521,685
	70,000			—	714,330
	12,000			W. M. Gillow & R. Holt (Manchester)	26,084
	9,000			Taylor & Simister	28,299
				Garrett & Simister and Buckland & Farmer (Birmingham)	106,349
110	50,000	55,000		McDonnell & Reid (Dublin)	—
				E. E. Fetch (London)	20,332
	70,000			T. E. Cooper	118,160
				—	3,110
	6,000	8,000		J. A. Williamson (Edinburgh)	8,799
	4,000			—	10,440
	20,000	18,500		P. H. Topham	50,614
		113,000		Briggs, Wolstenholme & Thorneley (Liverpool)	133,052
	60,000	95,000		Ashley & Newman (London)	81,678
				A. G. Hornsell (London)	27,980
				E. Cratney	17,155
				C. T. Adshead (London)	15,044
				Briggs, Wolstenholme & Thorneley (Liverpool)	78,504

Index

References in bold type are to page numbers of illustrations

Index

Index